Advance Praise for *Black Immigrants in the United States: Essays on the Politics of Race, Language, and Voice*

"What makes the Black immigrant and refugee experience unique? How does it feel to be a Black immigrant or refugee? How is being African American different from being a Black immigrant or refugee? This timely and relevant volume answers these and many more questions by capturing the diversity of Black immigrant and refugee populations. Conceived at the intersection of race, politics, language, culture, education, social justice, and immigration, this book provides a voice for a largely silent (and silenced) population and reveals its complexities in a variety of contexts. It bridges the gap between academia and the lived experiences of Black immigrants and refugees. By taking an inclusive, multidisciplinary approach, Cooper and Ibrahim broaden the focus on immigration to shine a much-needed light on this overlooked and misunderstood population. The result is an invaluable resource for educators and learners alike."

Mary Romney, MA, MA, EdM
ESL Educator

Black Immigrants
in the United States

This book is part of the Peter Lang Education list.
Every volume is peer reviewed and meets
the highest quality standards for content and production.

PETER LANG
New York • Bern • Berlin
Brussels • Vienna • Oxford • Warsaw

Black Immigrants in the United States

Essays on the Politics of Race, Language, and Voice

Edited by Ayanna Cooper and Awad Ibrahim

PETER LANG

New York • Bern • Berlin
Brussels • Vienna • Oxford • Warsaw

Library of Congress Cataloging-in-Publication Data

Names: Cooper, Ayanna, editor. | Ibrahim, Awad, editor.
Title: Black immigrants in the United States: essays on the politics of
race, language, and voice / edited by Ayanna Cooper & Awad Ibrahim.
Description: New York: Peter Lang, 2020.
Includes bibliographical references and index.
Identifiers: LCCN 2020000318 (print) | LCCN 2020000319 (ebook)
ISBN 978-1-4331-7396-7 (hardback) | ISBN 978-1-4331-7397-4 (paperback)
ISBN 978-1-4331-7393-6 (ebook pdf)
ISBN 978-1-4331-7394-3 (epub) | ISBN 978-1-4331-7395-0 (mobi)
Subjects: LCSH: Africans—United States—Social conditions. |
Africans—Race identity—United States. | West Indians—United
States—Social conditions. | West Indians—Race identity—United States.
| Latin Americans—United States—Social conditions. | Latin
Americans—Race identity—United States. | Blacks—United States—Social
conditions. | Blacks—Race identity—United States. | Immigrants—United
States—Social conditions. | United States—Emigration and
immigration—Social aspects. | United States—Race relations.
Classification: LCC E184.A24 B53 2020 (print) | LCC E184.A24 (ebook) |
DDC 973/.0496073—dc23
LC record available at https://lccn.loc.gov/2020000318
LC ebook record available at https://lccn.loc.gov/2020000319
DOI 10.3726/b16536

Bibliographic information published by **Die Deutsche Nationalbibliothek**.
Die Deutsche Nationalbibliothek lists this publication in the "Deutsche
Nationalbibliografie"; detailed bibliographic data are available
on the Internet at http://dnb.d-nb.de/.

I dedicate this book to four women who have had a great influence on my life as a teacher, researcher and advocate; to my mother Deborah J. Wornum and to my cousin the late Paula C. Pope with whom I spent countless hours after school at Legal Services in Jamaica Plain, MA. Now I realize the significance of being in that space, around educated women working in and for their communities. To my sister, Kimberly M. Artez, one of my first teachers. To my daughter, Breanna R. Cooper, whom I lift up on her own journey. I love you all dearly.

-Ayanna Cooper

I dedicate this book to my brother Hassan Hamadeen who taught me what an economy of unconditional hospitality might look like and what loving unconditionally might feel like. We will meet at the rendezvous of victory where we will hug and laugh as we always do. I miss your beautiful, loud and genuine laughter. I hope you are resting. To the African kings and queens; ya makin' it BIG. Keep the hope! To my daughter, Baian, this one is for you!

-Awad Ibrahim

Table of Contents

Figures

Tables

Acknowledgments

A special thank you to my husband Ronnie Cooper, and our children Ronnie and Breanna Cooper. Thank you for being so supportive of my writing projects by asking questions and listening to the details as they unfolded. Thank you for making any and all small milestones worthy of celebration.

To my co-author, Dr. Awed Ibrahim, thank you for your contributions to the field of TESOL and beyond. I especially appreciate your guidance, for sharing the stories of Black immigrants in Canada, and for crossing the border to help me share their stories here in the United States.

I would like to thank Dr. Anthony Van Der Meer a faculty member at the University of Massachusetts at Boston. Thanks to Attorney Leila Yassin who first suggested I consider a career in education. Dr. Libya Gil for highlighting the K–12 population of Black English learners while serving the U.S. Department of Education Assistant Deputy Secretary, and Director for the Office of English Language Acquisition (OELA). Thanks to Mary Romney and Mawakana Onifade for their support and ongoing encouragement. Thanks to Laura Gardner and Gabrielle Jackson for their time and contributions to this publication.

-Dr. Ayanna Cooper

I would like to thank first and foremost continental African youth with whom I have been working and whose lives I have been tracking for the last two decades. They struggle but they triumph as well. I would like to thank my sister Aziza for her love. Osailat, you have been an inspiration. Let us all keep the hope! Our best is here, but our absolute best is yet to come.

-Dr. Away Ibrahim

Drs. Cooper and Ibrahim would like to thank the contributors to this publication. We are extremely grateful for your time and dedication to this project.

Thank you for sharing your vision. The authors are listed here in alphabetical order: Nimo Abdi, Melissa L. Alleyne, Ayanna R. Armstrong, Ebony Bailey, Martha Bigelow, Kisha C. Bryan, Babatunji Ifarinu, Mary Lou McCloskey, Isabella Alexander-Nathani, Bic Ngo, Pedro Noguera, Teni-Ola Ogunjobi, Amy E. Pelissero, Patriann Smith, Enzo Silon Surin, S. Joel Warrican and Alex Kumi-Yeboah.

Foreword

AWAD IBRAHIM, CO-EDITOR
University of Ottawa, Canada

What happens when Blackness meets the syntax of immigration? Let us not anticipate a simple answer to such a complex question, but we must try an answer. As the chapters in *Black Immigrants in the United States: Essays on the Politics of Race, Language, and Voice* show, when Blackness meets the syntax of immigration, the two categories desilence an oft-silenced voice and discourse and create a cartography where the book *Black Immigrants* is possible. Like Offred, in Margaret Atwood's novel *The Handmaid's Tale* (1985), who gave birth out of frustration, we too conceive this book out of frustration. As people who live (or lived) in the East Coast of the United States (where a substantial number of Black immigrants live) and work, among others, in the field of teaching English as a Second Language (ESL), our classes are filled with ESL learners who are Black immigrants, primarily continental Africans, and we know, talk to and have an ongoing conversation with Black immigrants. However, outside class, their voices and stories are not heard, neither in the academy nor in the popular media discourse. Our hope in *Black Immigrants* is to open a crack – moving between the autobiographical and the biographical – so that the word and the world of Black immigrants can be connected.

Chimamanda Ngozi Adichie's novel *Americanah* is the closest we got to addressing what can be called "The Black Immigrant Question." Using episodic style, the novel introduces two terms which are used interchangeably: "Black immigrants" and "non-American Blacks." In its totality, the novel is a tour de force deciphering the ever-complex identity, cultural, linguistic and psychic process of "becoming American" for a Black immigrant. *Becoming American for a Black immigrant*, the novel explains, *is becoming Black American.* "In America," Adichie (2014) writes, "you are black, baby" (p. 273). In her letter to Black immigrants or non-American Blacks, she writes:

> Dear Non-American Black, when you make the choice to come to America, you become black. Stop arguing. Stop saying I'm Jamaican or I'm Ghanaian. America doesn't care. So, what if you weren't "black" in your country? You're in America now. We all have our moments of initiation into the Society of Former Negroes. Mine was in a class in undergrad when I was asked to give the black perspective, only I have no idea what that was. (Adichie, 2014, p. 273)

Clearly, when the Black body encounters the syntax of (im)migration and displacement, a "complicated conversation" (Ng-a-Fook, Ibrahim, & Reis, 2016; Pinar, 2007) seems to come into existence. Here, Blackness becomes a second language and Adichie is its translator. Following in the footsteps of Adichie, we certainly set *Black Immigrants* as a fuller translation of this complicated conversation, which includes how and what it means to "speak Blackness." To speak Blackness, for non-American Blacks, is becoming aware of its syntax, which includes the smallest acts, which in *Americanah* include the head nod, using the word "strong" every time one speaks about a Black woman, tipping generously, brushing off the accusation that one got into an Ivy League college because of Affirmative Action when one is the top of his/her class, etc. To speak Blackness, moreover, is to say you have little to no knowledge of what it means *to be Black* in United States; after all, as I have argued elsewhere, there are no Blacks in contexts where Blackness is the majority. There are no Blacks in Africa; for example, there we are Fulani, Dinka, Ivorian or Malawian. In other words, Blackness is not your defining characteristic, however, once in the United States, these descriptors become secondary to your Blackness. You thus enter the process of becoming Black (Ibrahim, 2014).

On the other hand, as this book is about Trumpistan (Rushdie, 2018), students of migration studies must be tearing their hair out as they listen to Donald Trump talking about "immigrants." First because of his mistaken use of the term "immigrant." *Immigrants are not refugees*, the latter term is what Trump is referring to most of the time (see Ibrahim, 2020). Refugees are those who are fleeing violence, wars and the brutality of famished lives; those who have been knocking "on other people's doors since the beginning of time" (Bauman, 2016, p. 1). Immigrants, on the other hand, have no fear for their lives, tend to be highly educated, with a stable income, and migrate from their homeland to their new "home" voluntarily (Kymlicka, 2010). Yet, for the purpose of this book, we will hold on to the term "immigrant" for its recognizability (and to subvert it from within instead of doing away with it). Second, Trump links "immigrants" with South and Latin Americans. This link obscures the population under investigation in this book, Black immigrants – from the continent and the Caribbean – as well as Black Latin Americans. Pedro Noguera's chapter is set purposefully as the opening chapter for this book to make this point; that is, to talk about Black immigrant experience on the one hand and to complicate both the categories of Blackness and South/Latin America on the other. South and Latin America do include Blackness. Third and finally, one may argue that Trumpistan is the perfect exhibit of what Zygmunt Bauman (2016) calls "migration panic." This migration panic lays bare the West despite its Enlightenment and Kantian cosmopolitanism. Built around the notion that a large number of "foreign" people are threatening the very fabric of society, the danger of the migration panic is that it exploits fears and anxiety, especially among those who already lost so much, namely the poor.

There is a need, therefore, for further research to fully grasp how Black immigrants deal with this migration panic. What is happening now to Black immigrants, especially with Trump's policy on deportation? Little is known about this and with *Black Immigrants*, we hope to open up the discussion. Besides the second editor's work (e.g., Ibrahim, 2014, 2020), who himself was a refugee from the Sudan, we know only a handful of researchers who are attempting to paint the picture of Black immigrants in North America. In doing so, these researchers are showing challenges and struggles as much as they are showing hope, joy and triumph. After all, we have Ilhan Omar, a Somali-American refugee who has arrived in the United States at the age of 12, in the U.S. House of Representative. She, among so many others, is bearing witness to our human possibility and interdependence. Our humanity, if it is to survive along other species, has to build not walls but mutual respect, cooperation and solidarity. Only then can Black immigrants capture their full subjectivity and create a better, more rich and hopeful future, which we should all help bring into existence.

References

Adichie, C. (2014). *Americanah*. Toronto: Vintage.

Atwood, M. (1985). *The handmaid's tale*. Toronto: Random House.

Bauman, Z. (2016). *Strangers at our door*. London, UK: Polity.

Ibrahim, A. (2014). *The rhizome of Blackness: A critical ethnography of Hip-Hop culture, language, identity, and the politics of becoming*. New York, NY: Peter Lang.

Ibrahim, A. (2020). *Black immigrants in North America: Essays on race, immigration, identity, language, Hip-Hop, pedagogy, and the politics of becoming Black.* New York, NY: Myers Education Press.

Kymlicka, W. (2010). *The current state of multiculturalism in Canada and research themes in Canadian multiculturalism 2008–2010.* Ottawa: Citizenship and Immigration Canada.

Ng-A-Fook, N., Ibrahim, A., & Reis, G. (2016). *Provoking curriculum studies: Strong poetry and the arts of the possible in education.* New York, NY: Routledge.

Ogbu, J., & Simons, H. (1998). Voluntary and involuntary minorities: A cultural-ecological theory of school performance with some implication for education. *Anthropology & Education Quarterly, 29*(2), 155–188.

Pinar, W. (2007). *Intellectual advancement through disciplinarity: Verticality and horizontality in curriculum studies.* Rotterdam: Sense.

Rushdie, S. (2018). Truth, lies, and literature. *The New Yorker.* Retrieved February 25, 2019, from https://www.newyorker.com/culture/cultural-comment/truth-lies-and-literature.

Introduction

AYANNA COOPER, CO-EDITOR
A Cooper Consulting

This book serves as conversation booster, one that hopes to shed light on a population that has been traditionally misunderstood, marginalized, and misrepresented. Black immigrants and refugees, who have come to the United States by choice for most (or not), as a result of opportunities sought for different, if not a better, life in a country other than where they were born. Examples of these experiences have been captured in the television miniseries *Roots* (Haley, 1977), the comedic movie *Coming to America* (Landis, 1988), books *Desert Flower* (Dirie, 1998), *Escape from Slavery: The True Story of My Ten Years in Captivity and My Journey to Freedom in America* (Bok, 2003), *Problematizing Blackness, Self-Ethnographies by Black Immigrants to the United States* (Hintzen & Rahier, 2003), *Color, Race, and English Language Teaching: Shades of Meaning* (Curtis & Romney (Eds.), 2006), Trevor Noah's (2016) autobiography *Born a Crime*, and the like. More recently, Bryan, Cooper, and Ifarinu illustrated the complexity of the Black, immigrant experience in *From Majority to Minority Advocating for English Learners from the African Diaspora* (2019) and offered ways that K–12 teachers, administrators, and teacher education programs can support and advocate for this population.

The chapters in this book are an exclusive collection of autobiographies and qualitative and ethnographic research practices to continue providing a voice to the often voiceless. It has been years since a publication solely dedicated to the lives and experiences of Black immigrants in Canada (Ibrahim, 2014). Now, the influence of Ibrahim's research has "crossed the border" interjecting itself into the discourse around Black people in America, immigrants, refugees, and the spaces where those identities intersect. It is at the intersection, the center, where we engage in the richness of politics, race, language, multiculturalism, and, ultimately, what it means to be Black in America.

Noguera's chapter serves as the precursor for framing out the realities of identifying as a Black person in the United States while having immigrant parents from the Caribbean. Part autobiographical, part critique of existing research, Noguera touches upon the marginalization of Black voices from "the struggle," which ultimately afforded some Black immigrants access and opportunities but not afforded to working-class Black Americans. He also discusses the decisions Black immigrants must make and the implications of those decisions, what he refers to as a political act, as part of navigating one's social status and cultural identity as being Black in America.

In the second chapter, Ayanna Armstrong shares her experiences as a Black female immigrant. This autobiographical account explains how her intersecting identities, Barbadian by birth, West Indian by identity, and African American by education shape her experiences in and outside of the United States. Finding safety in educational settings, Armstrong went on to study in Canada and the United States, ultimately settling at one of the largest historically Black universities in the United States. One of her goals is to develop students to be global citizens with an understanding of both macro and micro immigration policies.

Pelissero, McCloskey, and Ogunjobi's Chapter 3 starts off a subsection of the book with interviews of the students who attended the Global Village Project (GVP). Founded in 2009, the GVP serves as a school for refugee girls and young women who have experienced interrupted education. The narrative interviews presented in this chapter serve to study (1) the experiences

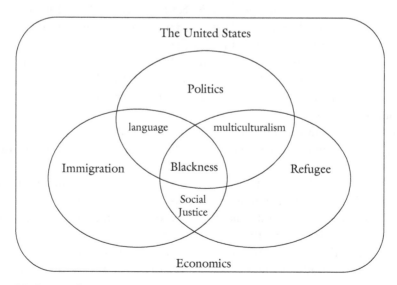

Figure I.1: Intersections

and multiple challenges of these young women and (2) what supports the resilience they have displayed and resilience that has kept them in school and prepared them for the lives they imagine for themselves.

Chapter 4, by Abdi and Ngo, further explores how the experiences of high school Somali-American immigrant students have been shaped at the intersection of race and religion. The interviews conducted relied on the student's memories of selected events and situations they experienced. Some of the follow-up questions inquired about the emotions experienced by the students, their surroundings, and, if others were around, how they seemed to act or behave in response to the incident at hand. The female authors, Somali-American and Vietnamese-American, acknowledged the influence of their own immigrant backgrounds on selection of data, analysis, and writing.

Warrican, Kumi-Yeboah, Smith, and Alleyne continue exploring student experiences in Chapter 5, through a lens, which highlights culture, linguistic diversity, and past educational backgrounds of Senegalese adolescent immigrant students. Specific attention is paid to how students negotiate their own identities and position themselves in their new environmental life in the United States. Their findings directly align to the need for more to be done in order to meet the standards expected of classrooms and schools that truly embrace and sustain culturally relevant learning environments. Additionally, the call for attention to the needs of Black immigrant students must be incorporated nationwide into preservice teacher education.

Chapter 6, by Bigelow, highlights the experience of a Somali female immigrant student with limited or interrupted formal education (SLIFE). Bigelow describes that the strong Somali community student is a member of which ultimately translated into the student having "social capital," a notion which is well defined in the chapter. The student's family received resettlement assistance from the government, a receptive policy. However, socially the Somali immigrants were likely to have experienced prejudice, among other challenges, especially since they are assumed to be Muslim. In addition to community assets, the importance of SLIFE having learning opportunities that meet their language, literacy, and social-emotional learning needs is affirmed.

Chapter 7, by Ifarinu, concludes the subsection on student experiences by addressing the need for culturally responsive pedagogy with an African-centered perspective. Ifarinu describes the difference between three distinct immigrant groups of African descent: first Continental African immigrants, second those from the Caribbean and Latin America, and next African Americans. The latter refer to those who were forcibly bought and brought to the United States. Ifarinu further explains the convergence of all three subgroups, Black student population, as it relates to the urgent and critical need for culturally responsive pedagogy with educators who know and understand the similarities and differences between groups.

In Chapter 8, Bryan brings attention to the implications of teachers and teacher educators who do not acknowledge and consider the intersections of race and language of their students, especially those who teach Black immigrants. She draws from textbooks, non-academic, informative texts, organizations such as #BlackLivesMatter, to provide demographic, quantitative, and myth-dispelling information regarding Black immigrants in the United States. Bryan describes culturally sustaining strategies and course assignments that she implements as part of the ESL teacher preparation program at a mid-size HBCU in the mid-South region of the United States. Her chapter affirms the need for both culturally relevant and culturally sustaining pedagogy.

In Chapter 9, Bailey captures the experiences and lives of Black immigrants stranded at the border between Mexico and the United States. Black immigrants end up in Mexico due to recent immigration policy changes in the United States. Essentially they are conducting their lives just outside the border of where they intended to go. Blackness is not considered common in Mexico and has since attracted journalists, photographers and documentarians. Assuring her research is accessible by populations outside of higher learning academia, she, in her chapter, sheds light on the role of diaspora and decoloniality in the representation of Black people in Mexico.

Alexander-Nathani continues exploring issues around Black migration but from outside of North America in Chapter 10. With the influx of West and Central African migrants to Morocco, this chapter describes the political challenges related to race, non-citizenship status, and changes within the economy for different groups of Moroccans who identify as "Black" or "African" depending upon their social and economic status. Additional factors around culture, class, racial identity, and social and political inclusion or exclusion are explored. Bringing awareness to Black migrant experiences outside of the United States and North America is part of cultivating a sense of global advocacy for people of African descent. Besides advocacy, this chapter is meant to give the global perspective of the Black immigrant body.

Chapter 11 by Cooper serves as a resource, listing organizations that specifically support Black immigrant and refugee populations in the United States. These organizations, some well known and others not so much, are deserving of attention and recognition since they actively work to break down barriers and obstacles faced by those who want to live their best lives possible outside of their countries of origin. By connecting researchers, scholars, Black immigrants, and the like to these and similar organizations with shared missions and goals, we are able to build a bridge, instead of a wall, that supports advocacy, autonomy, and the access to the American dream.

In addition to the United States, the following is a list of some of the countries represented in this publication (in alphabetical order): Barbados, the Democratic Republic of the Congo, Eritrea, Haiti, Mexico, Morocco, Nigeria, Senegal, Somalia, and Sudan.

References

Bok, F., & Tivnan, E. (2003). *Escape from slavery the true story of my ten years in captivity--and my journey to freedom in America*. New York, NY: St. Martin's Press.

Bryan, K., Cooper, A., & Ifarinu, B. (2019). From majority to minority advocating for English learners from the African diaspora. In H. Linville & J. Whiting (Eds.), *Advocacy in English language teaching and learning* (pp. 190–201). New York, NY: Routledge.

Curtis, A., & Romney, M. (Eds.). (2006). *Color, race, and English language teaching: Shades of meaning*. Mahwah, NJ: Lawrence Erlbaum Associates.

Dirie, W., & Miller, C. (1998). *Desert flower: The extraordinary journey of a desert Nomad*. New York, NY: Virago Book.

Haley, A. (Writer). (1977, January 23). *Roots* [Television series]. Burbank, CA: ABC.

Hintzen, P. C., & Rahier, J. M. (2003). *Problematizing blackness: Self-ethnographies by Black immigrants to the United States*. New York, NY: Routledge.

Ibrahim, A. (2014). *The rhizome of Blackness: A critical ethnography of Hip-Hop culture, language, identity, and the politics of becoming*. New York, NY: Peter Lang.

Landis, J. (Director). (1988). *Coming to America* [Motion picture]. United States: Paramount Pictures and Eddie Murphy Productions.

Noah, T. (2016). *Born a crime stories from a South African childhood*. New York, NY: Spiegel & Grau.

"Voyager"

ENZO SILON SURIN

Voyager
You are a speck
azure & dust
in a galaxy
called potential

potential to bust
in that what have
you done for me
lately milky way

weight of the wait
says stop caring
before the world
does—in that you

are not going to
amount to anything
worth remembering
like a rogue planet

immigrant & black
second born, brother
of your father's son, a

speck through the lens
of ephemeral gazes &
constant stares—you
master constellations
like mazes—their eyes

heralding blue planets
& others filled with
oceans—in awe
of the possibilities—

galaxies light years
away—while at home
cities become oceans &
black moons become dust

& every day something
threatens to launch you
into the interstellar space
of your very own body.

1 On Being Black but Not American: Bringing Politics Back to the Study of Race

PEDRO A. NOGUERA
Distinguished Professor, University of California, Los Angeles

Twenty years ago, scholarly treatises on race sought to be relevant to race politics – the civil rights movement, anti-colonial struggles, Black Power, etc. There was a tacit understanding that those of us who held faculty appoints in colleges and universities obtained these as a result of the struggle of others – students who took over buildings, activists who marched boycotted and in some cases rioted, to demand access and representation within the university. Many of those who put their lives on the line in the 1960s and 1970s, did so with the understanding that while they might not benefit directly from their efforts, future generations would reap rewards from their sacrifice.

Today, in many academic circles, including departments of African, Black and Ethnic Studies, there is increasingly relatively little connection between the scholarship produced by the academicians to contemporary racial politics. Instead, contemporary race scholars are more likely to engage in a mode of analysis and scholarship that is increasingly detached from the lives of most Black people, including Black immigrants and refugee populations. This is a most unfortunate and troubling trend. We are living at a times when Black people in the United States and throughout the diaspora, are increasingly marginalized, exploited and subjected to relentless attack. In such times the need for race scholars, particularly those who work in Black and Africana Studies Departments, to connect their scholarship to the plight of Black people is of critical importance.

History would suggest that re-establishing the connections between scholarship and struggle should not be difficult to accomplish. After all, the early traditions of Black Studies were rooted in protest. The first Black Studies department in the nation at San Francisco State University was created through a protracted struggle and a strike involving students, faculty and community allies. Over time, the departments evolved, often moving away from their radical roots. However, the need to understand the Black experience and meaning of racial identity and oppression in a society where Black people occupy the status of the despised and feared, the ultimate "other" (Dubois; Woodson; Hurston; Drake and Cayton 1945) is as relevant today as it ever was. In the not too distant past, among both social scientists and humanists, there was an intimate and direct connection between Black scholarship and to what we once referred to as the "Black struggle" – the fight against racism, for social justice, and for the betterment of Black people. While the term "Black struggle" might seem anachronistic because it implies a degree of uniformity in outlook and action that certainly does not exist today, and perhaps never did in the past, it is important to recognize what we have lost. Black scholars such as Angela Davis, Sonia Sanchez, Asa Hilliard and many others, dedicated much of their scholarship to the challenges confronting Black people, and they often imagined themselves as participating in a collective struggle that would lead to liberation, self-determination and freedom.

In academic circles, the politics of race in America is increasingly marginalized as a topic of study having been replaced by scholarship most closely tied to what is now called "cultural studies." In this genre, scholars write books and articles generally read exclusively by other scholars in their field, in which they may ponder the dilemmas faced by Black people, but their ties and responsibilities to their people are rarely interrogated or explored. There is generally little mention of how the experience of Black immigrants, many of whom are exploited as guest workers or treated as fugitives in the US because of their undocumented status, relates to the plight of Black people in America or beyond. "Black lives matter" may resonate as a call for ending police killings of Black people, but there is insufficient attention to how and why they matter in other contexts.

This is not to say that all scholarship done under the banner of Black studies should have relevance to efforts aimed at understanding the meaning and significance of race in American society. To be so prescriptive would deprive Black studies of the dynamism and creativity it needs to thrive. However, there are too many Black immigrant scholars who express anguish and ambiguity about being rendered invisible because they are frequently lumped in with Black Americans rather than recognizing the need for solidarity. There seems to be an unstated fear that if they are unable to maintain their status as something other than Black Americans they will fall victim to all the stereotypes, discrimination and abuse heaped upon this group. In some respect it is hardly surprising that these scholars would seek to separate themselves. After all, in a society that has equated all persons defined as Black with inferiority and savagery, and that has for over three hundred years struggled with how to exploit and exclude members of this group simultaneously (Wacquant, 2001), most persons learn quickly that it is better to be *anything but Black* (Morrison, 1993). Sadly, this includes many contemporary Black scholars. Given that Black immigrants invariably become linked to the history of Black Americans, even when they feel no particular affinity, it is not surprising, but most unfortunate, that many go out of their way to make it known that they are not one of "them." With the exception of Haitians, who may be the only group that actively seeks to be identified with Black Americans because the society from which they come is even more despised, very few Black immigrants to the United States welcome losing their distinctive national identities (and accents) and being subsumed under the broader identity heading of "Black."

I know this tendency all too well because the effort to distance oneself from Black Americans was a social stance that was foisted upon me by my parents. As Trinidadian and Jamaican immigrants, they too desperately sought to distinguish themselves from Black Americans. Their efforts to free their children from what they regarded as an ignominious categorization were based upon an understandable desire to escape at least some of the discrimination that Black Americans endured. As West Indians, they were sometimes held in higher regard than Black Americans by employers, teachers and other authorities who approved of their strong work ethic, their facility with the "King's" English, and excellent table manners. By imparting such distinctions to us, their children, they hoped that whites would be less likely to hold us in contempt, and, better still, that we would be less likely to be hated by them.

Of course, this was more often a dream than a reality. As a young man in the Coast Guard and Merchant Marines, my father learned that white racists are often incapable or unwilling to make distinctions among Blacks. After he was nearly stabbed by racists who were steadfast in their unwillingness to comply with President Truman's order to integrate the armed forces, his mother turned to her Congressman, Adam Clayton Powell (D-Harlem), for assistance in obtaining release from military service. Later, when he served as a bodyguard to Paul Robeson in Peekskill, New York, and he witnessed firsthand the violent racism of the mobs sought to thwart Robeson, he was reminded yet again that distinctions based on nationality were irrelevant to the racist mobs. Experiences like these made him all too well aware of the fact that it was the skin he was in that they hated, and their racial hatred could hardly be avoided by claiming allegiance to distant Caribbean island.

The efforts of my parents to create a sense of difference in their children, all six of whom had been born in the United States, from their Black American counterparts had a different goal. While they knew that they couldn't shield us from white racism, they hoped they could at least buffer us from the sense of inferiority they perceived as prevalent among Blacks in the United States, and which they regarded as the most damaging effect of American racism. "You are not Black" my father would insist, "You are Brown." Of course, we understood the implication of this admonition; Brown is presumably better than Black. More importantly, if you think you're better and if you see yourself through a lens that has not been stained by the history of racial oppression in the United States, then perhaps you can avoid the stigma of race in America. In fact, beyond telling us that we were not Black, my father pointedly informed us that we were only Americans by accident of birth.

Despite the desire of my parents, each one of us learned in our own way that outside of our home we were most definitely perceived as Black. It was a realization that came quicker and easier for me, and my darker skinned siblings, than for the lighter ones. With Spanish first and last names, the lighter ones could easily pass for Puerto Ricans. In fact, my younger brother passed for Puerto Rican throughout much of high school.

My own racial awareness was largely political almost from the start. I was nine years old on the day Martin Luther King Jr. was assassinated. When I walked to school with my friends on the morning of the assassination, we met up with other kids who told us that Black students were not going to school that day because King had been shot. With my friends happily returning home, I did the same, only to be told by my mother that the boycott did not apply to my siblings or me because we were not Black. I tried without success to explain to her that everyone else thought I was Black. But as she proceeded to search for a belt with which to enforce her order to go to school, I realized that my assertion of Blackness would have to wait for another day.

The process of my racial awakening was furthered through conversations with my cousin Ronald Frazier, who at the age of 11 was wise beyond his years on these matters. Being the son of Trinidadian parents, Ronald also had to contend with the racial confusion his parents tried to impose upon him. However, unlike me, Ronald had figured out the politics of racial identity fairly quickly, and he readily shared his insights. Having grown up midst the racial violence of the East Bronx, Ronald had drawn the conclusion that racial identity had very little to do with national origin or even color. He explained "Pedro, there are only two races – Black or white. It's not about what color you are or whether or not you're West Indian, it's about which side you're on."

He went on to explain that there were whites and Puerto Ricans who sided with Blacks, and some Blacks who sided with whites. Having witnessed racial violence first hand from his intolerant Italian neighbors, Ronald explained that when fights broke out you had to know which side you were on, otherwise you would get hurt. "When the Italians go after Blacks they don't stop to ask if you're West Indian first." He assured me that race was a political stance, and that it was possible to maintain our Caribbean identity, which we associated largely with the music we listened to and the food we ate at home. The public face we wore to the outside world demanded utter clarity. This was the early 1970s, and with Black Power raging and white backlash responding there was increasingly no room for safety in ambiguity.

As fate would have it, Ronald was murdered at the age of 14 by three Black boys not much older than him. His refusal to relinquish his leather jacket to his knife-wielding assailants; a prized possession he bought for himself with savings from his newspaper route, resulted in his murder. His senseless death at the hands of other Black teenagers provided me with yet another lesson about race – despite all its proclaimed importance, the bonds created by racial solidarity actually meant very little to many of us in our everyday lives.

Understanding race as a political construct allows us to think critically about the meaning of racial solidarity and to maintain a healthy skepticism about the nature of racial categories. At the same time, critical race scholarship should also help us to understand the potential it holds as a source of mobilization and solidarity. We need not engage in romanticized and essentialist notions of race in order to appreciate the political significance of race in the US. As an imposed social category, it is clear that race does not serve as an inherent source of solidarity or the basis for unity. Divisions rooted in conflicting class interests, ideology and self-interests, often trump race-conscious behavior. Moreover, Black people who are criminally inclined are generally more likely to prey upon Black communities (Noguera, 2001). Similarly, there are also numerous examples of Black politicians and leaders who manipulate Black voters and constituents to advance their careers and line their pockets, and there are relatively few Black celebrities who use their wealth and prestige to demonstrate genuine solidarity or commitment to downtrodden Black communities. All of these examples serve as living proof of the limitations of race as a basis for social organization.

However, it is precisely because of these limitations that it is imperative to bring politics back to the study of race. The politics of race compels us to question the social responsibility of Black elites, and to seriously contemplate where individuals with privilege, including Black scholars, stand in relation to the less fortunate Black majority. That is as true for the authors in this volume, as it is for Colin Powell, Oprah Winfrey or Michael Jordan. Talking Black or playing the race card when it is convenient as we have seen from the likes of Supreme Court Justice Clarence Thomas and Bill Cosby, is perhaps the most convincing evidence of the limitations of racial rhetoric. Such figures stand in stark contrast to individuals like LeBron James who refused to accept an invitation to the White House due to the racist actions and beliefs of President Trump, and who invested significant sums of money to create a school for Black children in his home town in Akron, Ohio. The same could be said of Beyonce, the recently murdered rapper Nipsey Hussel and Colin Kaepernick, the NFL football player who refused to stand and salute during the National Anthem and was subsequently banned from practicing his profession. Like Paul Robeson, such individuals understand that standing on principle even when it means risking rewards and acclaim, is important at certain moments in history. We need more Black scholars to operate with a similar sense of social and political responsibility.

Bringing politics back to the study of race is not a call for others to stand in judgement of who is authentically Black on the basis of some narrow-minded, politically correct criteria. However, in society where racism is still pervasive in its interpersonal, ideological and structural forms, race politics compels us to recognize that it would be a mistake to retreat from race. This was the fatal flaw of Paul Gilroy in his book, *Against Race* (2000). In his convoluted analysis of racial politics and history, Gilroy spent more time castigating Black people for perpetuating the myth of race by pointing out that the race categories were created for the purpose of naturalizing domination and exploitation. Ironically, while Gilroy was clear about his opposition to the construct of race and its uses, he was virtually silent about the pernicious effects of racism. In fact, Gilroy like too many other contemporary Black scholars operate on the assumption that if Black people would simply let go of race and begin to see themselves as merely human, racism would fade away.

As the rise of Trump has shown, and the racist attacks carried out by neo-fascists and Klansmen who now feel emboldened by his presidency remind us, we have not entered a post-racial phase in American society. For this reason scholars whose work is rooted in post-modernist, post-structuralist discourse must do more than merely deconstruct, dismantle and destroy race as a social construct. We who enjoy the benefits of affirmative action must remain connected to the movement against police killings, the defense of the undocumented, and the effort to end mass incarceration and voter suppression. Rather than silence we must seek out new ways to connect our scholarship to the struggles of Black people.

However, as burdensome as such hassles and hardships may be, such experiences are for me precisely the reason why I believe that keeping politics in our analysis of race is so important. Twenty years ago, despite considerable confusion and discord about how to combat racism and racial oppression, there was greater awareness about the need for scholarly analyses of race to be linked to a larger political project. For many, this was a project that sought to unite the oppressed majority against the oppressive minority. Though ideology and even language often made such efforts difficult to actually bring about, the desire to connect scholarship to questions of equality, justice and freedom was evident and ever-present.

Such an approach continues to be present in the work of a small number of race scholars today. *The Miners' Canary* (2001), by Lani Guinier and Gerald Torres, is perhaps the best example of this trend. Rather than retreating from race, or rejecting it on the basis of biological determinism, the authors carefully examine how race can be used as a basis for organizing and challenging various forms of injustice. They demonstrate a healthy skepticism about how race is used in popular discourse and recognize that racial categories have been imposed for the purpose of rationalizing domination. However, they also recognize that race can be used as part of a political project that brings various subordinate groups together and that responds to the genuine sensibilities of ordinary folk who continue to see themselves through racial lenses.

It is not my intention to offer these comments as an attack against Black scholars who are content with apolitical work. Rather, this is a call for Black scholars to once again see themselves as responsible to the Black struggle and the fight for Black freedom. Consider *Black Power* by Charles Hamilton and Stokely Carmichael (1967) or Charles Tabb's *The Political Economy of the Black Ghetto* (1970). Both works offered sophisticated analysis of race and racism that went well beyond tirades against prejudice. Hamilton and Carmichael explained the significance of the call for Black Power, linking it to the struggle for self-determination in Black communities in the United States and throughout the world. They also introduced the concept of institutionalized racism, demonstrating through their analysis how racist practices and the ideology of white supremacy become manifest within the operations of institutions and the law. Or Tabb, whose analysis of conditions in the inner-city, built open the work of Robert Blauner (1970) to show how persistent poverty, crime and unemployment were by-products of the material and social relationships that exist between white elites and Black functionaries.

Unlike much of today's "critical race theory," these works not only offered powerful critiques and analysis but also consciously and pointedly showed how and why social science and social theory could be employed to combat racial oppression were ready and willing to use their work to support and further the Black struggle. These were organic intellectuals who in the Gramscian tradition saw their intellectual work as political (Gramsci, 1971). They understood fully that privileged academics have to be accountable to those who made it possible for them to hold the comfortable university professorships they now enjoy – the Black masses.

As a first generation African American, born to Caribbean parents but raised in Black communities in the United States, I operate with one foot foreign and more at home in the Caribbean than the United States, and the other firmly rooted in the dismal reality of America. Although I have often found that I see things differently than my Black immigrant colleagues, I understand perhaps more than most Black immigrant scholars that the privileges we enjoy in academy were won through the struggle of Black people in this country. I know that while talent and merit are important, I also know that at most it deserves only partial credit for the "success" of many Black immigrant scholars. The rewards we enjoy from the comfort of the Ivory Tower are the product of a history of struggle waged over the course of centuries by Black people in America whose fight for freedom and justice has historically been the strongest impetus for democracy in the United States.

I was made aware of the difference place of birth can create in how one thinks about race a few years ago while conducting interviews with Caribbean immigrants. I was interested in probing the notion that West Indians constitute a model minority due to their relative success in education and employment (Ogbu, 1988), at least as compared to Black Americans. During the middle of one interview with a couple from St. Lucia, I probed what they felt were some of the differences between themselves and the Black people they knew. Both explained that unlike the Black Americans they worked with, they managed to maintain friendly relationships with their white co-workers. Both husband and wife described Black Americans as "standoffish" and unnecessarily hostile toward whites, and suggested that their negative attitudes hurt their performance on the job and the likelihood that they would advance in their careers.

Upon hearing this invidious comparison, their 12-year-old daughter who had been watching television in the adjacent living room interrupted the conversation to blurt out "Well you can't forget history Daddy." Struck by her comment, I turned to the 12 year old to ask for elaboration. I was particularly interested in what history she was referring to. The 12 year old explained "Look at what happened during slavery and with all the lynchings that followed. It's not easy to put all of that aside and just forget."

Unlike her parents, this 12-year-old girl had been born in the United States. Even with two immigrant parents who claimed greater tries to their native St. Lucia than to the United States, the child had already adopted an African-American identity, and embraced a history and sense of political and social responsibility that distinguished her from her parents.

I suppose my outlook on racial identity is more like that of this 12 year old than that of many Black scholars today. We don't have an "invisible identity." We must proudly claim out Black identities that are inextricably tied to the plight of the 12 million Black people who reside in the United States. This does not mean that we should reject our connections to the Diaspora. Rather, we must recognize that to identify as Black in America is an inherently political act, one that connects us organically to the plight of Black people throughout the world.

Racial identity has always been political in America and it still is. Scholars who study race, especially Black scholars regardless of where they might be born, must understand these politics, and like my cousin Ronald Frazier they must decide where they stand and which side they're on.

Discussion Questions

1. The author describes experiences in school, wanting to be part of his peer group despite how his parents defined his "brownness." How might those experiences be similar or different to what Black immigrants in school settings experience today?
2. What types of decisions must Black immigrant and refugee populations make as they navigate intersecting identities in the United States? How might those identities be "invisible" or not, as noted by the author?
3. Is there a sense of urgency and advocacy that resonates with you after reading this chapter? If so, describe.
4. How are the traditionally marginalized groups, Black Americans, Black immigrants and Black refugees similar yet different when it comes to advocacy issues?

References

Blauner, R. (1970). Internal colonialism and Ghetto revolt. *Social Problems, 16*, 393–408.

Carmichael, S., & Hamilton, C. (1967). *Black power; The politics of liberation in America.* New York, NY: Vintage.

Essed, P., & Goldberg, D. T. (2002). *Race critical theories.* London, UK: Blackwell Publishers.

Gilroy, P. (2000). *Against race*. Cambridge, MA: Harvard University Press.

Gramsci, A. (1971). *The prison notebooks of Antonio Gramasci*. New York, NY: International Publishers.

Guinier, L., & Torres, G. (2001). *The Miner's Canary*.

Morrison, T. (1993). On the back of Blacks. *Time Magazine*, Fall p. 57.

Noguera, P. (2001). The trouble with black boys. *Harvard Journal of African American Public Policy, VII*, 23–46.

Ogbu, J. (1988). Cultural diversity and human development. *New Directions for Child and Adolescent Development*, 42, 11–28.

Tabb, W. (1970). *The political economy of the Black Ghetto*. New York, NY: W.W. Norton Company.

Wacquant, L. (2001). Deadly symbiosis: When Ghetto and prison meet and mesh. *Punishment and Society*, 2–3 Fall.

2 The Continuing African Journey to America: Continuity and Change: Struggles, Overcoming, and Celebrating

AYANNA R. ARMSTRONG
North Carolina Agricultural and Technical State University

Barbadian by birth, West Indian by identity, African American by education, and global citizen by socialization and experience, this identification came from my father's understanding and description of the uniqueness of our identity. I was born in the island of Barbados, but each one of my family members were born in a different Caribbean state, one family 4 passports, Barbados, Jamaica, Trinidad and Tobago, and Guyana. My paternal aunts and grandparents emigrated to the United States well before I was born, and I look back at childhood trips to New Jersey, Florida, Washington D.C., and New York, with fond memories filled with new and exciting experiences, like ice cream trucks and Disneyworld. Immigration and movement across borders has almost always been a part of my socialization – passport pictures, long lines, customs checks, etc.

At 16, I received a national scholarship to go to a United World College in Victoria, British Columbia, and Canada, and after that I was accepted to study economics at the historically Black, all-women's Spelman College, in the city of Atlanta, GA. Like many young people at that stage in my life, I had no idea what I wanted to do with my future, but it had always been instilled in me that education and expanding my global footprint was a blessing that I had to take advantage of. On reflection, had I been a little braver or perhaps more self-aware, I may have chosen a different path. Ironically, it is not exactly knowing what I wanted to do that kept me in academia. I felt safe while in school, my visas were in status, my parents were happy, and I could avoid major life choices. In undergraduate Graduate school offered the promise of being able to work on campus in capacities beyond the 20-hour mandate for undergraduate work-study. Before time in graduate school, I spent every semester and summer working as hard and wherever I could, from data entry for an optometrist to tutoring, grading papers, residential assistant, and Director for one week, I worked in the office of admissions, student affairs, public safety, and counselling services. I worked every single job I could on that campus; my all-time record is having six jobs at one time. As a graduate assistant in my Master's program, I gained valuable knowledge of statistical analysis; as a teaching assistant in my PhD program, I found my calling as a teacher, establishing true meaning in shaping young Black minds, immigrants, and African Americans alike. It is because of hustling with all of those different jobs in undergraduate and given the space to grow scholastically in graduate school, I was able to develop a strong work ethic and understanding of self through. I am currently Associate Chairperson of the Department of Political Science and History at one of the Largest Historically Black Universities in the United States.

As an educator, I think it is important to develop students to be Global citizens. In order to understand the implications of large concepts and changes in immigration and how it affects them, sometimes we need to start at the micro-level having discussions about the immigration process itself and the people who go through the process. This begins the socialization process. For myself I have a reputation as one of the more challenging instructors in my Department, but perhaps it is my example as a Professional Black female instructor with a Ph.D. that seems to resonate most with my students. There is a sameness in many of my experiences having been educated at historically Black colleges and universities (HBCUs), but it is always my identity as a Black immigrant that defines me and guides as to be an example for them.

There are many other Black immigrants who have settled in the United States and like me, their narratives are colorful and variegated, often steered by need and want of educational and employment opportunities. The identity of any Black immigrant is a unique tapestry brought together by the nuances of countless experiences, places, people, and things. This tapestry, more specifically, is woven together by a number of dynamic factors including discrimination, inequality, the pressures of upward social mobility, isolation, language barriers, legal and illegal employment, detention, and education, just to name a few. This essay seeks to explore some of the seminal experiences of Black immigrants in the United States over the past 20 years especially through my perspective as an educator and Afro Caribbean immigrant. It also articulates some lessons of successfully transitioning into and mutual acceptance and full celebration of the African-American community.

Relevance and Importance

The ongoing discussion about Black immigrants to the United States is critical to the strengthening of the "Tapestry of the Black community" in America. In this chapter, the following areas stand out as being relevant and important. Firstly, we attempt to explore the theoretical underpinnings of transition, acceptance, and integration of Black immigrants into the African-American community. Secondly, we articulate some of the potential barriers and areas of miscommunication for foreign-born Blacks. Thirdly, there is need to share individual stories of the journey from Africa and the Caribbean into America, and the global Black community and I share mine. We then need to draw out the lessons, not only of barriers and problems, but also of successes in the journey of breaking down the walls of prejudice, misunderstanding, and ego, and to assist others who are making that journey. Finally, there is discussion and celebration of the completion of the full circle of coming home to the global Black community that is emerging and must grow stronger into the future.

Theoretical Framework

It is important to underpin our perspectives on a specific phenomenon with theory, because theory allows scholars to build on the ideas of other scholars. The identity of the Black immigrant is herein framed by a theoretical *framework of Double-consciousness. This concept* is social philosophy referring, originally, to a source of inward "twoness" experienced by African Americans because of their racialized oppression and devaluation in a white nationalistic society: African Americans have to identify as Black first and Americans second (Pittman, 2016). The concept is often associated with William Edward Burghardt Du Bois, who introduced the term into social and political thought, famously, in his groundbreaking *The Souls of Black Folk* (1903). For the purposes of this chapter, Double-consciousness is contextualized as that of the "twoness" experienced by Black immigrants because of their status as both immigrant and a person of color in this highly racialized and nationalistic country like the United States of America.

It is with this conceptualization of double-consciousness that this chapter seeks to briefly explore how Black immigrants navigate the current political, economic, and social environment's hostility toward both their immigrant status and their Blackness. The chapter also explores the immigration process itself and some of the nuanced dynamics between African Americans and Black immigrants, and the importance of socialization and language, mental and emotional challenges of being a Black immigrant and some of the advantages and challenges for their American born children.

Black Immigration to the United States and Appraisal

According to the Pew center for research, the United States has long had a sizable Black population because of the transatlantic slave trade beginning in the 16th century. But significant voluntary Black migration is a relatively new development – and one that has increased rapidly over the past two decades (Anderson & Lopez, 2018). A record 3.8 million Black immigrants live in the United States today, more than four times the number in 1980, according to a Pew Research Center analysis of U.S. Census Bureau data. Black immigrants now account for 8.7% of the nation's Black population, nearly triple their share in 1980 (Anderson, 2015).

Pew Center statistics further assert the modern wave of Black immigration to the United States began when U.S. immigration policy changed in the 1960s, becoming more open to a wider variety of migrants. Just like other immigrants, foreign-born Blacks were aided by the Immigration and Nationality Act of 1965 that emphasized family reunification and skilled immigrant labor (Anderson, 2015). In addition, the Refugee Act of 1980 loosened immigration restrictions by allowing more immigrants from conflict areas such as Ethiopia and Somalia to seek asylum in the United States. Additionally, the U.S. Immigration Act of 1990 sought to increase the number of immigrants from underrepresented nations, and although the act was initially intended to increase the flow of European immigrants, Africans have benefited from the program, as well (Anderson, 2015).

This act, also known as the diversity visa program, has been an important way for African immigrants to gain entry into the United States. About one-in-five sub-Saharan African immigrants (19%) who gained legal permanent residence between 2000 and 2013 entered through this program (Anderson, 2015).

During the same period, about three-in-ten (28%) sub-Saharan African immigrants arrived in the United States as refugees or asylum seekers. That share was only 5% for Caribbean immigrants and 13% for the overall immigrant population (Anderson, 2015). Caribbean immigrants are much more likely to enter the United States through family-sponsored Caribbean, and sub-Saharan African immigrants are less likely to have been granted admittance via employment-based visa programs than immigrants overall.

While there are a number of avenues to legally or illegally immigrate to the United States, there are some immigration advocates who have long sought to highlight how impossible it can be to navigate the U.S. immigration system. For many immigrants, there is an intrusive process of showing bank accounts, waiting in long lines, spending large sums of money, proving English language proficiencies, educational requirements, finger, and hand-prints and signing away rights of your original national identity. For many other Black would-be immigrants, there is no "turn" they can wait for, and no line to stand in. It is simply not a possibility for them. The process is not only complicated but it can be statistically rigged against Black nationals from specific countries. The President of the United States Donald Trump has been cited as referring to African Countries and Haiti as "Shit-hole" countries, a sentiment that unfortunately may be shared by other Americans (Dawsey, 2018).

African Americans and Foreign-Born Black People: The Common/Different Realities

On arrival in America the Black immigrant unlike any others must then navigate the American Criminal Justice system. The American Criminal Justice system has for too long been cited for rampant abuses and disproportionate incarceration of Black and Brown peoples (Goodwin-White, 2008). Black people in the United States face constant challenges as they are profiled and disproportionately seen as a threat to persons around them. There are too many examples of young Black people being gunned down for appearing suspicious because of their Blackness, including Travon Martin, Tamir Rice, Freddie Grey and so many others. The Criminal Justice system does not physically see the existential difference between Black immigrants and African Americans. Racial prejudice does not wait to ask if English is your first language. Most recently in the news, Botham Jean, a young man from St. Lucia residing in Dallas, Texas, was shot in his apartment by a white officer because of his being Black. His national identity played no part in his senseless death (Sanchez, 2018). It is noteworthy that almost all of the Afro-Caribbean organizations, from across the United States, that issued statements on the murder, referred to the assault on Black people, and Our Black communities in America Customs and Immigration services also fall within the structure of this broken Criminal Justice system and can also be cited for rampant discriminatory practices (Raff, 2017). It has been argued and documented that U.S. immigration law historically has operated and continues to operate to prevent poor and working noncitizens of color from migrating to, and harshly treating those living in the United States (Johnson, 2009). While not all my experiences with the immigration process and officers have been traumatic or difficult, too often as an international student I recollect the raw and uncomfortable feeling of being escorted to the awful rooms beyond the long immigration queues, to further check my immigration credentials or luggage. It was not until a recent finger printing exercise with a colleague in the Criminal Justice Department at my University that I realized how the process of constantly going through immigration had stayed with me and not necessarily in a positive way. Constantly being reminded through the media, what a threat the Police can be to Black people, I reflected on how the exercise made me feel and how the process can be stressful. The incident in question happened during a class exercise where my co-worker being both a Police Officer and professor asked me to volunteer to take my prints so that the students could identify what pattern of prints they were. During the activity I began shaking uncontrollably, much to the amusement of the students and my colleagues. A simple exercise brought on profound emotional distress and a frightening reality. I have lived in the United States for 19 years, I currently have a Green Card, My husband and son are both National born U.S. citizens. I am highly educated and have good standing in the community. These facts however do not separate me in any way from the awareness that both my Blackness and my status as an immigrant national will always be the source of insecurity for me. My status in the United States can be questioned and has to be verified at any given moment.

Reflecting on response to the incident in that class, I can only imagine to be a Black illegal immigrant could only be that much more stressful an experience, especially those with language barriers. These Black Immigrant communities can be especially affected by racial profiling; discrimination; exposure to gangs; immigration raids in their communities; arbitrary stopping of themselves and family members to check their documentation status; incarceration; returning home to find their families have been taken away; and deportation resulting in isolation from family.

Transitions to Citizenship

For the purposes of our analysis, an African American can be identified as a Black person with long generational lines in the United States, with slave ancestors. As people of the African Diaspora African Americans and persons identified as Afro-Caribbean share a common heritage with Africans (Jackson & Cothran, 2003). While some Americans see immigration as a cornerstone of the success of the nation, some believe immigration should be drastically limited. Others propose restrictions for specific countries.

Black Immigrants often have the challenge of explaining their Black identity, especially to African Americans. Many of us find great pride in our national identity and some even have challenges identifying as Black despite pheno- and geno-typical characteristics showing features of African identity or heritage. This idea of national affiliation before racial identity is very different from that of the experiences of our African-American brothers and sisters (Waters, 1994). As an educator at a historically Black University and student of life who is constantly learning and internalizing an African-American consciousness, it becomes incredibly important to address this difference inside and outside of the classroom structure. Too often socialization can frame very dogmatic concepts of racial and cultural self even for young people; it is important for immigrant and American alike to see the difference in perspective of Blackness and what it means allowing for a deepening of their understanding and empathy of one another.

This deepened understanding and comradery is especially important when we refer to the importance of freedom for all Black people in a racially unjust system and governmental structure like the one that exists currently in the United States. Social movements have played a major part of the history and freedom in the United States of America, and this freedom has been shaped by African-American and Black immigrants alike. On the behalf of the Black immigrants in the forefront of these movements, it is their consciousness of the need to fight on behalf of all Black peoples and not just some that has strengthened many of these movements. One such example is with Civil Rights Activist, Stokely Carmichael who in the 1960s originated the Black nationalism rallying slogan, "Black Power." Stokely is considered along with Malcolm X and Martin Luther King to be "the Great leader of the greatest grassroots movement for liberation in history – The Black Freedom Struggle in the US" (Joseph, 2014). Born in Trinidad, he immigrated to New York City in 1952 and became a naturalized American citizen at the age of 13. While attending Historically Black Howard University, he joined the Student Nonviolent Coordinating Committee and was jailed for his work with Freedom Riders. Carmichael, an Afro-Caribbean student, is one of many Black immigrants who began to understand and fight against the hostility and oppression of the American Political, Economic, and Social landscape toward all Black lives in the United States (History, 2009).

It is fair to apply this same paradigm to the double-consciousness of any Black immigrant in the United States. African and Afro Caribbean people were also involved globally in the Black struggle throughout the 18th, 19th, and 20th century in their own Anti-Slavery revolutions and Organizations. It was DJ Kool Herc, a Jamaican immigrant, who is credited as the founder of hip-hop. Louis Farrakhan, the leader of the Nation of Islam, a Black national-ist movement, was the son of a woman from St. Kitts and Nevis and a Jamaican father. Marcus Garvey was Jamaican. Politician Shirley Chisolm, whose par-ents were from the Barbados and British Guiana, and who spent much of her childhood in the Caribbean, became the first Black woman elected to U.S. Congress in 1968, going on to become the first major-party Black candidate for the President, as well as the first woman to run as a president for the Democratic party (Rivero, 2016).

Recently, the emergence of the BLACK LIVES MATTER Movement that has been the center of the resurgence of Black Civil rights activism. The movement has articulated that "Black humanity and dignity requires Black political will and power. In response to the sustained and increasingly visible violence against Black communities in the United States and Globally, a col-lective of more than 50 organizations representing thousands of black people across the country have come together with renewed energy and purpose …"-#-BLM-an affirmation and embrace of the resistance and resilience of Black people Challenges (Platform, 2018).

There a number of challenges that affect all immigrants, but there are three main challenges that I would like to highlight as being important when discussing the lives of Black immigrants and their navigation through life in the United States. These challenges include the need to create commu-nity and not be isolated with no support system, the pressure to succeed and obligations – these obligations include but are not limited to sending home money, the expectation of hosting relatives and friends in your home for extended periods of time or even possibly filing for family members to also come to America.

Being away from family and familiar places and things can cause severe stress and depression. Building a sense of community can often be easy in places where large groups from the same part of the world live. In the United States, places like New York, Florida, Washington D.C., and California have large Black immigration populations of African, Afro-Caribbean peoples; these groups often live in the same areas and establish their sense of commu-nity with people from the same regions or countries, in these areas foods and products are easily imported to support these large groups.

This is not the case for some Black immigrants who find themselves in areas isolated from so many of the people or things that they grew up around. Finding a sense of community is important for the mental and emotional development for most people. Places of worship, work, school, and organiza-tions can be good to find people who you build with. I arrived in Greensboro as a young, unmarried professor with no roots here, and now I am wife and mother with a growing family. I do not know what I would do without my church community and network, many of whom are African Americans; at any time, they have provided everything like childcare and counseling, and sometimes just a hug or a home-cooked meal has made the difference for me. Establishing roots and a healthy environment would have been lost to me if I harbored a "me versus them" attitude toward my African-American brothers and sisters. This experience for me has taken away from many of familiar things I grew up with and I often miss. Despite an immigration experience more blessed than stressed in many ways, I understand the struggle of obligation and a healthy maintenance of work-life I have now created for myself in the United States. As a Black immigrant woman in the United States I have always felt obligated whether it be to myself or my family to work and study harder than my peers which unfortunately can bring about anxiety and pressure.

Several circumstances have sparked rekindled immigration of Blacks from the Caribbean and Africa beginning in the 1970s. New laws opened legal channels for people wanting to immigrate to the United States. Cheaper and more frequent air travel reduced the physical and psychological distances. Better telephone and eventually email communications connected immigrants to their families back home, and sent news of job opportunities to potential immigrants (Kent, 2007).

Poor economic prospects, political instability, and violence in some areas were powerful "push" factors. The strong U.S. economy and the United States' long history as an immigrant country was among the factors attracting additional newcomers from these regions. Some analysts also point to a less welcoming atmosphere for Africans in Europe as encouraging potential immigrants to come to the United States (Kent, 2007). The pressure to succeed and send resources home can be a major source of obligation and stress for many immigrants. Remittances (sending money back to your home country) help bolster economies all over the world, but can lead to performance anxiety and health consequences (Ambugo & Yahirun, 2016). In their 2016 article, Ambugo and Yahirun assert that the obligation to send remittances back to one's family and community can actually be a source of depression, sadness, and economic hardship.

Second and Future Generation

There are a number of theories that discuss what factors differentiate first- and second-generation immigrant children from homogenous African-American children. Most of these theories underline the statistically higher success rates first- and second-generation immigrant Blacks have. Some argue that they have high academic standards because of a belief in the relationship between education and the American Dream of success, interpreted through the sacrifices by their families. Differently, there is the argument that African and Caribbean Blacks have a strong belief in their ability to succeed because they had first hand examples of Black professionals in their native lands. The impact of seeing everyday Black professionals such as dentists, nurses, and schoolteachers can be very powerful (Valentine, 2012) – whatever the reasons this success must be seen to be at the service of and strengthening of the Black community to which we now belong.

There are a number of examples of first- and second-generation immigrant children excelling and becoming successful at the service of the Black community in America. Former Attorney General Eric Holder's family emigrated from Barbados, before he became the first Black man to hold that position. Former Secretary of State Colin Powell's parents are from Jamaica. He too was the first Black man to serve in that position. Barbados native Rihanna Fenty is major player in global popular culture. The president of Howard University, one of the nation's most prestigious historically Black universities, is Trinidadian. President Obama's origin tale also fits into this similar storyline (Rivero, 2016). Differently, during the 2019 Super bowl weekend, popular rapper 21 Savage was picked up by the United States immigration and customs enforcement agents and detained, despite his distinctly Atlantean Socialization and persona, fans seemed put-off that the entertainer they so admired was in fact an American citizen (Samuel Getachaw, 2019). While these are examples of celebrated Black immigrants and some of their children, once again I think it becomes most important to acknowledge the diversity within each individual's experiences and identities to understand Black immigrant identity.

This growing diversity of the Black community is both a potential strength and a weakness for us. African-American and foreign-born Blacks must now navigate and master survival and success in a country and world where the differences between us are becoming less and less apparent and our similarities more and more important. Our families are integrating through marriage, children, and experiences. This integration is good and will accelerate in a world where communication is on steroids and a movie like Black Panther has caught the imagination of the entire global community in general, and the Black global community in particular. As I watch my son Zaire growing up, I understand that he will be faced with numerous obstacles as a Black man in the United States, but one of his greatest strengths and that of the Black community, to which he fully belongs, is his Global network of cousins, church members, and relatives, both African American and foreign born. While there will remain miscommunication and tension within the diversity of this emerging global Black community, we must celebrate the strengthening of the bonds of the Black community – no matter what route we have each taken to becoming a part of it.

Discussion Questions

1. Other than this idea of double consciousness what are some useful theoretical ways framing the transition of Black immigrants into American society in general, and the African-American community in particular?
2. What are the major barriers for Black immigrants transitioning into the United States?
3. How might these barriers be part of a Black immigrant's school and/or work experiences?
4. How can we facilitate Black Immigrants who reject their Black identity?
5. What are some of the positive experiences of this transition into America in general, and Black America in particular? Are there allies who are part of those experiences? If so, what role might they play?
6. What are some of the practical lessons that we can articulate on this transitioning that will help those going through it, and those yet to go through it, to make the road a little easier?
7. What role does education and/or choice of profession play in the Black immigrant's experiences?

References

Anderson, M. (2015). *A rising share of the U.S. black population is foreign born.* Washington, DC: Pew Research Center. Retrieved from http://www.pewsocialtrends. org/2015/04/09/a-rising-share-of-the-u-s-black-population-is-foreign-born/

Anderson, M., & Lopez, G. (2018). *Key facts about black immigrants in the U.S.* Washington DC: Pew Research Center. Retrieved from: http://www.pewresearch. org/fact-tank/2018/01/24/key-facts-about-black-immigrants-in-the-u-s/

Ambugo, E., & Yahirun, J. (2016). Remittances and risk of major depressive episode and sadness among new legal immigrants to the United States. *Demographic Research, 34,* 243–258. Retrieved from http://www.jstor.org.ncat.idm.oclc.org/stable/26332034

Dawsey. J. (2018). Trump derides protections for immigrants from "shithole" countries. Retrieved from https://www.washingtonpost.com/politics/ trump-attacks-protections-for-immigrants-from-shithole-countries-in-oval-office-meeting/2018/01/11/bfc0725c-f711-11e7-91af-31ac729add94_story.html?utm_term=.e0549beb2625

Goodwin-White, J. (2008). Placing progress: Contextual inequality and immigrant incorporation in the United States. *Economic Geography, 84*(3), 303–332. Retrieved from http://www.jstor.org.ncat.idm.oclc.org/stable/40377264

History.com Editors. (2009). Stokely Carmichael. Retrieved from https://www.history.com/topics/black-history/stokely-carmichael

Jackson, J., & Cothran, M. (2003). Black versus Black: The relationships among African, African American, and African Caribbean persons. *Journal of Black Studies, 33*(5), 576–604. Retrieved from http://www.jstor.org.ncat.idm.oclc.org/stable/3180977

Johnson, K. (2009). The intersection of race and class in U.S. Immigration Law and Enforcement. *Law and Contemporary Problems, 72*(4), 1–35. Retrieved from http://www.jstor.org.ncat.idm.oclc.org/stable/20779033

Joseph, P. E. (2014). *Stokely: A life*. New York, NY: Basic Civitas.

Kent, M. M. (2007). Immigration and America's black population. *Population Bulletin, 62*(4), 1–16.

Pittman, J. P. (2016). "Double consciousness", *The Stanford Encyclopedia of Philosophy*, Retrieved from https://plato.stanford.edu/archives/sum2016/entries/double-consciousness/

Platform. (2018). Retrieved from https://policy.m4bl.org

Raff, J. (2017). The double punishment for black undocumented immigrants. Retrieved from https://www.theatlantic.com/politics/archive/2017/12/the-double-punishment-for-blackimmigrants/549425/

Rivero, D. (2016). The Rihanna generation: How black immigrants are reshaping America. Retrieved from https://splinternews.com/the-rihanna-generation-how-black-immigrants-are-reshap-1793855054

Sanchez, R. (2018). Man fatally shot by police officer mourned from Texas to St. Lucia. Retrieved from https://www.cnn.com/2018/09/07/us/dallas-police-shooting-botham-shem-jean/index.html

Waters, M. (1994). Ethnic and racial identities of second-generation black immigrants in New York City. *The International Migration Review, 28*(4), 795–820. doi:10.2307/2547158

Valentine, C. (2012). Rethinking the achievement gap: Lessons from the African diaspora. Retrieved from https://www.washingtonpost.com/blogs/therootdc/post/rethinking-the-achievement-gap-lessons-from-the-african-diaspora/2012/09/04/eebc5214-f362-11e1-a612-3cfc842a6d89_blog.html?utm_term=.6753fb67ba5f

3 Black Voices from the Global Village

AMY E. PELISSERO, MARY LOU MCCLOSKEY,
AND TENI-OLA OGUNJOBI
Global Village Project

Introduction

In this chapter, we share the stories and reflections of three young women with refugee backgrounds, who were resettled in the Atlanta area and previously attended the Global Village Project (GVP) in the state of Georgia, United States. They share their experiences as refugees; as voyagers among cultures, places, languages, and religions; and as Black women newly arrived in the United States. They also share something about their educational histories and what has supported them toward success in seeking their dreams. Our intent is to use narrative interviews (1) to study the experiences and multiple challenges of these young women and (2) to learn what supports the resilience they have displayed, resilience that has kept them in school and prepared them for the lives they imagine for themselves. We believe that these stories show how educational and relational support help to maintain and develop these women's resilience.

GVP is a non-profit, free, special-purpose middle school for refugee girls with interrupted education. The mission of the school is to develop a strong educational foundation for each student within a caring community using a strengths-based approach, and the organizational vision is to ensure that refugee girls and young women with interrupted schooling have access to the education necessary to pursue their dreams. Every young woman has the potential not only to change her life and that of her family's, but also to that of her community and even the world. At GVP, she finds space to grow into an empowered, confident young woman and the support to make that happen. The school provides careful, scaffolded programming to meet the individual needs of students with interrupted education, a strength-based approach that takes advantage of the talents, knowledge, and skills students bring to the classroom, and close and safe relationships with caring adults who serve as cultural interpreters and a support system for these young women in reaching their educational goals. The current 45 students at GVP come from 1 of 12 African or Asian countries and collectively speak 15 languages—from French to Kinyarwanda and Kirundi to Arabic, Swahili, and Matu Chin. On average, students at GVP have missed three years of formal schooling, but some have never had access to school before.

Key elements of the program include intense English language development, small-group guided classes, weekly meetings with a counselor with expertise in addressing issues of trauma and transition, and thematically organized STEAM (science, technology, engineering, the arts, and mathematics)-based content. STEAM partners in the community offer weekly drama and music classes, individual instrumental instruction, and many opportunities to explore the arts and sciences in the community. Over 100 weekly volunteers assist with classes, music lessons, one-on-one tutoring, and in many other ways. The GVP mentor program, which has created over 200 student-adult partnerships, provides an educational mentor for every third year student at the school. Mentors support students at GVP, in high school, and beyond, helping students and families navigate the complex transitions into and through high school and into college and careers.

- 78 GVP alumna are in high school and 35 have graduated from high school.
- 20 are in college and the first 2 graduated in the spring of 2018.
- 93 alumnae and current students currently participate in the GVP Mentor Program and are supported by 65 mentors.
- 96% of students who were enrolled in the all-day academic program for at least two years and matched with a mentor have continued their formal education.

Over the 10 years of its existence, the student body at GVP has changed with the shifting patterns of resettlement from countries experiencing conflict and war. In recent years, displaced families fleeing Afghanistan, Burma, the Democratic Republic of the Congo, Central African Republic, Rwanda, Somalia, Syria, and many other countries have arrived in the Atlanta area with teenage daughters, who may have experienced serious interruptions to their education. The 3000 or so refugees who come to Atlanta each year represent a tiny percentage of the 70.8 million people who live as refugees or displaced people in the world today (UNHCR, 2020), more than half of whom are under 18.

Limited access to schooling perpetuates and magnifies the challenges of life in exile – finding work, staying healthy, holding on to dignity and hope. It also limits the potential of refugee women and girls to rebuild their lives, protect themselves against abuse and take a lead in shaping the lives of their communities. (UNHCR, 2019a)

GVP teachers and staff work to understand the cultures of origin of these students and to help them address the myriad challenges they face: being refugees; potentially having experienced extreme trauma and war; having many interruptions to their learning, beginning to learn, and learn in new languages; and being Black in a new culture that is not consistently welcoming. They experience multiple, diverse oppressions on overlapping local and global levels, what Grewal and Kaplan (1994) call "scattered hegemonies."

It is important to note that these students' stories are set in the American South. Historically, this part of the United States has been haunted by a legacy of ongoing racial tensions between Whites on the one hand, and on the other hand, the Blacks whose ancestors had been brought in as slaves. Additionally, the South remained largely isolated and unchanged in the past, so that between 1850 and 1970 it was home "to a smaller percentage of immigrants than any other region" of the country (Bankston, 2007, p. 24). Since the 1990s, however, the region has seen a steep increase in immigration, and the foreign-born population rose more than 200% in the state (Hooker, Fix, McHugh, & Migration Policy Institute, 2014). Winders (2007) concluded, "Southern locales have become strategic sites where borders and national security are enacted and performed with a growing tenacity" (p. 933). Such conclusions reinforce the need for better understandings of how social and political processes come to bear on the everyday lives of refugee women of color.

Refugees, who may already be multilingual, often arrive in English-speaking countries with little to no English (Capps, Newland, & Migration Policy Institute, 2015; Hatoss & Huijer, 2010) and limited educational and print literacy experiences (Bigelow, 2010; Capps et al., 2015; Martin, 2004; McBrien, 2005). McBrien (2005) found that refugee students with heavy accents were ridiculed in schools; students who used their native languages were punished; there was a demand for English-only instruction; and refugee students often did not understand or have past experiences with academic English. In addition, Piller and Takahashi (2010) concluded, "the linguistic factor has increasingly been acknowledged as one of the most crippling obstacles to the social inclusion of migrants" (p. 550). Language, at least to some extent, defines who and what we are and who and what we believe we might be. It is critical to explore the discourses that circulate and powerfully connect language, community, and citizenship and the ways in which gender, race, and being refugee intersect with these discourses.

In order to learn more about the experiences of Black refugee young women, the authors purposefully sought interviews with past students at GVP who had come as refugees from Africa. The guiding questions during interviews were created to elicit participant stories of resettlement as refugee women of color. The stories that Hamda, Abramie, and Leonie share can inform educators about what practices are effective with newcomers to the United States.

Hamda

Interviewed by Amy E. Pelissero

Hamda (pseudonym) drove to school to meet with me on our first day back from winter break. Classes at the local college had not yet started, so she had some time for a talk. As we greeted one another, she commented on how much she had needed the break and the rest before going back to finish up her final semester of school. She wore hijab, a long skirt and a Girl Power sweatshirt. I immediately noticed her posh oversized purple glasses. She was smiling and excited to see the old school looking so new and different after the renovations. She wanted a full tour before we started the interview.

Hamda's Journey

Hamda was among the 30 students in the Global Village Project (GVP)'s very first class when it opened nearly ten years ago. She came to the school soon after her aunt discovered its existence. As a refugee resettlement caseworker born in Somalia, her aunt understood the value of a small school devoted to serving refugee young women like Hamda who were newcomers to the country with limited English and limited or no formal schooling. She was quick to visit, withdrew Hamda from public school, and enrolled her in this new independent school. During our interview, Hamda noted, "I couldn't even write my own name when I first started school."

Hamda was not eager to share the story of her journey to the United Sates. She was the only child from among her many siblings to come here. Her aunt brought and raised her alone, and Hamda's contact with her parents, brothers, and sisters has been maintained mostly online and through the Internet. Like many refugee women, Hamda's everyday life is transnational. She lives across space and time through her family, social media, and online experiences. Hamda explained that it was difficult coming here and credits her aunt for keeping her going through the tough times.

Hamda's Layered Challenges

While Hamda and I talked about the strides she had made since coming to the United States and the successes she has had—graduating high school, earning multiple scholarships, and internships, and managing to make it into and through college, the multiple "scattered hegemonies" she faced came more clearly into view (Grewal & Kaplan, 1994). Hamda explained that as a Black, Muslim, refugee women and a non-native English speaker, she experienced ongoing challenges and doubts here in her new home, and even fears. When I asked Hamda about her feelings as a person of color living in the United States, she was quick to say, "It is very scary here." She had not noticed or paid attention to her skin color before because everyone in Somalia looked like her, but here she said, "People hate you just because you have more color on your skin." She went on to say, "What I'm most scared of is walking on the street and being harassed or being pulled over. It is very scary what you see on the news. I think if somebody will harass me on the train on the way to school."

Hamda also expressed worry about her accent and the way that her language might influence what people think about her. She said, "Whenever I'm talking to someone, I wonder what do they think about you? Is your accent too strong?" Language and accent act as immediate markers of difference and often are used to signify "otherness." Language shapes actual and imagined communities (Anderson, 2006), and language use is often an indicator of membership, integration, and inclusion. Language difference, on the other hand, is often equated with ignorance, signaling that the user is an outsider and does not belong. As Lippi-Green (2012) noted, "It is crucial to remember that it is not all foreign accents, but only accent linked to skin that isn't White, or which signals a third-world homeland, which evokes such negative reactions" (p. 253).

Hamda noted that like her language and black skin wearing "hijab adds another barrier." She explained that as a Muslim choosing to wear hijab, she feels people often view her as "negative" and as someone who makes them "uncomfortable." She said that she worries about "how Muslims are portrayed in the media. People are watching all of this bad media. It keeps you on guard."

Women of color, like Hamda, who resettle as refugees in this region of the United States face distinct challenges, in that the powerful racial, cultural, and linguistic norms that dominated for so long also served to keep traditional and often discriminatory roles and views in place. Recent and rapid changes in the South, including rising numbers of refugees, have had complex consequences. As Hamda described her experiences here, she recalled both the difficulties and doubts she constantly fought against as well as her sense of accomplishment at overcoming them. She talked about the way that some people made her feel here in her new home. She said, "As soon as they get under your skin, and make you feel like less of a person, it can destroy your soul." It was clear that Hamda already experienced opposition and had to contend with multiple and overlapping forces of oppression in her young life. However, she refused to accept the limitations placed on her and persisted. Three times during our interview she repeated a similar refrain, "I keep going. Keep trying. Stay positive and don't give up."

Hamda's Resilience

Hamda came to this country as an 11-year-old girl from Somalia. She endured the loss of her country, most of her family, and much more. She came with no previous formal schooling and "had to start from the basics like a little kid going to Pre-K, learn my ABC's and go from there." Today, Hamda is bilingual, manages a part-time job, internship, college classes, transnational family relationships, and so much more. She is a transnational woman, living across cultures, spaces, and communities. She embraces and embodies aspects of her homes here and there and lives beyond the boundaries and borders, those around her often seek to create and strengthen. Hamda epitomizes the hope of what is possible when we reach across and beyond the borders. She said, "I look back at where I started, and I see how far I have come. I smile. There is room to grow, but I have come so far." When asked about the challenges ahead, Hamda told me, "I'm scared of going into the work environment, but I think I have overcome so many challenges. This will just be another hurdle and once I get in, I'll adapt. I know it will be challenging, but I think I can do it."

Hamda is among the 1% of refugees around the world who gain access to tertiary education (UNHCR, 2020). She is a Somali Muslim woman in a country where Executive Orders explicitly seeking to stop immigration and refugee resettlement from Somalia have been issued and where the movement of Muslims broadly into the country is strongly contested. Despite the multiple layers of oppression and bias Hamda faced and still contends with, she continues to pursue her dreams. She will graduate from college in May and plans to work in the growing Health Informatics field. When I asked about any advice she would share with other women of color who face similar situations, she said, "I would tell them to do what my Auntie said. To keep trying and also to be tough. A lot of things will happen and it might not get easier, but you can get better at dealing with these things. I would tell them to keep going and not give up."

By sharing her story, Hamda makes visible her practices of resistance and agency. Resistance and agency exist in the everyday practices of remembering and storytelling where openings and opportunities to imagine exist. As a newcomer and with her aunt's support and encouragement, Hamda has imagined a future for herself in which she is educated, competent, capable, and engaged in meaningful work. She has resisted attempts to "make [her] feel like less of a person" because of the color of her skin, religious beliefs, or language.

Abranie

Interviewed by Mary Lou McCloskey

Abranie (pseudonym) is a strong, bright, imaginative young woman, now a junior in high school. She loves to sing, dance, and play soccer. She intends to finish high school next year and hopes to go on to study nursing. Her life and her educational path have not been easy, however. She has experienced multiple changes and challenges in her life – including moving among many cultures, living in multiple countries where she didn't speak the language, experiencing the effects of war and family separation, attending numerous schools with many interruptions to her education, facing the relentless challenges of hunger and poverty, and experiencing a new culture in which being Black is not just something normal and beautiful, but something she is made conscious of.

Abranie's Refugee Story

Abranie's parents come from different areas of the Democratic Republic of the Congo (DRC) – "the big Congo," as she calls it. Her mother and father belong to very different cultures and speak different mother tongues, but communicate in Swahili, which is Abranie's first language. Because of war in the DRC (Reyntjens, 2009), they left the country for Malawi, and then to Tanzania, where Abranie's older sister was born. But the war continued to interfere, and first the father and then the mother left for Mozambique, where Abranie was born. They lived first in the town of Lichinga, and later relocated to Maratani Refugee Camp in Mozambique. Life there was challenging.

In the rainy season, our tent would get full of water and fall down. We didn't get to eat every day. We grew our own food, so there was plenty to eat in the rainy season, but in the dry season we had no food. Sometimes trucks came with food, sometimes not.

Abranie's worst memory is hunger was of mothers who didn't have enough food for themselves and couldn't feed their infants. "As a young child," she said, "it's hard to experience that."

By 2010, Abranie's family had begun the intricate process of relocating to the United States as refugees, which involved much paperwork and several trips to Maputo, the capital of Mozambique. Even after they were approved, they had to postpone the trip after the birth of their third child, and the five of them finally left the United States in August, 2012. It was an endless trip – from Maputo to Pretoria, South Africa, to Miami, and finally Atlanta, and Abranie was unable to eat the whole time. On August 8, they finally arrived Atlanta, and were warmly met by their refugee agency caseworker, who brought them to their new apartment in the middle of the night.

All the way, Abranie had been imagining the wonders of America. Based on the movies she'd seen, she expected a new car in the driveway, a swimming pool in the backyard, and a big TV. The night she arrived, everything seemed so beautiful. But when she woke up in the morning, the reality of her apartment complex was not what she had dreamed of. The family was grateful for the help they received from their caseworker – the food in the fridge (though it was strange), help with the utilities, the furnished apartment, help finding jobs, signing up for Medicaid and Supplemental Nutrition Assistance Program (SNAP, formerly Food Stamps), some initial instruction in English, and registering for school. After a few short weeks, however, they didn't see their caseworker much anymore and they were basically on their own. Refugees in Georgia are provided a loan for their airfare to the United States (which they must repay), and support for the first three months (International Rescue Committee, 2019). After that they are expected to be self-sufficient. Her sister and mother figured out how to manage the bills and communicate with the rental agency, etc. and now they're teaching Abranie. Her next challenges are to take the test for her driver's permit and to apply for citizenship.

Now that they are in the United States, no one is hungry, but Abranie's parents must work very hard to provide for the family, standing for 8 hours a day in a very cold factory, processing seafood. Her mother works days, from about 7 am till 5 pm. "I feel sorry for them," says Abramie. Her father works nights, taking care of the two newest members of the family, ages one and three during the day. Abranie is responsible for the childcare from the time she gets home until her mother arrives.

The family has grown in the United States. When they arrived, they were five, but four more children have been born, and the family now numbers nine. They had a scare that they would be homeless in 2018, when the manager of their rent-controlled apartment told them that they could not have a family of nine remain in a 3-bedroom apartment because of a Housing and Urban Development (HUD) requirement, and threatened not to renew the family's lease. Eventually, they were allowed to stay, but to prepare for the future, they are now in the difficult process of saving the down payment and finding a lender so they can purchase their own home, with room for all and no restrictions on how many live there. It is difficult to learn how to accomplish this when everyone is working so hard and parents are limited in English. Abranie reports that the family has not yet developed strong connections in the Congolese community in their city that might help them with such challenges.

Abranie's Educational Story

Abranie went to elementary school for a while in Mozambique, first to a French language school. Then, suddenly, because of a government mandate, the language changed to Portuguese (Varela Canhanga & Banda, 2017). She never felt that Portuguese became her language, and it made everyday life and school difficult. When they ended up in the refugee camp, the family had no money at all for books or uniforms and the children could not go to school. Abranie remembers a Swahili-speaking volunteer at the camp who used to sit with the children under a tree and tell stories, and that's how they learned what they could. In the United States, at 12, she was placed in a middle school in the seventh grade. Because she had so little foundation, and almost no English, she felt like she was in Pre-K and she had to learn everything over again. In Mozambique, she had considered herself a good student, but in the U.S. school was very difficult. Even math had changed – when she came, she thought she could add and divide, but the way they did it in U.S. classrooms was so strange that she couldn't do it anymore. She was angry and frustrated. After a year and a half in middle school, Abranie still struggled with reading and she knew she wasn't going to be ready for high school. When a friend told her about the Global Village Project, she thought it sounded like the place for her. Abranie believes that she never would have made it in high school without the Global Village Project, which she attended for two years. Learning was not easy, but with small classes and an individualized reading program, she did learn to read, and she began to understand math. She received much support from patient teachers, kind volunteer tutors who gave her individual help, and the mentor who has supported her in so many ways in high school. Getting along was not always easy, though. Her anger and frustration did not end immediately and she sometimes vented her feelings through conflicts with other students and teachers. With patient help and support, Abranie feels that now she has learned to better manage her emotions.

In the second term of her sophomore year, Abranie's mentor helped her get a scholarship and transportation to attend a Montessori high school. Everyone was kind to her at the new school, and Abranie had a good experience there, though she hated the long commute. But she never felt like, as a Black student and an African, she really belonged.

> When I went to Montessori, everywhere I walked it was just bright. They were nice, but I didn't feel comfortable. There was one Black girl, but she'd been at Montessori forever and she was more like the white kids than like me.

After one semester at the Montessori school, Abranie's transportation was no longer available, so she transferred back to the public high school in her area. She has been successful there, though she struggles sometimes with math and physics, and with courses that require a lot of dense reading. She's even added her fifth language, Spanish. "I was surprised that my school counselor expected me to learn another language, when I was still learning English, but now I'm doing just fine in Spanish, my Portuguese that I learned in Mozambique helped me."

Abranie's experiences are invaluable in informing teachers of refugee learners from Africa and around the world of the multilayered challenges these students face, and the need to acknowledge, account for, and teach in consideration of the refugee experience, which is likely to include displacement, trauma, dealing with new languages, educational absence or interruption, family separations, and cultural alienation, multiplied by the challenges of poverty and living in a culture where racial prejudice and discrimination continue. Abranie also illustrates the amazing resilience that these students demonstrate in the face of all their challenges, and demonstrates how their resilience, met with thoughtful, careful programming designed with their needs in mind, and the support of caring adults who can serve as cultural and educational interpreters, can lead to learners' success in achieving their dreams.

Leonie

Interviewed by Teni-Ola Ogunjobi

Leonie (pseudonym) and her family fled her home country, the Central African Republic (CAR) to Chad as refugees in 2012. They left Chad after a few months and Leonie, age nine, arrived in the United States in 2012 with her mother, father, three sisters, and one brother. After only a few months in the country, Leonie's mother died unexpectedly. As a result, over the past seven years Leonie has been separated from her siblings on and off and she has moved around several times living between homes with her father, sisters, or a family friend. Her refugee journey and circumstances compelled Leonie to become independent at a young age. This was very difficult in the beginning because she was so young when her mother died, and because disconnecting from her siblings was isolating. Over time, she got used to the lifestyle and it became her new normal. She explains:

> Something I learned is to trust the journey and always keep going. It will be a day where everything will be normal. I feel like I'm still with them (my mom and sisters) and things are normal.

Leonie's Educational Journey

In parallel with her journey as a refugee and her integration into America, Leonie also started her educational journey to learn English and a new culture. She went to public school for a year and then she attended the Global Village Project (GVP) from 2014 until 2017. Like many GVP students and English Language Learners, Leonie tested into the school with both low English proficiency and lower academic levels than her age mates due to gaps in her education. She started learning English in the public primary school and at the International Center (a county program for newcomers), but it was not until after about one year and half at GVP that she really felt she got the grasp of English. The way GVP teachers introduced concepts and taught subjects with English Language Learners in mind helped her learn at an increased pace. She was also provided extensive one-on-one and small-group support from tutors that guided Leonie's learning experience. In her final year at GVP, she was paired with a mentor through the school's mentor program. This mentor has served as an academic and social support for her as she transitioned into and throughout high school.

Learning Language and Culture

Leonie speaks four languages: Arabic, Sango, French, and English. Learning English was easier. She feels so because she is multilingual person, and she started learning English around the age of ten. Leonie practiced her English skills by consistently speaking English at school and at home with friends. She also learned a lot about American culture at GVP. The teachers would observe the students' behavior and explain the differences from their home cultures and U.S. culture. During her past seven years in the United States, Leonie has developed an advanced knowledge of American culture and the multiple cultures of her diverse community. She learns from other cultures within the larger refugee and immigrant communities surrounding her in her highly ethnically diverse hometown. She explores the different cultures by being immersed in them: going to social events, learning various dances, eating traditional food, and listening to international music. Leonie considers herself special as a multilingual person, because the more languages she speaks and cultures she experiences, the more she knows and understands.

Leonie identifies with youth refugees and other African immigrants because they share experiences with displacement from their homelands, integration into a foreign culture, and learning a new language. When she initially experienced U.S. culture, the focus was on the comparison and contrast of her culture and U.S. culture. In the United States, she had extended boundaries as a youth and fewer limitations as a woman than she experienced in her Central African culture. For example, in her culture, looking someone in the eyes, especially a child looking at an adult in the eyes, is disrespectful. But in America, it can be considered disrespectful when you do *not* look into someone's eyes when communicating.

Leonie's family religion is Islam and as Muslims, there were certain interactions that she came to know as inappropriate for women and men in her Islamic tradition, such as women and men shaking hands with one another. However, Leonie noticed men and women shaking hands regularly in America and came to understand that it was normal in her new culture. In America, she would see women working in career fields that were not common or permitted for women in her culture and women having the right to go wherever they wanted to go without limits. While Leonie has been able to take-in these new-found freedoms and positive aspects in U.S. culture, she understands that having so many choices in the United States can have negative outcomes for some people. She has tried to choose wisely and this wisdom has worked for her so far.

Leonie's Experiences as a Woman of Color

Leonie is very aware of her experience as a young Black teen girl growing up in America. She knows that she has been treated differently and unfairly both because she was an African and because she was Black in America. She has been grouped into stereotypes about Black Americans and Africans by some White American youth and by fellow refugee/immigrant youth. Leonie states:

Most of the time people judge you because you don't have the same skin color as them. My first time coming to the United States at the International Center, there were only Spanish, Asian, and mostly white people. It was not a lot of Black people so it was hard to get used to it there. Some Mexicans laughed at you because your skin is more darker. It was hard to stay there, but we had to get used to being treated different … Some of the Asians were feeling like they were in a more higher level than the Africans because they feel like their countries' not in Africa. A lot of people think Africa is 'ratchet' [meaning ghetto, poor, uncivilized in this context], but it's not all like that.

As a teenager Leonie admits that she does not know everything there is to know about the racial and gender inequality she hears about in the media and that racism is not always detected in her day-to-day life. She views the discriminatory treatment she has seen and received from her multicultural/immigrant peers as irrelevant, because she believes that, in the end, we are all the same. She believes that others had to suffer and we all have to suffer. She does not take these kinds of comments or tactics seriously. She takes the energy from the negativity and lets it fuel her. The same goes for the adversity that Leonie has experienced. Her challenges made her the person she is now. Her challenges are fewer because she's pushed through a lot and she made it through to the other side of it. She is now self-motivated and has lifted her spirits with practices and her own words of inspiration when facing discrimination and hardships.

I prove them wrong by doing better than them. No matter what situation you're in, if you can get through one situation, you can get through the next situation. Believe in yourself. Nobody is you.

Leonie has been able to carry onward and upward as an independent, determined, and strong young woman. She still faces challenges within her ever-changing living situation and family dynamics. She struggles to balance the cultural and religious expectations placed on her as a Central African Muslim girl and the reality of life for a Black refugee/immigrant teenage girl in America and her school coursework and a part-time job. Leonie is currently a sophomore in high school and she hopes to be a lawyer one day. She is just getting started, but because she now has a solid foundation and community of supporters, she has the best chance of finding success in the world. She has the right state of mind and the willpower to fulfill her dreams. In her words, "You got to work for it … you want it, you got to work for it!"

Discussion

As we have seen from their stories, the challenges faced by young woman refugees are many, layered, and intersecting. They are women, often coming from cultures where women have less agency outside the home than in the United States. They are women of color, in these instances, in a setting in the southern United States with a long legacy of racial oppression and discrimination. They are women with interrupted education, because of war or because of traditional cultural views about the value of educating women. Some of them are Muslim in a country where negative assumptions have been made about them solely because of their religion or their choice to wear hijab. And, they are just beginning to learn English, the language of power in this culture. Yet these women have persevered and are in the process of completing the education that will provide them with choices for the future. The following discussion focuses on 1) the nature of these challenges, and how they might actually play a part toward developing the strength these students have and 2) the evidence these stories provide about what makes a difference in their education to help them developing the resilience they needed to persevere against all odds.

Challenges

All of these young women described challenges they experienced in displacement and resettlement. They struggled to catch up in education because of the many interruptions to their schooling: Hamda described starting school unable to even write her name; Abranie told about how division made no sense to her in the new language in the new school. They had to learn in a new language that they found difficult: though they all arrived multilingual, they have struggled with learning English and with self-consciousness when speaking with a different accent. They had to learn how to function in a new culture, to survive and have a roof over their heads, to face discrimination because they were Muslim or wore a hijab. All of these young women reported the new awareness of their race in the United States. In their home countries, they didn't see themselves as different; in the United States their lives became racialized: they were perceived as women of color; they met people who seemed to hate them just because of their skin color; they found themselves in settings where no one looked like them and they felt no one understood them.

Some scholars view intersectionality as the multiple forms of oppression, or intersecting systems of power that create layers of inequity in the lives of refugee women (Pittaway & Bartolomei, 2001). Although it is important to uncover the scattered hegemonies that refugee women experience, Fong (2004) differently draws upon conceptions of intersectionality in order to understand the complexity of multiple social group memberships and identities that are interconnected in everyday lives. Fong (2004) views intersectionality as part of an ecological perspective that does not necessarily limit agency or possibilities but rather can support additive approaches such as biculturization or multiculturization. In fact, Fong (2004) views intersectionality as key to seeing the resources and strengths refugees possess as well as the challenges they face. The intersections of oppression in the lives of refugee women are important to explore, yet as Fong (2004) suggests and as one can see in the 3 stories here, these intersections may also reveal resiliency, resources, strengths, and spaces for resistance and agency (p. 311). Fong (2004) contends that perspectives of intersectionality are important to culturally competent, strengths-based practices.

For refugee women of color, who are too often excluded from research and referred to as illiterate and uneducated (see Minh-ha, 2010; Piller & Takahashi, 2010; Pittaway & Bartolomei, 2001; Sarr & Mosselson, 2010; Semlak, Pearson, Amundson, & Kudak, 2008), the sharing and spreading of their success stories is desperately needed. Reframing refugee women as transnationals—capable of crossing and breaking down borders and holding multiple ways of knowing, being, and doing in tension – -in our research and stories may create more space for resistance and reimagining conceptions of race, identity, and citizenship.

Resilience

In these interviews and stories, Hamda, Abraine, and Leonie shared the resilience and efficacy they have developed, perhaps in the process of meeting their challenges.

> I was surprised that my school counselor expected me to learn another language, when I was still learning English, but I'm doing just fine in Spanish, my Portuguese that I learned in Mozambique helped me. (Abranie)
>> I know I will be challenged but I think I can do it. (Hamda)
>> I prove them wrong by doing better than them. (Leonie)

Each of these women told about important adults who supported and inspired them: teachers (all), an aunt (Hamda), or mentors (Abranie and Leonie). Those relationships appear central to the development of resilience. Focusing on the resilience evidenced in these stories can provide routes for educators to change their beliefs about students like these. Truebridge (2014) sees resilience as, "the dynamic and negotiated process within individuals (internal) and between individuals and their environments (external) for the resources and supports to adapt and define themselves as healthy amid adversity, threat, trauma, and/or everyday stress" (p. xvii.). Or, put more simply, resilience is "the ability to spring back from adversity"; and is "a process, not a trait" (p. 13). Truebridge (2014, 2016) further suggests that education is also about "problem solving, perseverance, empathy, flexibility, creativity, confidence, decision-making, self-awareness, relationships, collaboration, and navigating to mine resources" (p. xvii).

Teachers' beliefs and expectations can preclude or encourage student success. Often, school is perceived as "a place that perpetuates stress" (Truebridge, 2014, p. 39). Instead, schools must help teachers and students develop a conceptual framework of resilience that includes a more inclusive definitions of success in school and of wellness, ones that are not solely based on grades or standardized tests. Teachers must not see students like Hamda, Abraine, and Leonie as deficient. Instead, an additive and intersectional perspective will allow teachers to see them as successful students, who have developed a passion for learning and as creative, innovative, and persistent problem solvers and thinkers: "individuals who are whole—academically, socially, physically, emotionally, and spiritually" (p. 33). Educators must find ways to model positive relationships and interactions in schools and find ways to scaffold learning so that students' experiences of success will lead to more success. Schools must provide students with platforms to tell their stories and use what they know as a resource to transform themselves toward resilience.

Conclusion

Resilience and relationships emerge as significant factors in the success of the young women profiled in this chapter. They are successfully overcoming obstacles and challenges, achieving their educational dreams, and navigating a very complex process of integration and acculturation. Each one shares a story that stretches across cultures and national borders and reveals the resources, relationships, and resilience they have developed through adversity. The scattered hegemonies they experience have proved to empower these young women.

Unfortunately, in schools and in society refugees and women of color often are portrayed as deficient and incapable. Approaches to education are too often subtractive and come from a deficit perspective. Instead, these stories show the strength and resources these young women possess and use to position themselves as capable, strong, and transnational women. Relationships emerge as key to this. Supportive, caring teachers who believed in students' capabilities were essential: Allen, Kern, Vella-Brodrick, Hattie, and Waters (2018) found teacher support to be one of the strongest predictors of students' sense of belonging and connectedness in school. Adults who cared and supported students inside and outside of school and who helped them navigate the complexities of learning to operate in a new culture also were essential: Suárez-Orozco et al. (2009a, 2009b) argue that strong relationships are the highest predictor of engagement and achievement among immigrant youth.

We have shared the voices and the stories of three young women with refugee backgrounds who have multilayered experiences as refugees, as women of color, as students with interrupted education, as newcomers to a very different culture, as women who have lost everything and are regaining their place in a new country. Their stories show them as emerging resilient and en route to success in achieving their educational and vocational goals. We believe that these stories show how school connectedness – the belief by students that adults and peers in the school care about their learning as well as about them as individuals and relational support – caring adults who provide emotional, educational support and help in learning to manage their lives and learning in a new culture – are keys to the resilience that leads these young women toward self-confidence and the kind of educational success Truebridge (2014) describes that goes beyond grades and scores.

Discussion Questions

1. What is revealed in the stories of these girls about how their education has supported them in becoming resilient?
2. What are the meanings of "intersectionality," and "scattered hegemonies"? How do these experiences factor in the lives of these girls? How do they incorporate the experiences of being Black in the United States?
3. How have mentors made a difference in helping these learners navigate a new language and a new multidimensional culture?
4. Based on what you learned from their profiles, how are these young women different from one another?
5. What are your recommendations for a quality program to develop the resilience of students with interrupted education?

References

Allen, K., Kern, M. L., Vella-Brodrick, D., Hattie, J., & Waters, L. (2018). What schools need to know about fostering school belonging: A meta-analysis. *Education Psychology Review, 30*(1), 1–34. http://eric.ed.gov/?id=EJ1170234

Anderson, B. (2006). *Imagined communities: Reflections on the origin and spread of nationalism* (Rev. ed.). New York, NY: Verso.

Bankston, C. L. (2007). New people in the New South: An overview of Southern immigration. *Southern Cultures, 13*(4), 24–44.

Bigelow, M. (2010). *Mogadishu on the Mississippi: Language, racialized identity, and education in a new land.* Chichester, West Sussex, UK: Wiley-Blackwell.

Capps, R., Newland, K., & Migration Policy Institute. (2015). *The integration outcomes of U.S. refugees: Successes and challenges.* Washington, DC: Migration Policy Institute. Retrieved from: https://www.migrationpolicy.org/research/integration-outcomes-us-refugees-successes-and-challenges

Fong, R. (Ed.). (2004). *Culturally competent practice with immigrant and refugee children and families.* New York, NY: Guilford Press.

Grewal, I., & Kaplan, C. (1994). Introduction: Transnational feminist practices and questions of postmodernity. In I. Grewal & C. Kaplan (Eds.), *Scattered hegemonies: Postmodernity and transnational feminist practices* (pp. 1–33). Minneapolis, MN: University of Minnesota Press.

Hatoss, A., & Huijser, H. (2010). Gendered barriers to educational opportunities: Resettlement of Sudanese refugees in Australia. *Gender and Education, 22*(2), 147–160.

Hooker, S., Fix, M., McHugh, M., & Migration Policy Institute (2014). *Education reform in a changing Georgia: Promoting high school and college success for immigrant youth.* 333 Retrieved from http://www.migrationpolicy.org/research/education-reform-changinggeorgia-promoting-high-school-and-college-success-immigrant-youth

International Rescue Committee Atlanta. (2019). *How does the IRC help refugees in Atlanta?* Retrieved from https://www.rescue.org/united-states/atlanta-ga#how-does-the-irc-help-refugees-in-atlanta

Lippi-Green, R. (2012). *English with an accent language, ideology and discrimination in the United States* (2nd ed.). London, UK: Routledge.

Martin, S. F. (2004). *Refugee women.* Lanham, MD: Lexington Books.

McBrien, J. L. (2005). Educational needs and barriers for refugee students in the United States: A review of the literature. *Review of Educational Research, 75*(3), 329–364.

Minh-ha, T. T. (2010). *Elsewhere, within here: Immigration, refugeeism and the boundary event.* New York, NY: Routledge.

Piller, I., & Takahashi, K. (2010). At the intersection of gender, language, and transnationalism. In N. Coupland (Ed.), *The handbook of language and globalization* (pp. 540–554). Malden, MA: Blackwell.

Pittaway, E., & Bartolomei, L. (2001) Refugees, race, and gender: The multiple discriminationagainst refugee women. *Refuge, 19*(6), 21–32.

Reyntjens. F. (2009). *The Great African War: Congo and regional geopolitics, 1996–2006.* Cambridge, UK: Cambridge University Press. Retrieved from: https://www.sahistory.org.za/sites/default/files/file%20uploads%20/filip_reyntjens_the_great_african_war._congo_andbook4you.org_.pdf

Sarr, K. G., & Mosselson, J. (2010). Issues in teaching refugees in U.S. schools. *Yearbook of the National Society for the Study of Education, 109*(2), 548–570

Semlak, J. L., Pearson, J. C., Amundson, N. G., & Kudak, A. H. (2008). Navigating dialectic contradictions experienced by female African refugees during cross-cultural adaptation. *Journal of Intercultural Communication Research, 37*(1), 43–64.

Suárez-Orozco, C., Pimentel, A., & Martin, M. (2009a). The significance of relationships: Academic engagement and achievement among newcomer immigrant youth. *Teachers College Record, 111*(3), 712–749.

Suárez-Orozco, C., Rhodes, J., & Milburn, M. (2009b). Unraveling the immigrant paradox: Academic engagement and disengagement among recently arrived immigrant youth. *Youth and Society, 41*(2), 151–185.

Truebridge, S. (2014). *Resilience begins with beliefs: Building on student strengths for success in school.* New York, NY: Teachers College Press.

Truebridge, S. (2016). Resilience: It begins with beliefs, *Kappa Delta Pi Record, 52*(1), 22–27.

United Nations High Council for Refugees. (2019a). *Her Turn: It's time to make refugee girls' education a priority.* Retrieved from https://www.unhcr.org/herturn/

United Nations High Council for Refugees. (2019b). *UNHCR figures at a glance.* Retrieved from https://www.unhcr.org/figures-at-a-glance.html

Varela Canhanga, M., & Banda, M. (2017). Education language policy in Mozambique: A critical view. *International Journal of Humanities Social Sciences and Education (IJHSSE), 4*(5), 12–21. Retrieved from https://www.arcjournals.org/pdfs/ijhsse/v4-i5/2.pdf

Winders, J. (2007). Belonging in the contemporary US South. *Antipode, 39*(5), 789–955.

4 "No one wanted to play with me": Somali-American Students' Memories of Racism in Elementary School

NIMO ABDI AND BIC NGO
University of Minnesota

Introduction

Threats to racial and religious minorities have long been a history of the United States. At the time of this writing, racial prejudice and discrimination are rising across the nation, with immigrant communities facing virulent racist nativism. In Kansas, three militia members were convicted of domestic terrorism by a federal jury for plotting to bomb an apartment complex home to Somali refugees (Smith, 2018). Against the backdrop of the 2016 anti-immigrant discourses of Donald Trump's presidential campaign, the militia members also targeted government officials, news media, and landlords who leased to refugees and immigrants with a nativist manifesto that warned, "If you have anything to do with the sellout of this country your homes, your businesses, your families are at risk" (Smith, 2018, para. 3). In Minnesota, home to the largest population of Somali immigrants in the United States, community members responded to plans of Somali Americans to build a mosque with xenophobic emails such as, "Islam is a direct threat to our national security. They MUST be stopped" (Du, 2016, para. 25). Another email contended, "If the Somalis can't accept our clothing style, our laws, our religion, then get out of Dodge" (Du, 2016, para. 26). More recently, the owner of Scream Town, a popular Minneapolis-St. Paul area Halloween attraction, enacted anti-Somali racism with a policy targeting Somali-Americans: "Note that we are having a zero-tolerance policy with Somalis. (Other guests, you can make your best judgment call.) But absolutely zero tolerance with Somalis" (Zamora, 2018, para. 2).

These events illustrate the ongoing, urgent need to examine the experiences of Black, Muslim, immigrant students, and the intersection of race, religion, and immigrant status. The research literature on Somali immigrants' education in the United States and Canada has shed important light on the impact of racism and Islamophobia in the educational experiences of Somali-American, and Somali-Canadian young people. Some research highlights the ways in which Somali children navigate and negotiate multiple and intersecting identities such as race (Forman, 2001; Ibrahim, 1999, 2004), religion (Collet, 2007; Zine, 2000, 2006), language learner (Ibrahim, 1999), and immigrant status (Roy & Roxas, 2011). Research conducted in pre-9/11, often highlighted the challenges Somali students faced as they navigated North American social and racial relations (Forman, 2001; Ibrahim, 1999). In the aftermath of 9/11, research about Somali students brought attention to the importance of considering the intersection of race, religion, and immigration status, particularly as Islamophobia became more prevalent (Bigelow, 2010; Collet, 2007; Jaffe-Walter, 2016, 2017). The multiple identities of Somali-origin young people as Black, Muslim, and immigrant puts them in a unique position as they grapple with marginalization (Forman, 2001; Ibrahim, 1999, 2014; Roy & Roxas, 2011), racialization, and violence (Bigelow, 2010; Zine, 2006).

While research has contributed to our understanding of Somali immigrant students' experiences with racism and racialization, the focus has been on the experiences of older students (e.g., middle school, high school). There is a need for research that explores the elementary experiences of Black immigrant children shaped at the intersection of race and religion. This chapter draws on data from a phenomenological study with Somali-American high school students to explore the elementary school racial experiences of one female and one male Somali-American student. It illustrates the gendered dimensions of their racialized experiences, the role of teachers in moments of inclusion and exclusion, and the role of language-use in their meaning making. The chapter contributes to the dearth of research on Somali-American children's experiences with race in school and the role of memory work in the development of Somali-American children's identity.

Theoretical Framework

In this study, we draw on interpretive phenomenology both as a conceptual framework and as a methodology. Interpretive phenomenology is mainly concerned with how humans perceive and interpret the social world within which they inhabit. One of the main characteristics of interpretive phenomenology, as developed by Heidegger (1998), is that human understanding moves away from epistemology (of Husserlian phenomenology) to ontology. This emphasis on being in the world is prioritized over that of knowing the world. Being in the world has implications for the body in relation to time and space (Merleau-Ponty, 1995, 2012). Both Heidegger (1998) and Merleau-Ponty (1995, 2012) understood time and space to be something that the body is always in living relationship with and not a succession of stream of events passing by at the moment (see also Dahlberg, Drew, & Nystrom, 2001). This leads us to our conception of memory as embodied and as negotiated. The embodied nature of memory highlights that "the body is the medium of our temporal and spatial communications and therefore significant in the function of memory" (Dahlberg, Drew, & Nystrom, 2001, p. 52). Memory can be conceptualized as an attempt to engage with time (or past events) based on current significance (Merleau-Ponty, 1995, 2012).

In this chapter, we rely on Merleau-Ponty's (2012) conception of memory as embodied as well as a space for epistemological ambiguity that is contrary to common belief in which memory is conserved and can be recalled by the subject's choice. Instead, if we consider the realm of memory to be neither constructive, nor conserved but rather an intersection of "remembrance and oblivion" (Merleau-Ponty cited in Krell, 1982), then we can utilize memory to better understand the possibilities for meaning making (see also Shotter, 1990) and identity work. We are interested in memory both as a piece of information that is recalled and the processes in which memory is worked through by participants as they draw from past experiences in order to engage with identity work. Amy Cole explains:

> The memory of a specific event has the potential to be highly malleable in order to suit the purpose of the moment and help the individual make meaning of the event's relationship to other events within the individual's existing framework of understanding. (2010, p. 225)

This suggests that what we remember is not only selective, but also the context in which we recall certain experiences matter. In other words, memory provides a repertoire of meanings to deal with the present. However, this does not mean that which is remembered always gives us a readymade set of information to help us figure out the present, but rather that memory of a particular event can enhance our understanding of a current happening. Hence, the underlying assumption in memory work highlights the subjective nature of both reality and production of knowledge. And which according to Haug and colleagues (as cited by Cole, 2010) leads to, "multiple realities shaped by social, political, economic, ethnic, gender, and disability (Cole,

2010, p. 225). Therefore, if knowledge production is contingent on a constantly shifting social world, so is our understanding of this social world.

Speaking to the relationship between perception and the perceiver, Dahlberg and Dahlberg (2003) draw on Merleau-Ponty to explain that "our perception, or experience of the world is associated with both the "world itself and us as subjects" (p. 39). According to this view, the relationship between subject (knower) and the object (knowledge) is a more dynamic relationship, and central to the emergence of meaning making (Dahlberg & Dahlberg, 2003). An important concept in phenomenology is that epistemology is drawn from the lifeworld. The lifeworld is understood as how we live and experience the world. This means the lived world is replete with "multiplicity and ambiguity" (Dahlberg & Dahlberg, 2003, p. 36), that of constantly changing relationships between the subject and object. This view calls for an epistemological orientation that considers multiplicity and ambiguity as central not only to how we perceive the world, but our being in the world.

Contrary to common belief in which memory is conserved and can be recalled by subject's choice, we view memory as taking place at the intersection of "remembrance and oblivion" (Merleau-Ponty cited in Krell, 1982). This implies that the way we talk about memory, or what we remember happens within the discursive field that is socially constructed that are also influenced by embodied experiences of the world. According to Shotter,

> [I]t is because our ways of talking about our experiences work, not primarily to represent the nature of those experiences in themselves, but to represent them in such a way as to constitute and sustain one or another kind of social order. (1990, p. 122)

This suggests that our language-use about our experiences are critically significant, because it is through our discourses that we enter in dialogue with an already existing social world, while at the same time shaping and co-creating it. According to Shotter (1990) we speak not to present the world, but rather "we speak in order to create, maintain, reproduce and transform certain modes of social and societal relationships" (p. 124).

Methodology

This research draws on interview data from a larger study that examined the experience of 1.5- and second-generation Somali immigrant students in U.S. school systems in a mid-sized Midwestern city. In this chapter, we explore the racialized experiences of two students, Asli, and Yahya. At the time of the study, Asli was in 11th grade, and Yahya was in 12th grade. We employed ethnographic methods, where the first author spent a total of 10 weeks at the school site, which we call Sugan Academy. The study explored: 1) how childhood stories of schooling that were remembered and told by students were understood and interpreted from current perspectives and 2) how the current context shaped students' identity. The first author asked the students to share, and/or reflect on experiences in which they felt different. Interviews with 11th and 12th grade students lasted between 1 and 1:30 hours, followed by follow-up interviews that lasted between 1:15 and 1:45 hours. An example of the questions the first author asked is: "Can you tell me a story from your school that you will always remember?" She asked follow-up questions that inquired about how students felt at the time of the incident, their emotions, and surroundings, and if there were others around, and if so how others seemed to act or behave in response to the experiential incident at hand.

The analysis of the interview data paid particular attention to the stories told from early childhood experiences, and the context in which stories were told. For instance, at times we relied on our field notes in focusing on critical incidents that took place prior to an interview session, in order to explore why and how certain experiences were recalled and interpreted by students. First author conducted follow-up interviews with most of the students at least once during the duration of the study. Each follow-up interview was initiated by a selection of a particular incident that was shared previously by each student. The analysis drew on van Manen's (2014) highlighting approach, which considers whole-part-whole approach analysis. Hence, emerging themes were considered separately as well as their relationship to the overall data. In making sense of the data, we relied on Dahlberg and colleagues' (2008) concept of bridling rooted in interpretive phenomenology, which acknowledges the back and forth between the researcher's identity and experiences and those of the participants (see also Vagle, 2016). Put differently, bridling acknowledges researcher positionality regarding data interpretation. Hence, as two women of color (Somali-American and Vietnamese-American), our own immigrant backgrounds influenced our selection of data, analysis, and writing.

Findings

Somali children's school experiences are shaped by the intersection of Black racial identity and Muslim identity in multiple and varied ways. Asli and Yahya recalled incidents that happened during elementary school that emphasized the ways their intersectional identities of race, religion, gender, and immigrant status shaped their schooling experiences. The memory moments in which Asli and Yahya drew on, emphasized how lived experiences of schooling were connected to larger discourses that tend to marginalize Muslim immigrant children in U.S. educational contexts. In this chapter, we focus particularly on two main themes, which build on one another. These include: 1) dialectic memories of exclusion and inclusion in early schooling and 2) remembering school through the prism of race and racialized identities. Next, we explore the stories of two Somali-American students, Asli an 11th grade female student, and Yahya a12th grade male student.

Asli: Young, Female, and Muslim

Asli came to the United States at the age of one, as a first-grade student; she went to a neighborhood school with very few Somali children. Asli's early memories on schooling are as follows:

> [In elementary school] I didn't play with anyone because I first thought no one wanted me because of all the experiences I had back then but also, I didn't have this welcoming presence, you know. You know you are not wanted just by the look on their faces.

Nimo: What do you mean by experience?
Asli: Just being Somali, Muslim and all. In recess, I'd rather walk around, kick some mulches and even though the teachers over there were just talking, they never came up to me and said, 'Hi, how are you doing?' all that. I even remember when we had this fieldtrip to a pool and I'm not, I didn't wana go to the pool, even though my mom was like, oh, you can have fun that day. Here is a swim suit and all that. I'd say I don't want to. So, I'd splashed in the water, with my feet, just watching all the kids having fun. And none of them, none of the teachers came up to me. That's what I wonder, why didn't they?

In this excerpt, Asli is not only recalling incidental experiences, but is also attempting to make sense of her elementary schooling: "I first thought no one wanted me because of all the experiences I had back then." This suggests that her own sense of self is understood through her racial, ethnic, and religious differences as Somali and Muslim, and how these differences are received by others. Her statement, "You know you are not wanted by the look on their faces," suggests an insight that was probably felt as a child, but could only be articulated as an adult, namely her readings of the facial expression, which communicated that her body was not desirable in that particular space.

Asli's experiences of loneliness and exclusion are not unique, but rather common among young immigrant children, particularly, those coming from nonwhite communities (Vaught & Castagno, 2008). However, and significantly, Asli's language-use holds her teachers accountable for not taking the initiative to include her in the class community. She emphasizes, "they never came up to me and said, 'Hi, how are you doing?' and all that." This suggests that the teachers noticed but ignored Asli's daily social marginalization. At the same time, Asli wished that the teachers acted differently. She wonders "and none of them, none of the teachers came up to me. That's what I wonder, 'Why didn't they?'." Her repetition of "none of them" implies that teachers are ethically positioned to assume responsibility for the well-being of the children in their charge. Her question, "Why didn't they?" insists on holding teachers accountable for their willful neglect.

Although Asli struggled with making connections and being different from other children at school, the school community's acceptance was highly desired by her:

Asli: I did not understand it. I questioned it a lot, and I was like, maybe they didn't know that I knew the language that well. Or maybe they thought that I just felt like the need to be left alone. Because I tried to fit in. I so tried to fit in, and even my mom used to tell me, like, oh you are Somali and all that, I didn't know what that meant. I did not know the Somali language, until I went to Kenya for a visit. Since, because of that I grew into my shell, had low self-confidence, low self-esteem and all that. And I, when you start learning how to speak in public is when you're 5th 6th, or 7th grade. I used to fail in those classes because my experience in elementary school. Because I used to sit in the back of the class because I knew that I could not fit in. I knew that if I could sit next to them, they'll be asking me questions and I'll not talk to them because that's how shy I was. I had a shy personality. So, and then I won't be like discriminated against, or subjected to racism, but the way kids were back then. They'll be asking weird questions and all that, their parents too.

Nimo: Like what sort of questions?

Asli: Like they'll be oh, do you wear that towel inside the shower and all that .... I have a long way to go because I still struggle, in making decisions very well.

Asli links early experiences of pain to current challenges she has as a high school student. She explains: "because of that I grew into my shell, had low self-confidence, low self-esteem and all that." Additionally, the comment "They'll be asking weird questions and all that, their parents too" suggests that even though Asli differentiates between students and their parents, it does not change her feeling and imagining the Othering gaze of both parents and children. Both students and their families are categorized as "they." She explains "They'll be like, 'Oh, do you wear that towel inside the shower and all that'." The word *towel head* is a common pejorative term used against Muslim women and girls who wear the hijab or headscarf as a religious and spiritual observance. Asli's story is her own sense-making of her experience as a young hijabi (girl in headscarf) in a mainstream school with no other veiled girls, as much as it is about the exact words or terms used against her in her elementary school that shaped her sense of alienation.

In particular, Asli connected her experiences of exclusion in elementary school to her being visibly Somali, and hence the reason that she could not belong. She explained, "I so tried to fit in, And even my mom used to tell me, like, 'Oh, you are Somali'." This suggests that Asli's desire to fit in was not an option for her mother, since Asli's Somali background was a marker of difference. It could be argued that Asli's mother wanted to instill in Asli a healthy Somali identity, even though Asli did not necessarily understand the racial and religious markers of her difference at the time.

Yahya: Young, Male, and Black

Yahya a 12th grade Somali student, who came to the United States at the age of five, recalled the following experiences about elementary school:

Yahya: No one wanted to play with me and honestly, sometimes, it's just that I think it was because of my skin color. I went to like a school with a whole, a lot of white, people. I think, I was maybe the fourth or the third Black boy in the entire school .... In the playground, they used to call me names.

Nimo: What sort of names, do you mind sharing?

Yahya: Things like monkey, [n-word]. There was this mean kid, who also rode the bus with us [my sister and I] that used to always call us these things and then everyone will laugh. They was just bunch of mean kids, especially him, that's all.

Nimo: It sounds terrible, did you tell anyone, your parents perhaps?

Yahya: That's why my father said we are moving to [this midwestern state], to be around other Somalians.

Nimo: What was it like living there?

Yahya: My mom still talks about it that people used to stop and look at them everywhere they went. They [people in town] have never seen Somalians before my family and few others were moved there.

Nimo: What was it like for you and for your family to be in that town?

Yahya: I remember that we lived close to some Ruush [Russian] people, and we [the children], never got along. Those niggas kept stealing my bike.

Yahya's narrative reflects an immigrant story of experiencing racism and bullying in a small rural town in the Southeast of the United States. Yahya did not readily share that he was called "monkey, [n-word]." He did so only after the first author asked him. From the tone of his voice, the first author could sense that recalling this incident made him a bit upset. Yahya referenced the use of the words "monkey" and "n-word" as "things," which sheds light on the dehumanizing and racist nature of the terms.

Further, the memory work engaged here does not differentiate between Yahya as an informant and the memory itself (Cole, 2010). In the above example, Yahya is using racial discourse in the United States to frame his own encounter with racism and bullying. In addition, Yahya is also engaging cross-generational memory, by borrowing from his mother's stories of racism. He comments that "people used to stop and look at them" suggesting that the family's experience become part of Yahya's past and memory, despite the fact that he was only five at the time and most likely could not remember the Othering gaze that his mother felt. For Yahya, the racism and sense of alienation he and his family experienced center around their racial and immigrant status. His recollection of childhood experiences is thus also imbedded within a larger story of becoming Black (Ibrahim, 1999, 2014) in the southern United States.

This is significant in Yahya's discomfort with being called [n-word]. The usage of the racial epithet of the n-word versus *niggas* is important for at least three reasons. First, Yahya's discomfort with the n-word implies his understanding of its use is connected to a legacy of enslaving Africans, and that as a Black male in the South, there were implications for such usage that were beyond a mere insult. The context and the user of a racial epithet matter as much as the terms themselves (Hom, 2008). Hence, the use of language "like monkey, [n-word]" reinstates the Black male to the demeaning social status of a slave. Significantly, it was a white boy who called Yahya the n-word. Second, Yahya's use of "niggas" to refer to the Russian children draws on the meaning and usage of the term within hip-hop culture (Alim, 2007; Ibrahim, 2014). Within hip-hop culture when the term "nigga" is used pejoratively it does not carry the same weight as the n-word, and especially when it is used among Black and other urban youth of color (Hom, 2008). Yahya is thus not engaging the same dehumanizing practice that he was subjected to by the white boy in his story. Unlike adolescent black immigrants who come to North America and invest in learning to be Black through language-use and dress style, Yayha's experiences of racialization from a very young age in the United States socialized him in Black English for most of his life (see Ibrahim, 1999). Lastly, Yahya's use of Black English suggests that as a Black immigrant, he not only identifies with Blackness, but utilizes Black English (e.g., to refer to the Russian boys) as a mechanism against racism. This allows Yahya to draw on Black American collective memory to make sense of his social position as a Black male.

In contrast to Asli, for Yahya race and gender were salient signifiers of difference rather than race and religion. While Asli's early schooling experiences were characterized by alienation, Yahya's experiences shifted between those of exclusion and inclusion as certain incidents emerged in his recollection of elementary school. For example, Yahya shared the following about a caring ESL teacher. Yahya explains:

> Yahya: I used to spend a lot of time with the ESL teacher. I remember him, especially later in second and third grade. He was very friendly and I remember that he was very nice to the Somali kids.
>
> Nimo: What was his race?
>
> Yahya: He was an old white guy. I remember this particular day. I used to fight a lot with the other boys.
>
> Nimo: Why did you fight?
>
> Yahya: I used to fight to help my younger sister and other Somali girls. One day, this kid was throwing food on one of the Somali girls, and he would not stop it. So I went over and pushed him down of his chair. He fell on the ground and we got into a fight. Then the teachers came and broke the fight. I remember the ESL teacher used to tell me that you can't fight in school, even if you are upset. He told me that it is not good to fight, even when you are upset.
>
> Nimo: Why do you think he was so nice to you, the Somali kids?
>
> Yahya: I don't know, I just remember him being there and talking, when my parents were called to the school. They always called him [the ESL teacher] whenever I was in trouble and the like .... I even remember him coming to our house and talking with my mom.

Here, Yahya shares that he "used to fight a lot with the other boys" to defend his younger sister and other Somali girls from students who harass and throw food at them. This suggests the ESL teacher was an ally and advocate. The statement "I just remember him being there" is important for highlighting that the teacher was "there" as a resource for Yahya and his family, particularly as a mediator and advocate for him and his family. Yahya's comment, "I even remember him coming to our house and talking with my mom" suggests that it was out of the norm for his teachers to pay home visits, but this teacher took the time to visit Yahya's family. This "old white guy" made a positive contribution to the elementary school experience of a black immigrant boy marginalized by race and ethnicity. It is pertinent to note that Yahya's first response was about his pain of being excluded. However, in his later responses more positive experiences of being cared for seemed to emerge as significant for Yahya's sense making.

Yahya's recollection of his ESL teacher was in response to his feeling lonely among his peers. Yahya remembered the kind gestures of this teacher. In the story, although other teachers intervened to stop the fight, they were not as significant as the ESL teacher. His comment, "I remember the ESL teacher used to tell me that you can't fight in school, even if you are upset" suggests a role the ESL teacher played as a mentor to provide Yahya with an understanding of acceptable school behavior. While school staff often do not understand Somali immigrant and refugee children's tendencies to physical altercations (Roy & Roxas, 2011), the ESL teacher understood to some degree that as a refugee child coming from a civil war context, Yahya needed help understanding the cultural context of the school in the United States, that prohibited physical conflicts.

Conclusion

The findings from this study suggest that the marginalization of Somali-American students in school starts early in the schooling process. The students in this study highlighted incidents in which they were made to feel that they did not belong in the school community through exclusionary practices by teachers and their peers. In addition, the results from this research also speaks to the role of discourse and language-use ways in which these memories of alienation were articulated and interpreted. Students' stories reveal incidents of marginalization and exclusion manifested through racial epithets, physical altercation, or the racializing gaze of Islamophobia. Feelings of loneliness were attributed to the visibility of race, religion, and invisibility of linguistic ability.

For some both race and religion were factors that shaped perception of selfhood. For others like Yahya, exploring initial understanding of past experiences led to a more nuanced and complex comprehension of early school memories. For instance, at times this complexity was articulated through language use. Somali-American youth connected their experiences of racism to larger struggles of Black and brown people in the United States. This indicates not only are these young people aware of their racialized identities, but also, they were actively engaging modes of resistance within an already existing collective Black consciousness through use of Black language (Alim, 2007; Ibrahim, 2004).

While at other times it was through Yahya's relationship with a caring ESL teacher, which contradicted his primary feelings of being excluded, hence opening up more nuanced meaning making. Meanwhile, for Asli, engaging with memories of past schooling experiences led to asking a series of questions about her teachers' role in her exclusion. Her quest to make sense of her exclusion speaks to the ambiguity inherent in memory and what is remembered (Merleau-Ponty, cited in Krell, 1982). This is relevant in thinking about memory as a tool for not only accessing past experiences but also ways of articulating and working through aspects of lived experiences that may lead to a "potential social transformation" (Moorsi, 2011, p. 210). Memory fosters opportunities to put language in dialogue with lived experience. As we have noted above, the act of remembering and recalling certain experiences has more to do with the extent the language we use to talk about experiences as connected to larger discourses of meaning making than the experiential incident itself.

As we showed above, the narrated schooling experiences of the youth in this study reflect deeply ingrained memories of childhood experiences in school that are shaped by how they imagine and think about schooling, which is closely linked with their perception of intersectional identities of being black, Muslim, immigrant, and gendered subjects. But more importantly, Asli and Yahya's stories of remembering their early schooling raise a set of ethical and moral questions for adults in charge of caring for and teaching young children. The type of relational experiences children are exposed to daily in their schools are significant and influence learning and identity development. Hence, children's memories of early school experiences are about their senses of belonging, which are associated with learning.

Discussion Questions

1. In what ways do the stories of Yahya and Asli expand our understanding of the ethical and moral obligations teachers have toward their students?

2. What lessons can you draw from Asli's experiences of marginalization and alienation that can inform your pedagogical commitment to building a classroom community? What strategies can you develop to ensure that students like Asli and Yahya feel a sense of community in your classroom?

3. In our above conceptualization of memory as negotiated and embodied, how will you want to be remembered by your students? What

types of stories do you want your students to tell about your practice in a decade from now?

References

Alim, S. H. (2007). Critical hip-hop language pedagogies: Combat, consciousness, and the cultural politics of communication. *Journal of Language, Identity, and Education*, *6*(2), 161–176.

Bigelow, M. H. (2010). *Mogadishu on the Mississippi: Language, racialized identity, and education in a new land* (Vol. 60). Malden, MA: Wiley-Blackwell.

Cole, A. L. (2010). Object-memory, embodiment, and teacher formation: A methodological exploration. In C. Mitchel, T. Strong-Wilson, K. Pithouse, & S. Allnutt (Eds.), *Memory and pedagogy* (pp. 223–238). New York, NY: Routledge.

Collet, B. A. (2007). Islam, national identity and public secondary education: Perspectives from the Somali diaspora in Toronto, Canada. *Race, Ethnicity, and Education*, *10*(2), 131–153.

Dahlberg, H., & Dahlberg, K. (2003). To not make definite what is indefinite: A phenomenological analysis of perception and its epistemological consequences in human science research. *The Humanistic Psychologist*, *31*(4), 34–50.

Dahlberg, K., Dahlberg, H., & Nystrom, M. (2001). *Reflective lifeworld research*. Lund, Sweden: Studentlitteratur.

Dahlberg, K., Dahlberg, H., & Nystrom, M. (2008). *Reflective lifeworld research* (2nd ed.). Lund, Sweden: Studentlitteratur.

Du, S. (2016, January 20). St. Cloud is the worst place in Minnesota to be Somali. *City Pages*. Retrieved from http://www.citypages.com/news/st-cloud-is-the-worst-place-in-minnesota-to-be-somali-7976833

Forman, M. (2001). "Straight outta Mogadishu": Prescribed identities and performative practices among Somali youth in North American high schools. *TOPIA: Canadian Journal of Cultural Studies*, *5*, 33–60.

Haug, F., Anderson, S., Bunz-Ellferdeng, A., Hauser, K., Lang, U., Laudan, M., Ludemen, M., . . . Thomas, C. (1987). *Female sexualization: A collective work of memory* (E. Carter, Trans.). London, UK: Verso Books.

Heidegger, M. (1998). *Being and time* (J. Macquarrie & E. Robinson, Trans.). Oxford, UK: Blackwell Publishing. (Original work published 1962).

Hom, C. (2008). The semantics of racial epithets. *The Journal of Philosophy*, *105*(8), 416–440.

Ibrahim, A. E. K. M. (1999). Becoming rap and hip-hop, race, gender, identity, and the politics of ESL learning. *TESOL Quarterly*, *33*(3), 349–369.

Ibrahim, A. (2004). One is not born Black: Becoming and the phenomenon(ology) of race. *Philosophical Studies in Education*, *35*(1), 77–87.

Ibrahim, A. (2014). *The rhizome of Blackness: A critical ethnography of Hip-Hop culture, language, identity, and the politics of becoming.* New York, NY: Peter Lang.

Jaffe-Walter, R. (2016). *Coercive concern: Nationalism, liberalism and the schooling of Muslim youth.* Stanford University Press.

Jaffe-Walter, R. (2017). The more we can try to open them up the better it will be for their integration: Integration and the coercive assimilation of Muslim youth. *Diaspora, Indigenous and Minority Education, 11*(2), 63–68.

Krell, D. F. (1982). Phenomenology of memory from Husserl to Merleau-Ponty. *Philosophy and Phenomenological Research, 42,* 492–505.

Merleau-Ponty, M. (1995). *Phenomenology of perception* (C. Smith, Trans.). New York, NY: Routledge.

Merleau-Ponty, M. (2012). *Phenomenology of perception* (D. A. Landes, Trans.). New York, NY: Routledge.

Moorsi, P. (2011). Looking back: Women principals reflect on their childhood experiences. In C. Mitchel, T. Strong-Wilson, K. Pithouse, & S. Allnutt (Eds.), *Memory and pedagogy* (pp. 209–222). New York, NY: Routledge.

Roy, L., & Roxas, K. (2011). Whose deficit is this anyhow? Exploring counter stories of Somali Bantu refugees' experiences in "doing school". *Harvard Educational Review, 81*(3), 521–542.

Smith, M. (2018, April 2018). Kansas trio convicted in plot to bomb Somali immigrants. *The New York Times.* Retrieved from https://www.nytimes.com/2018/04/18/us/kansas-militia-somali-trial-verdict.html

Shotter, J. (1990). The social construction of remembering and forgetting. In D. Middleton & D. Edwards (Eds.), *Collective remembering* (pp. 120–138). London, UK: Routledge.

Vagle, M. D. (2016). *Crafting phenomenological research.* Walnut Creek, CA: Left Coast Press, Incorporated.

van Manen, M. (2014). *Phenomenology of practice: Meaning-giving methods in phenomenological research and writing.* Walnut Creek, CA: Left Coast Press, Incorporated.

Vaught, S. E., & Castagno, A. E. (2008). "I don't think I'm a racist": Critical race theory, teacher attitudes, and structural racism. *Race Ethnicity and Education, 11*(2), 95–113.

Zamora, K. (2018 October 12). Scream Town reopens after deal with Carver County. *Star Tribune.* Retrieved from http://www.startribune.com/scream-town-to-reopen-this-weekend/497262511/

Zine, J. (2000). Redefining resistance: Towards an Islamic subculture in schools. *Race Ethnicity and Education, 3*(3), 293–316.

Zine, J. (2006). Unveiled sentiments: Gendered Islamophobia and experiences of veiling among Muslim girls in a Canadian Islamic school. *Equity & Excellence in Education, 39*(3), 239–252.

5 Fostering Senegalese Immigrant Students' Language and Literacy Learning Experiences and Academic Achievement

S. JOEL WARRICAN
The University of the West Indies

Alex Kumi-Yeboah
University at Albany, State University of New York

PATRIANN SMITH
University of South Florida

MELISSA L. ALLEYNE
The University of the West Indies

Introduction

Over the last 50 years, there has been significant racial and ethnic transformation in the United States. Paul Taylor (2014), writing for the Pew Research Center, posits that in the United States, modern immigration is different from the late 19th and early 20th centuries. During those early periods, he reported that approximately 90% of immigrants were from Europe, compared to the 12% today. Meanwhile, the African immigrant population in the United States has jumped from 30,000 in the 1960s, 80,000 in the 1970s, and 176,000 in the 1980s, to approximately 1.6 million in 2010 (McCabe, 2011). This transformation in the racial and ethnic makeup of the general population is reflected in the socio-cultural and ethno-linguistic mosaic that now exists in the country. For example, available research evidence indicates that about 20% of school-aged children in the United States speak a language other than English at home, while 55% speak English with difficulty (National Center for Education Statistics, 2012). Although the school population in U.S. schools is becoming increasingly multiethnic, the primary concern is that many teachers have little understanding of the experiences of the multilingual and multicultural immigrant youth, or how to adapt their classrooms to the new diversity in language and culture (e.g., Kumi-Yeboah & Smith, 2016; Roubeni, Haene, Keatley, Shah, & Rasmussen, 2015).

In this chapter, we focus primarily on one group of immigrant youth (from Africa) who, as with other immigrant youth, appear to struggle as they position themselves in classrooms in the United States (Ukpokodu, 2013). As is the case with other immigrants, for the African youth, language learning (in this case, English) plays a critical role as they work through the process of acculturation into their newly adopted home. Language learning has been identified and emphasized as a significant factor in the educational success of immigrant youth (Suarez-Orozco, Rhodes, & Milburn, 2009).

Even with our broad interest in the African youth, for this study, we focus primarily on a sub-group, Senegalese immigrant youth, about whom not much is known with regard to the factors that promote language and literacy learning experiences. The educational systems from which they originate are based on the colonial French traditional educational system, where the curriculum involves little student participation in the classroom (Rideout & Bagayoko, 1994). As with other countries that experienced European colonial rule (Thompson, Warrican, & Leacock, 2011), imposed upon Senegal was a system established for the interest of France (Naida, 2016), a system that ensured that the Senegalese people were controlled and even dominated by the French. Language played a very important role in ensuring this dominance, with French promoted above all indigenous varieties as the official language. Interestingly, even after independence, French has been maintained as the official language.

The dominance was not always done overtly in a way that evoked among the masses a need for resistance. Instead, the French used structures such as education to establish their control. During colonial rule, through the schools, the Senegalese population was indoctrinated to love and accept the French language and culture (Naida, 2016). Naida stressed that French teachers taught not only the French language and culture but also used French textbooks to teach all other subjects. This sent a not-too-subtle message that "high culture" and values were all things in French. In many ways, this was quite an alienating process, resulting in students facing an ethnic identity crisis (Diallo, 2011).

In this study, we set out to investigate how 65 youth raised in Senegal with a culture of dependence on teachers as their source of knowledge adapt to a U.S. school system that is seemingly more open and lends itself to the co-construction of knowledge in the classroom. In essence, we study the experiences of these immigrant youth as they navigate through a new and unfamiliar environment. We recognized that there is a noticeable dearth of knowledge in the literature about language and literacy learning experiences of Senegalese immigrant youth. We, therefore, thought that this study of the 65 Senegalese immigrant youth (38 males and 27 females ranging in age from 17 to 20 years) provides an excellent opportunity to commence the building of a body of work.

The participating Senegalese immigrant youth in this study resided in Atlanta (Georgia) and attended six public high schools within two school districts. They all spoke French and one or more of the Senegalese local language varieties. To conduct this study, we sought help from the Senegalese community in the Atlanta metropolitan area to identify youth that were still in school. The 65 students were, therefore, purposively chosen (Leacock, Warrican, & Rose, 2015).

Having consented to participate in the study, we then conducted two rounds of interviews, each lasting 60 to 90 minutes, at the residences of the participants. In general, for the first round of interviews, we sought to identify classroom or school activities that facilitate their language and literacy learning experiences, as well as the factors that they found to affect their learning of English and their overall academic performance. We followed up with the second round of interviews to clarify any of the previous responses that the participants provided. To analyze the interview data, we used open coding, as described by Miles, Huberman, and Saldana (2014) to select and then group the codes by themes. The themes that emerged from the transcripts were then categorized to reflect the participants' ways of understanding, viewing and constructing meanings from their experiences in the new world.

Theoretical Framework

Taking into consideration the possible linguistic and cultural challenges that the 65 immigrant youth may face in their newly adopted home of the United States, we decided to frame this study using complementary pedagogies: Paris's (2012) culturally sustaining pedagogy and the earlier and foundational work of culturally relevant pedagogy by Ladson-Billings (1995). In the framing of the study, along with the pedagogies, we also considered the related concepts of identity and positioning.

Culturally sustaining pedagogy has the "explicit goal [of] supporting multilingualism and multiculturalism in practice and perspective for students and teachers" (Paris, 2012, p. 95). It goes beyond the cultural experiences of minority youth in that it "seeks to perpetuate and foster – to sustain – linguistic, literate, and cultural pluralism as part of the democratic project of schooling" (Paris, 2012, p. 95). The two primary tenets of culturally sustaining pedagogy are to focus on the plural and evolving nature of youth identity and cultural practices, and a commitment to embracing youth culture's counter-hegemonic potential while maintaining a clear critique of the ways in which youth culture can also reproduce systemic inequalities. Through the lenses of culturally sustaining pedagogy, we are, therefore, able to explore how the 65 immigrant Senegalese youth's identities and cultural practices evolved as they navigate the education space in their adopted country. In doing this exploration, we pay close attention to the responses of these youth to the new cultural and linguistic environment to which they are exposed.

Similar to culturally sustaining pedagogy, Ladson-Billings's culturally relevant pedagogy (1995) is concerned with maximizing the academic potential of the youth by valuing and affirming their cultures. The focus of culturally relevant pedagogy is (a) students' learning to be relevant while they become more proficient at understanding their cultures; (b) cultural competence which helps to identify excellence within the context of the students' community and cultural identities; and (c) critical consciousness, which challenges inequitable school and societal structures (Ladson-Billings, 2009).

In looking at this study through the lenses of culturally relevant pedagogy, we are able to consider the classroom environment created by the teacher in terms of whether or not attention is paid to the home context of the immigrant youth and how it affects the way they learn and adapt in the U.S. classroom context. We examine whether teachers use the cultural identities of the immigrant youth to promote spaces that recognize and even celebrate differences as opportunities of learning and enrichment. It also provides us with the opportunity to see to what extent the teachers help the immigrant Senegalese youth to question the cultures and values being promoted and discussed in the classroom. Through the lenses of culturally relevant pedagogy, we are able get a sense (as suggested by Boutte, 2002) as to whether teachers reflect on their perceptions of cultures, race, building relationships, and engaging diverse students in informed conversations. Teachers, Boutte suggests, need a sufficient in-depth understanding of students' cultural backgrounds to make learning meaningful and transformative.

Aligned to the analyses with theoretical considerations to culturally relevant and sustaining pedagogy, we pay particular attention to how the immigrant Senegalese youth negotiate their own identities and position themselves in their new environment according to the contexts. The concepts of identity and positioning share a close relationship, one in which both are used in the explanation of each other. Positioning is linked to the early work of Harré and Langenhove (1999). They define positioning as "the study of local moral orders as ever shifting patterns of mutual and contestable rights and obligations of speaking and acting" (p. 1). This concept demonstrates a level of fluidity of social interactions that is dependent on how individuals are positioned by others or how these individuals position themselves based on context. As such, the identities of these individuals do not assume a fixed form but a mutability that is linked to contexts (Smith, 2019; Smith, Warrican, Kumi-Yeboah, & Richards, 2018). It is this mutability that leads many researchers to the conclusion that identity is a complex concept that cannot be easily defined using one simple phrase (Yoon, 2012).

With the perceived interrelatedness to positioning, Moje and Luke (2009) suggest that "one sees identity less as an interpretation of the person who has the identity and more dependent on other people's recognitions of a person" (p. 418). Moje and Luke's conception demonstrates the interplay between identity and positioning, a relationship that Yoon (2012) describes as "not excluding individual constructions but [that] it clearly shows the power and influence of others" (p. 975). To illustrate the point, Yoon suggests that the same immigrant students, in one context, may position themselves as active participants in the classroom, while in another setting, depending on their perception of how others view them, they may position themselves as passive learners. Linked to this perceived state of fluidity is the fact that positioning can apparently be intentional or interactive (Davies & Harré, 1990). Yoon (2012) illustrates the intentional positioning in this way:

> Immigrant students' stated beliefs about their relative world help to illuminate how they position themselves in the classroom. For instance, some immigrant students might position themselves as students who assimilate into mainstream culture by losing their own cultural identity. Others might position themselves as students who challenge the dominant power and sustain their own cultural identity (p. 974).

As the word "intentional" suggests, and as illustrated in Yoon's excerpt, there is a deliberateness about this form of positioning which in fact "guides their interactive approaches with teachers and peers in classroom settings" (p. 974). For interactive positioning on the one hand, the immigrants are positioned based on, for example, how they are perceived by others and how and where they are placed in a learning environment (Davies & Harré, 1990). With this interactive form, in the school context, peers and teachers wittingly or unwittingly position the immigrant students quite often on perceptions about language, culture, and race. As Yoon (2012) posits, the teacher and classmates may position the immigrant students as "others," a state which may limit the immigrants' sense of identity.

Be it intentional or interactive positioning, it seems important that teachers be attuned to the concepts, and how either forms can affect immigrant students' identities and ultimately their classroom interactions. For example, a show by teachers that they value the home language of immigrant students through acts such as providing literacy opportunities in the home language is strongly associated with ethnic identification, which in turn, contributes to academic achievement (Bankston & Zhou, 1995). Teachers can even go as far as where they create an environment where immigrant students can see positive images of their culture portrayed. This is particularly so for students from African countries such as those in this study. Traoré and Lukens (2006) contend that the media have made Africa unattractive to students and teachers in the United States by denying them "access to positive information about Africa and Africans" (p. 247). This has created "debilitating stereotypes" (p. 247) of Africa by both students and teachers as they learn, thanks to the media, to associate Africa with wild animals and dark imagery. They conclude that along with language difficulties, African immigrant youth identified discrimination as a major factor that influences their adaptation and academic achievement.

Without teachers' direct and thoughtful interventions to help the immigrant students to have positive experiences in their adopted countries, the possibility exists that they will be marginalized in the classroom. Cummins (2009) reports that such marginalization of immigrant children comes with concomitant deleterious effects, including the creation of stereotypes that lead them to a feeling of alienation. According to Cummins, the marginalization of immigrant students' home language and cultural background leads to coercive relations of power, which can cause immigrant students to relinquish their values and submit to the mainstream cultures and values. To support this assertion, Alidou (2000) states that the poor achievement of immigrant students in learning language and literacy can be due to "linguicism," that is, "the ideology and structure that is used to legitimize, effectuate, and reproduce an unequal division of power and a resource between groups ... based on the devaluation of one's linguistic heritage" (p. 2). Alidou (2000) argues that linguicism is "reflected in the refusal of schools to acknowledge the varieties of English that exist in the U.S. and globally" (p. 2), a refusal which naturally has direct impact on immigrant students.

This exploration of the theoretical perspectives helped us to bring into sharp focus some key issues that the 65 Senegalese immigrant youth faced in the U.S. classrooms. We were able to identify what on the surface appeared to be positive actions by schools to meet the needs of these immigrant students, but which after closer inspection showed how these actions were inadequate or even counter to best practice.

Discussion of Findings

On the surface, the Senegalese immigrant youth[1] appeared to be in school environments where attempts were being made to make their experience a welcoming one. The students generally reported environments where both non-immigrant peers and teachers communicated with them in a way that they thought helped to improve their language. Teachers, for example, provided them with activities that helped them to work on language and reading skills in English. They also reported being provided with opportunities to participate in class discussions. When asked how class discussions help to improve their language and literacy experiences, Kari had this to say:

> I will say that class discussion helped me to interact with my peers and teachers. The open communication allowed me to talk and express my ideas. It empowers me to speak out and to understand the transition from speaking and writing in English. I like when some of my teachers offer us the chance to discuss issues in class. I think classroom discussions changed my reading ability. It has been good for me to learn reading and writing faster. It helped me to get better grades at school.

Most of the students described a system with some level of openness where the teachers provided opportunities for them to participate in class activities such as discussions in a way that they perceived helped them to achieve better academic performance. Open activities are indeed commendable. When teachers provide avenues for open activities where students are given voice, the immigrant youth are able to use language to form social bonds through cultural exchanges while at the same time benefitting linguistically from the opportunity to speak in a safe environment (Lam, 2004; Nieto, 2009).

Another feature described by the participants which to some extent also speaks to openness was the use of technology in their learning. They expressed delight about access to the Internet, not only at school but also at home, hailing it as a significant factor that helped them to improve their language and literacy learning. For example, Jabarie had this to say:

1. All names used for the immigrant youth in this section are pseudonyms.

Internet and other technology in my class helped me to improve my reading and language learning process, and I'm wondering if there were no technology in my class ... my challenges would have been more this time. I have gained much from my teachers using technology in class. It helped me to get better grades at school.

Additionally, Abdul shared his experiences of having access to technology in school:

I would say that our teachers allow us to use tablets in class. It's awesome because you can watch short clips or videos about the books we read. There is audio version of it too. I like the apps because you can locate websites that can help you to read stories and watch short movies. In class, we get the chance to use iPad ... and would say that it has helped me a lot in my readings and language progress.

Infusing technology into the language and literacy curriculum for immigrant students in the way described in the above excerpts offers them the opportunity to improve their English through the exposure to models of English usage, as well as widen their experiences. From the students' voices on technology use, it seems reasonable to suggest that twenty-first century teaching skills require teachers to incorporate technology into the teaching curriculum to enhance understanding of concepts for immigrant students. This is in harmony with the numerous general calls for teachers to be not only knowledgeable about technology but also adept at integrating it into their regular practice (Kumi-Yeboah & Smith, 2014).

Overall, the participants reported that they received teacher and staff support in class. They highlighted that teacher support in classroom discussions and one-on-one teaching helped them to contribute in class. Participants discussed how the teachers' approach to teaching English language and reading, as well as other subjects, helped them to understand content taught in class. In making the point, Abubakar shared this:

My teachers provide support for me when I didn't know about some things in class. I like the support I get from ESSOL staff in school. They helped me to complete class and homework. I will credit my teachers for helping me to know how to read and write in English, and they helped me to overcome the challenges I had in the beginning when I moved to United States.

Some even reported receiving after-school help from teachers and counselors as they struggled to adjust to their new home. This support system points to a level of care by teachers and other staff members for the immigrant youth. Many have argued that care is a key ingredient to good pedagogy (Warrican, Down, & Spencer-Ernandez, 2008). This concept of caring seems at the heart of Ladson-Billings's (2009) view that the way teachers teach overwhelmingly impacts students' perceptions of the content of the curriculum. When teachers care, it is more likely that their practice will leave a positive mark on their students.

Notwithstanding the positives we highlighted, as we delved deeper into the interview data, it became apparent to us that although there appeared to be some positives, these were in some ways superficial. They did not go far enough to meet the standards expected of classrooms and schools that embrace culturally relevant or sustaining pedagogies. For example, no mention was made by the participants that the teachers gave them a voice to demand recognition of their home languages in the classroom. This lack of opportunity to utilize the students' home language in the school suggests a case of linguicism, that is a devaluation of their linguistic heritage (Alidou, 2000), as well as the grim reminder of the colonial experience of the Senegalese people. The difference is that in this instance, English rather than French is thrust upon them.

The system, it seems, focused more so on improving their use of English and general academics rather than Paris's (2012) suggestion of sustaining linguistic, literate, and cultural pluralism. For example, Sulley noted:

> The books we read in school are all American stories and no African culture ….
> I struggle to understand the meaning of what we read in class. I think I will do better if the books we read in school are based on African culture. I'm struggling right now because of the cultural and language differences. My grades are falling because of that.

Another participant, Hanif, shared:

> All of the stories we read in the books at school have no African story. I struggle to understand it. They are all stories about cultures in Europe or America. The pictures are all from here [U.S.] and the ones about Africa only show negative images. Other students ask me so many questions about the identity of the pictures.

The interview data suggest that the lack of culturally relevant materials in the classroom affects not just the participants' academic performance but also their cultural identities. As mentioned earlier, immigrant youth need to see their language and culture accepted in their classrooms (Cummins, 2009). Traoré and Lukens (2006) remind us of how difficult it is for the African immigrant youth who are mostly portrayed in negative ways in the media to fit into a new environment with its linguistic, cultural, and academic demands. For these youth, it seems imperative that classrooms and schools take extra measures to address that trend. While teachers may have no control over what is shown in the media, they do determine what happens in their classrooms.

As suggested by Ladson-Billings (2009), they can identify excellence within the context of the students' communities and cultural identities. It, therefore, seems incumbent on teachers to position immigrant students to feel free to challenge hegemonic inequalities in the classroom such as the linguicism mentioned earlier.

The stress of coping with learning new a culture and language where their cultures are not represented in the classroom by teachers can lead the immigrant youth to experience marginalization. Abukari, in describing the feeling associated with that of marginalization, said:

> I get upset when I don't understand the content of the books I read. I get lost with some of the stuff we read in class and some of my mates will also refuse to work with me because of my limited English speaking and accent. I feel lonely and it's like you are not part of the learning process in the classroom."

Cummins (2009) contends that marginalization of immigrant students' home language and culture forces them to abandon their cultural and linguistic values and ultimately accept the mainstream cultures. The issue of marginalization is also directly linked to how the teacher and the non-immigrant students positioned the Senegalese immigrant youth in the classroom. It shows that they are positioned in a space where their culture, languages, and identities are devalued. The immigrant youth in these classrooms seemed to be positioned as "others" where their sense of identity is limited (Yoon, 2012). Although they are presented with support from teachers and other staff, and they participate in somewhat open activities such as discussions and access to technology, their voices were within limits. For example, it seems that their voices were limited to seeking help or clarification, and presenting perspectives on discussion points within the limits of the materials for lessons. This suggests they were positioned to some extent as learners in need of special intervention, perhaps because of not being fluent English speakers or even linked to a perceived notion of what it means to be African. None of the Senegalese immigrant youth reported intentionally positioning themselves (Yoon, 2012), where they used their linguistic and cultural identities to challenge how they were cast in these classes. This perhaps is because the classroom culture of "otherness" was so powerful that the immigrant youth felt so overwhelmed or marginalized that any possibility of them asserting their cultural counter-hegemonic potential (Paris, 2012) was suppressed.

A number of the participants, in talking about the challenges they were encountering in U.S. classrooms, also highlighted coming to terms with an unfamiliar pedagogical approach. Participants indicated they were used to teacher-centered learning, where teachers deliver instruction and students participate as passive learners. Participants discussed that the instructional delivery in the United States is totally different from what they were used to in Senegal. The majority of the participants reported that learning to adapt to new curriculum was a challenge for them, especially as they were grappling with learning a new language, English. For example, Sally had this to say:

> It's like I'm in a different world, everything is different here [U.S.]. I mean learning and adapting to a new language is difficult and different, I must admit that I do lots of reading here [U.S.] than in Africa but the changes in the way I have to learn stuff was a big problem for me. These are challenging moment for me to learn all the new stuff at school. Changing from French to English language at this time is making me get low grades at school.

Alidou (2000) has stressed that African immigrant youth (as with other immigrants of different origins) are likely to face academic challenges because they have to learn the principles and semantics of the new language (Alidou, 2000). The Senegalese immigrant youth appear to have found themselves in classrooms that, though possibly well intentioned, the teachers focused predominantly on teaching the students the mechanics of the English language. The teachers' idea of openness was a focus on learning to use the English language in a very controlled context where actions such as discussions were restricted to the prescribed materials of the curriculum without taking into account other factors such as the students' cultural and linguistic backgrounds.

Out of this study, we had a major takeaway. It is not sufficient as a teacher to possess goodwill toward or care for immigrant students. Rather, teachers must recognize the need to value the immigrant youth as more than an "other" in the classroom. In so doing, teachers must recognize the immigrant youth as having cultural and linguistic identities. Consequently, the teachers should create classroom environments where the immigrant youth's language and culture is embraced to the point where pedagogical activities are deliberately planned around them. We concluded that goodwill and care is definitely necessary but certainly not sufficient as teachers strive to create safe environments which foster English language and literacy learning experiences and academic achievement among immigrant youth (in this case, youth from Senegal).

Conclusion

It can be argued that the study that formed the basis of this chapter is limited as it was conducted among a single nationality. However, when the findings are examined through the lenses of the theoretical frameworks of culturally relevant and sustaining pedagogies concomitant with positioning and identity theories, questions can be raised that can be applied to any context where immigrant students are being educated. In any such context, it has to be acknowledged that immigrant students come to the classroom with their own identities linked to their cultural and linguistic backgrounds. Such identities should not be denigrated either by overt or covert failure to acknowledge them or by presenting them in less than positive lights. With the many population challenges around the world such as wars, political, and economic instability, and persecution of minority groups, people continue to relocate in order to be secure. This movement of people has affected the makeup of classrooms just as it has done to the wider society. Reflective of these migration flows is that classrooms around the world are now becoming increasingly diverse, evidenced by factors such as greater levels of multiculturalism and multilingualism. Those charged with providing educational opportunities for the students must be helped to develop knowledge, skills, and attitudes that empower these immigrants to achieve their potential in their adopted countries, without eroding their identities and ways of being. We contend that this is a new challenge for teacher preparation programs globally. Teachers can ask the following questions as they work toward supporting immigrant learners.

Discussion Questions

1. What unique language identities are presented by Senegalese students in literacy and English language arts classrooms?
2. To what degree are opportunities provided for immigrant students' identities to be acknowledged in the literacy and English language arts classroom?
3. What pedagogical approaches in literacy and in English language arts are used to create spaces for immigrant educators to learn and to be heard?

References

Alidou, H. (2000). Preparing teachers for the education of new immigrant students from Africa. *Action in Teacher Education, 22,* 101–108.

Bankston, C. L., & Zhou, M. (1995). Effects of minority-language literacy on the academic achievement of Vietnamese youth in New Orleans. *Sociology of Education, 68*(1), 1–17.

Boutte, G. S. (2002). *Resounding voices: School experiences of people from diverse ethnic backgrounds.* Needham Heights, MA: Allyn & Bacon.

Cummins, J. (2009). Transformative multiliteracies pedagogy: School-based strategies for closing the achievement gap. *Multiple Voices for Ethnically Diverse Exceptional Learners, 11*(2), 38–56.

Davies, B., &, Harré, R. (1990). Positioning: The discursive production of selves. *Journal for the Theory of Social Behaviour, 20,* 43–63.

Diallo, I. (2011). 'To understand Lessons, think through your own languages'. An analysis of narratives in support of the introduction of indigenous languages in the education system in Senegal. *Language Matters, 42,* 207–230.

Harré, R., & Van Langenhove, L. (1999). *Positioning Theory: Moral contexts of intentional action.* Oxford, UK: Blackwell.

Kumi-Yeboah, A., & Smith, P. (2014). Blended learning in K-12 schools: Challenges and possibilities. In L. Kyei- Blankson & E. Ntuli (Eds.), *Practical applications in blended learning environments: Experiences in K-20 education* (pp. 25–42). Hershey, PA: IGI Global.

Kumi-Yeboah, A. & Smith, P. (2016). Factors that promote enhancement of critical multicultural citizenship education among Black immigrant youth. *International Journal of Multicultural Education, 18*(1), 158–182.

Ladson-Billings, G. (2009). The dreamkeepers: Successful teachers of African American children. San Francisco, CA: Jossey-Bass.

Ladson-Billings, G. (1995). Toward a theory of culturally relevant pedagogy. *American Educational Research Journal, 32*(3), 465–491.

Lam, W. S. E. (2004). Second language socialization in a bilingual chat room: Global and local considerations. *Language Learning & Technology, 8*(3), 44–65.

Leacock, C. J., Warrican, S. J., & Rose, G. S. (2015). *Research methods for inexperienced researchers: Guidelines for investigating the social world* (rev. ed.). Kingston, Jamaica: Ian Randle.

McCabe, K. (2011). African immigrants in the United States. *Migration Information Source*, Retrieved January 12, 2015 from http://www.migrationinformation.org/.

Miles, M. B., & Huberman, A. M., Saldana, J. (2014). *Qualitative data analysis: A methods sourcebook* (3rd ed.). Thousand Oaks, CA: Sage.

Moje, E., & Luke, A. (2009). Literacy and identity: Examining the metaphors in history and contemporary research. *Reading Research Quarterly, 44,* 415–437.

Naida, M. (2016). Senegal's language problem: A discourse of disparity. *Honors Theses.* 2714. https://scholarworks.wmich.edu/honors_theses/2714/

National Center for Education Statistics. (2012). Participation in education: Elementary/secondary education. Retrieved March 30, 2016 from Http://nces.ed.gov/programs/coe/2012/section1/indicator12.asp

Nieto, S. (2009). *Language, culture, and teaching: Critical perspectives for a new century.* New York, NY: Routledge.

Paris, D. (2012). Culturally sustaining pedagogy: A needed change in stance, terminology, and practice. *Educational Researcher, 41*(3), 93–97.

Rideout, W. M., & Bagayoko, M. (1994). Education Policy Formation in Senegal: Evolutionary Not Revolutionary. In D. R. Evans (Ed.), *Education Policy Formation in Africa: A comparative study of five countries* (pp. 183–204). Washington, DC: USAID.

Roubeni, S., Haene, L. D., Keatley, E., Shah, N., & Rasmussen, A. (2015). "If we can't do it, our children will do it one day": A qualitative study of West African immigrant parents' losses and educational aspirations for their children. *American Educational Research Journal, 52,* 275–305.

Smith, P. (2019). (Re)Positioning in the Englishes and (English) literacies of a Black immigrant youth: Towards a 'transraciolinguistic' approach. *Theory into Practice, 58(3),* 292–303.

Smith, P., Warrican, S. J., Kumi-Yeboah, A., & Richards, J. (2018). Understanding Afro-Caribbean educators' experiences with Englishes across Caribbean and U.S. contexts and classrooms: Recursivity, (re)positionality, bidirectionality. *Teaching and Teacher Education, 69,* 210–222.

Suarez-Orozco, C., Rhodes, J., & Milburn, M. (2009). Unraveling the immigrant paradox: academic engagement and disengagement among recently arrived immigrant youth. *Youth & Society, 41,* 151–185.

Taylor, P. (2014, April 10). *The next America.* Pew Research Center. Retrieved from http://www.pewresearch.org/next-america/#

Thompson, B. P., Warrican, S. J., & Leacock, C. J. (2011). Education for the future: shaking off the shackles of colonial times. In D. A. Dunkley (Ed.). *Readings in Caribbean history and culture: Breaking ground* (pp. 61–86). Plymouth, UK: Lexington Books.

Traoré, R. L., & Lukens, R. (2006). *This isn't the America I thought I'd find: African students in the urban U.S. high school.* Lanham, MD: University Press of America.

Ukpokodu, O. N. (2013). Fostering African immigrant students' social and civic integration: Unpacking their ethnic distinctiveness. In E. Brown & A. Krasteva (Eds.), *International advances in education: Global initiatives for equity and social justice* (pp. 215–236). Charlotte, NC: Information Age Publishing.

Warrican, S. J., Down, L., & Spencer-Ernandez, J. (2008). Exemplary teaching in the Caribbean: Experiences from early literacy classrooms. *Journal of Eastern Caribbean Studies, 33,* 1–30.

Yoon, B. (2012). Junsuk and Junhyuck: Adolescent immigrants' educational journey to success and identity negotiation. *American Educational Research Journal, 49,* 971–1002.

"The South Bronx Breaks Its Own Heart"

ENZO SILON SURIN

I did not know the pavements of cities
were so willing to be soiled – Martin Carter

Forty-one shots directed at Amadou Diallo,
fourteen days before my twenty-second
birthday, meant an accent was still a liability.

By day, he sold videotapes, gloves and socks
from the sidewalk along 14th Street. That night
his silhouetted wallet, a dour and lowly black

square, bid as proof his name did not belong
in the fallible mouth of a 226's threaded barrel.
What was prevalent in his Republic of Guinea:
torture, most pressing, at the hands of security
forces—an errant air demanding *show me your*
papers? So, he made what was a natural choice

—did not know it would lead to his body's
last inscription. In The Bronx, there were all
too frequent absences expressed as a newness.

In the vestibule where he died, a severe rain
soft-peddled and rumpled cards and letters
disclosing yet another change of venue.

That night, a name was tossed into the hush
of an omen: a deliberate wallet cannot make up
the difference spawned by a detective's clumsy feet.

6 The Case of a Somali Teenage Girl with Limited Formal Schooling: Seeing Assets and Poking Holes in Deficit Discourse

MARTHA BIGELOW
University of Minnesota

Introduction

High quality schooling experiences are essential for adolescents with immigrant or refugee backgrounds. This is particularly true if they arrive with little prior formal schooling and low print literacy. Students with limited or interrupted formal education (SLIFE) can actually experience continued gaps in their education after resettlement if they are not in programs that meet their language, literacy, and social-emotional learning needs. Imagine being placed in a class where the students are expected to read a novel while still being in the process of learning to encode and decode single syllable words. The important role of quality schooling for future employment and academic goals is documented in a number of ethnographies of high schools (Lopez, 2003; Olsen, 1997; Valenzuela, 1999). However, it is nearly impossible for educators to see or celebrate assets above gaps in literacy and formal schooling at the secondary level when they have little experience with or understanding of youth with this background and feel a sense of urgency or even panic with the mismatch between the students' skills and the mainstream curriculum.

In this chapter, I share what I learned from one refugee-background girl – Fadumo (a pseudonym) – and her family. I wanted to learn about Fadumo's home- and community-based social capital that she brought to her schooling experiences (Gibson, 1988; Portes & Rumbaut, 1996; Zhou & Bankston, 1994). By uncovering her home and community assets, I came to understand and appreciate her experience and hope to pass on the rewards of learning about the lives of refugee-background students. The goal is to foster more and better home-school connections and fight the constant onslaught of deficit thinking when it comes to SLIFE.

Fadumo's first formal schooling experiences were in a U.S. urban high school, as a ninth grader. I discovered how and why Fadumo's family and ethnic community are rich sources of social capital. However, while much of her success can be attributed to the social capital she brings to school, I aim to point out that she still needs capital that would give her access to more workplace and post-secondary educational opportunities. This is where educators and other keepers of cultural capital need to step in to broker this sharing of capital in the form of cultural knowledge and linguistic skills in the majority language as well as the native language(s).

The Social Capital of Immigrant Adolescents

Social capital is defined as "intangible social resources based on social relationships that one can draw upon to facilitate action and to achieve goals" (Coleman, 1990, p. 302). Cultural capital, on the other hand, consists of investment in a set of symbols and meanings reproduced by the dominant class of a society and passed down, or reproduced, through generations (Bourdieu & Passeron, 1977). The investment and reproduction of cultural capital serve to include or marginalize individuals in society, which in turn leads to unequal social and economic rewards. Discussions of what cultural capital consists of will be strategically restricted to what Fadumo does that seems to reproduce behaviors of the dominant class because these are behaviors that are likely to gain her access to higher status social and economic opportunities in a hierarchical society like the United States. Maintaining this definition of cultural capital will allow an analysis of what schools do "to help marginalized students gain access to cultural capital and ... to critique the inequitable system that distributes advantages on the basis of arbitrary cultural practices" (Lubienski, 2003, p. 34). Cultural capital is not to be confused with useful or supportive cultural practices or norms from the native or home culture. In other words, the support Fadumo receives from her Somali family and community, her narrative of strength in her story of migration and survival, and her fluency in Somali, are all assets, but are not cultural capital, according to Bourdieu and Passeron (1977). It is important for me to draw this line early in this chapter, but problematize it later.

Social capital, on the other hand, is a key source of capital for immigrants and can come from family and co-ethnic networks (Portes, 1998) as well as from people that belong to other networks. Social capital is often maximized when immigrant groups are heartily welcomed by the host community as well as their own co-ethnic community. Portes and Zhou's (1993) Modes of Incorporation Typology (p. 84) is helpful in thinking about how a new immigrant or refugee group can be (un)welcomed in a certain context, in general, as well as how Somalis in particular are received in Minnesota, USA the setting for the present study. This typology considers factors that affect newcomers such as governmental policies, societal factors, and qualities of the existing co-ethnic community. To be brief in my application of Poretes and Zhou's Modes of Incorporation typology, I see that most Somalis in the United States and in Minnesota experience a receptive *government policy* in that they receive resettlement assistance, albeit short term, and come as refugees or asylum seekers. This means that, in comparison to undocumented immigrants, Somalis may be viewed as having a legal and thus legitimate right to be in Minnesota. Following Portes and Zhou's typology, Somali immigrants' *societal reception* is likely to be prejudiced in U.S. society because they are not phenotypically white. Their societal reception may also be compromised by the overwhelming climate of Islamophobia in United States given that they are assumed to be Muslim. However, the challenges of living in a society that is unwelcoming in some or many ways may be mitigated by the fact that Somali newcomers have a strong and large *co-ethnic community* in Minnesota, the last criteria used in the typology. A strong Somali community offers the potential for newcomers to develop social capital, which can translate into positive effects for them and their children (Portes & MacLeod, 1996). A strong co-ethnic community consisting of large numbers of Somali families, and religious and societal organizations can offer newcomers logistical support upon arrival (Zhou & Bankston, 1994) and employment long after they resettle.

The literature from the field of sociology in the area of social capital has found native language proficiency to be important. Bankston and Zhou (1994) argue that native language proficiency "can facilitate access to the social resources of ethnic communities" (p. 6). One large-scale study that included immigrant youth (Dinovitzer, Hagan, & Parker, 2003) found that relational ties to parents predict higher educational attainment. The authors link students' close relational ties to their parents to be dependent on their maintenance of the native language. In other words, the ability to speak their parents' and, therefore, the co-ethnic community's language gives youth access to many sources of social capital. Studies done by White and Glick (2000) and White and Kaufman (1997) mirror these findings. In the field of second language acquisition, many decades of research has confirmed the value of the maintenance and growth of native language(s) in the development of a new language (Cummins, 1981). Therefore, Somali language literacy and fluency also benefits English language development.

The research on social capital in relation to immigrant adolescents is well established. Nevertheless, there has been no research that specifically focuses on how adolescent refugees with limited formal schooling use social capital to succeed at school. In fact, it is often assumed that the families of refugee adolescents may be barriers to education rather than a source of assets that facilitate obtaining an education. For example, a common assumption is that older adolescents are expected to help the family financially by working or take charge of domestic duties so that others may work and this results in low academic achievement. Perhaps the assumption is that because refugee adolescents have never been to school, their families do not value education. (I have never found either of these assumptions to hold across communities or individuals.) Obstacles for older refugee-background youth are more frequently related to structural challenges created by schools or immigration policies than anything else (e.g., they become too old to attend high school, they do not complete graduation requirements, and they are not able to be reunited with their family members who are still in a refugee camp). Nevertheless, many refugee-background youth do graduate and successfully move into the workforce or on to higher education.

The Study

In light of this overview of the literature on social capital and immigrant youth, there is a need for particularizing the experience of attending high school as a recently resettled adolescent immigrant with no prior schooling experiences. Equally important is to situate students' experiences in the ways that underscore the fact that youth are members of a family and a community. To explore how home and school connect around issues of social and cultural capital for adolescent immigrant and refugee youth, the following questions focusing on one individual will be explored:

1. How does Fadumo's social and cultural capital support her academic success in a U.S. high school?
2. What are the limitations to how Fadumo's social and cultural capital can be used to support academic success?

This investigation reveals to educators information that has the potential to inform curriculum and instruction as well as point to crucial ways schools must be charged with sharing social and cultural capital freely and equitably.

Methodology

The data from this chapter came from a larger ethnographic study carried out with Somali teens.[1] The data from one participant, Fadumo, is show-cased because her stories illustrate numerous instances of how she uses her social and cultural capital at school. The context of the data collection was a Saturday tutoring group with four Somali high school girls. For over two years, I met with the girls and we worked on homework, did reading and writing activities together and talked about school and life.[2] Data sources included copies of homework assignments, creative writing exemplars, personal narratives, five semi-structured, hour-long interviews, and written observations. The goal of this methodology was to understand and recognize the complexity of one girl's life and the power of her non-school associations. These associations are not easily captured by statistics and are often exaggerated by the media (Jankowski, 1991, cited in Rymes, 2001). The focus of this chapter is on "practice" – what one girl and her family do and what she says they do (González, 2005).

The stories I gathered in the form of field notes and periodic audio recording from Fadumo often came from individual conversations in the car, or informal chatting among us all. Because of the participants' low-to-intermediate levels of English, Somali was used often in the girls' group, although I do not speak Somali. I am certain that I missed a great deal of important information because of my lack of Somali language skills.[3] I did not have a systematic protocol for when to record, but when I did, I made it very clear that what they said would be part of the study. Usually, I was just hanging out with the girls doing homework, chatting, and practicing English. Retrospectively, I refer to it as "hanging out methodology" following Awad Ibrahim (2010, 2014). Member checks (Lincoln & Guba, 1985) with the focal student was

1. This study examined the U.S. schooling experiences of Somali youth with limited formal schooling, including, for example, their home and school uses of Somali and English oral and literacy skills, their perceptions of their classes, their school-related tasks, interpersonal relationships at school and out of school and the cultural adaptation processes they experience and watch others experience.
2. Others have gathered data this way (Rymes, 2001). It is convenient because it does not interfere with the school day and allows for interaction with participants that is not linked to school and testing.
3. Early in the research I considered involving an interpreter who was Somali and female; however, as the groups' rapport and trust developed, it seemed that bringing in an outsider would change the group dynamics and thus the quality of data gathered. Furthermore, the presence of an older Somali adult woman would likely influence how the girls chose to present themselves to me (and her), and limit conversations about such things as dating and marriage.

done by presenting, in English, simplified sections of the syntheses, orally and in writing, for verification, and with the option of removing anything she wished, as per their informed consent.

The Participant

Fadumo, the single participant in this chapter, is a member of the largest Somali community in the United States. Minnesota has an estimated 40,000 Somalis, with most living in Minneapolis or St. Paul. Fadumo is also a member of a very large family. She is the oldest of 10 children and these data were gathered when she was 18 years old and a senior in high school. At the time of the study, Fadumo's mother worked second shift as a janitor. When I interacted with her, I found that she has very limited English language skills. Fadumo told me she had not been to school.

At age 6, Fadumo fled Somalia with her mother and siblings due to the Civil war in the late 90s. They lived in a refugee camp in Kenya for eight years. She is not alone in having her life interrupted by civil war. Somalis are among many refugees who have spent many years in refugee camps in Kenya or Ethiopia waiting to be processed to resettle in third countries. Refugee camps are characterized by violence, exploitation, lack of schooling opportunities, scarcity of food, inadequate housing, and unsanitary living conditions. Due to these stark facts, Fadumo's first formal schooling experience was in the United States. She was enrolled as a freshman in a large urban high school, which had two main student populations at the time: Somalis and African Americans. She attended this school for two years. In her junior year, she transferred to an Afro-centric charter school[4] and then returned to the initial school she attended to complete her senior year and graduate. Because Fadumo was part of a large wave of Somali refugees that settled in Minnesota, she was afforded a couple of high-school content classes in Somali during her first year. As she progressed through school and learned English, her grades steadily improved. She met all of her graduation requirements and graduated in 4 years with a 3.85 grade point average. I speculated that her "good student" behavior may have contributed to high grades, but I also believe that Fadumo did indeed meet her teachers' expectations.

---

4. An Afrocentric curriculum typically provides a learning environment that includes content, role models, images and discussions that reflect the African-American communities. The world-view presented and encouraged link students to their African and African-American history, arts, literature, philosophy, etc.

Results and Discussion

Fadumo's family is large and they work as a unit to support each other. Fadumo's family is clearly the most important source of social capital Fadumo has and this is the support that she often leverages to do well in school. Fadumo sees her mother as a strong role-model and the expectation in the family is that Fadumo will study and get a good job. Fadumo and her sister both talked about how difficult it was to be in the refugee camp but that the family stayed together despite the hardship. When they resettled in Minnesota, the family continued to work together. Examples of this are working together to understand the daily mail and to manage their interactions with English speaking Minnesotans. Fadumo stresses that her mother never allowed her children to become in charge of the household, translating or take on parenting roles due to her own lack of skill in English, something often reported in immigrant families (Faulstich Orellana, 2003). In fact, Fadumo's mother has strong opinions about schooling and has her own way of interacting with her children's teachers and schools. In the quote below, Fadumo explains that her mother uses her friends as translators in\stead of the children.

M (*researcher*): So your mother is not afraid to go to school? Does she speak English?

F (*Fadumo*): No.

M: How does she talk to the teachers … does she bring someone to translate?

F: Yeah. She don't bring us cause she think like … she don't trust us.

M: Who does she bring?

F: Like you know she calls the people she knows and "can you come tomorrow for help me, like that." They say, "Ok."

M: You know I've heard a lot of people say parents are afraid to go to school because they don't speak English.

F: My mom, she do whatever she do. She go to school by herself. She do everything.

This transcript does not reveal the common embarrassment teenagers feel about their parents, rather it shows that Fadumo is proud of her mother: "She go to school by herself. She do everything." It is also clear that Fadumo's mom is in charge of her own communication with the school because she brings a friend with her to talk to teachers rather than rely on her children or school liaisons to be interpreters.

Fadumo also said that her mother is likely to go to her children's school at any time, not only when called for conferences. Fadumo told me, laughing, that she and all her siblings try very hard to be on time for the school bus. Otherwise, her mother will load everyone into the family minivan and drop each child off at their school and visit each teacher, impromptu. While this may not be a common or even a sanctioned way of interacting with teachers in the United States, the message to the children is clear: their mother is going to find out how things are going in school, in her own way. Her mom has a set of questions she asks each teacher including finding out where her children sit in class. Fadumo explains her mother's opinion about her sons sitting in the back of the class and her strategy for getting them to move forward:

> F: You know they [Fadumo's brothers] sit in the class in the back. She don't like when the people sit in the back.
> M: So she finds out where they sit and everything.
> F: If they do something, she repeat it like joke. She make like a joke.
> M: She teases them about sitting in the back or whatever?
> F: Yes.

Fadumo's mother clearly shows interest in her children's education and communicates her expectation that they do well in school. Needless to say, Fadumo's mother challenges commonly held assumptions that immigrant parents are not involved in their children's schooling (Lopez, 2001).

Another thing that Fadumo's mother does is closely monitor the children in terms of who their friends are. If they are not associating with "good" kids, the child may be transferred to another school. Fadumo's mother believes that it is better not to have friends in school, if those friends are not "good." This issue has applied only to the boys in Fadumo's family thus far, but the assumption is that the same thing would occur if a girl in the family began associating with "bad" friends. The following conversation began because Fadumo told me about an incident at her school where a gun was found in a student's locker.

> M: Do your brothers get in fights?
> F: Never.
> M: How do they stay out of fights?
> F: It's the parents.
> M: Because they are afraid of the parents. So what does your mother do to make them afraid?

F: She knows, "Why you to fight, what are doing in the house, xxx, I cook for you for food, I clean everything. Just go to school and learn.
M: School is their only job.
F: Yeah. Same for me. They get like that cause they scared for my mom because of that. For the boys, she go to school and talk to other teachers and she says to them now, "Why this happen and who was the side of the problem."

This excerpt illustrates again the fact that Fadumo's mother is solidly rooted in her parenting role and that she is respected by all of her children. She can exert this power in terms of their behavior outside of the home, including at school. These data contribute to the large body of literature (Dinovitzer, Hagan, & Parker, 2003) indicating that parental involvement and close monitoring are important for academic success.

About a year after this interview, Fadumo told me that her mother took two of the oldest boys in the family to a boarding school in Kenya. This decision was made when Fadumo's mother felt that the boys were in danger of getting into trouble with the law because they stayed out all night on a couple of occasions without permission. Fadumo tells about how the boys were given no notice, presumably in order to curtail any opposition to the decision. The months went by and Fadumo gave me frequent updates about how the boys "were growing up to be men," how they were speaking Somali, doing their Qur'anic studies and doing well in school. Fadumo was certain that her mother's decision to send the boys back to Africa was good for them. Nevertheless, educators may see this decision as extreme or educationally disruptive. According to Fadumo, it was the best thing her mother could have done and it ended well.

Knowing that Fadumo is the oldest of 10 children, one would expect her family responsibilities to have a powerful impact on her ability to get her homework done. These responsibilities, however, did not seem to hinder her ability to meet her teachers' expectations. Fadumo explained to me how she would go to a nearby library if she needed a quiet place to study and her sister or brothers would take over her tasks. On a separate occasion, Fadumo told me about how when she needed help with her homework, she would take a bus to a neighborhood where she could get help at a homework help program and that it was often possible to get bilingual help at this program. She also told about how some of the younger children who are somewhat more fluent in English often helped her with her homework. The description Fadumo depicts of her home with respect to education is that they all work together to help each other succeed. It is also evident that Fadumo is not the only one succeeding. It is also relevant to note that a child does not necessarily require a parent to sit with them to complete homework assignments, as is often assumed. This task can often be managed among peers or siblings.

So, while she is the oldest girl, in a large family that moves frequently and struggles financially, it is clear that this is a highly functioning family unit with a strong mother who is clearly in control of her children's upbringing and education. They pool their skills and resources in ways that clearly illustrate that they support each other's goals, and value all the sibling's success at school. Fadumo's family is clearly a main source of social capital for Fadumo. This portrait of family involvement may challenge the cliché of a refugee-background family without formal educational experiences as floundering, without agency, or following proscribed ways of parent involvement endorsed or expected by educators in the United States.

It comes as no surprise that Fadumo identifies as Somali and Muslim and, for her, these descriptors are almost completely interchangeable. These identity markers are meaningful in this context because of the large Somali community in Minnesota that identifies similarly. Fadumo wears a full length, traditional hijab, which further identifies her as Somali and Muslim. In all the time, I knew her, she never modified[5] her conservative-style hijab, nor did she experiment with taking it off, as some Somali girls I knew did. At the time of the research, I was learning about Islam, so this was a frequent topic I brought up. The following is what Fadumo said when I asked her about taking off her hijab:

F: If you don't like the hijab, you have to throw it away. Sometimes you wear it. If you don't like it, destroy it. You are big enough. You're not a kid.

M: If you decided that you didn't want to wear the hijab anymore would your mother be mad?

F: She say ok. You're not like a little kid.

One possible explanation for this absence of struggle is that Fadumo's family regularly goes to the mosque on weekends and observes Islamic prayer and eating requirements together. Fadumo studies the Qur'an and meets with a tutor (*duksi*) to do so. She is not experiencing a rapid assimilation process and has a great deal of cultural continuity in her life. Portes and Zhou (1993) argue that immigrant youths who remain firmly ensconced in their respective

---

5. Some Somali girls modify their head covering by wearing hats, hooded sweatshirts, tight scarves that cover their hair and tie into a low bun, or loose scarves that drape without full hair coverage.

ethnic communities may, by virtue of this fact, have a better chance for educational and economic mobility through use of the material and social capital that their communities make available" (p. 82).

Fadumo's community, given its size, is another source of social capital for her. The community grounds her as Muslim female in an overwhelmingly Judeo-Christian society and, in conjunction with her family, seems to give her strength to maintain her religious practices and rewards her with a respectable place in her society. Beyond using a bilingual homework help there are few examples of Fadumo using the Somali community as social capital. As explained previously, her mother uses her community network to recruit translators to accompany her to the children's schools. They are able to shop, worship, hear news, and socialize in Somali. It is likely that Fadumo will be able to cash in on the social capital she has in the Somali communities of Minnesota for work opportunities in the community and perhaps beyond it, in which case her Somali co-ethnics serve as brokers of cultural capital of mainstream culture knowledge (Willis, 1977).

An important mechanism that Fadumo and her family use to leverage social capital is through their use of the Somali language. Heller (1987) points out that "it is through language that a person gains access to – or is denied access to – powerful social networks that give learners the opportunity to speak" (p. 5). I argue that the Somali networks that Fadumo and her family leverage may not be viewed as a powerful group at the time Fadumo was in high school, but they were very important for gaining access to many important social networks and sources of social capital. The way in which Fadumo and her family operate as a unit and part of a larger social network of Somali families allows them to access a number of networks that call for Somali and English language skills. Their Somali language networks are tapped through Somali television, commerce, and a large network of family friends. Fadumo's family benefits greatly from the size of the Somali community in this metropolitan area.

I often asked to come to school with her so I could understand what Fadumo's school day was like, but she repeatedly found excuses for me not to come to see her at school. Information about who Fadumo was as school is a large gap in this study, but things she told me, point to a lack of friends as a gap in Fadumo's social network, and perhaps social capital. She said that she often spent the entire day at school alone, talking with no one. She resisted making friends because she thought that they could distract her from her one purpose of being in school, which was to graduate, or that they could put her in physical danger if they offended another group of students and caused a fight. It is also notable that Fadumo had few acquaintances who were not Somali. She said that the only white people she knew were her teachers and me. It seemed to me that Fadumo's policies about no friends at school seemed to be working for her, but given how important peer groups typically are for adolescents, it was something I kept questioning. There is a great deal of scholarly literature on this topic (Datnow & Cooper, 1997), much of which suggests the importance of peer groups for developing a sense of belonging, or being known at school.

Cultural Capital: Language, and Doing School

Fadumo and her family demonstrate that they are quickly acquiring cultural capital. The ability to master English and any other language should be seen as cultural capital (Trueba, 2002) in today's globalized economy. Fadumo's family is retaining Somali and at the same time learning English quickly. English skills are needed to navigate numerous institutions and systems and for this reason are termed cultural capital. Fadumo's family hears about social services and homework help programs through their social network (social capital) and often call upon their friends to help them navigate those services. One clear example is their enrollment in a program, which pays Fadumo a stipend for the care of her younger siblings. Enrolling in this program required knowing the program existed, knowing that they would qualify, and then getting on the waiting list. Managing bureaucracies in Minnesota, as well as the workings of schooling and immigration institutions require skills that tap into Fadumo's Somali social capital and then crosses over into displays of cultural capital that can turn into concrete financial gains.

In addition, a guiding question in my interactions with Fadumo was how does an adolescent refugee newcomer with no prior formal schooling enroll in a U.S. high school and know what to do? Fadumo had to make for herself a student identity without many references. As the oldest sibling, nobody in her family had done what she was doing, and she did not have the years of experience with formal schooling that adolescents her age typically have. Nevertheless, Fadumo was strategic in high school and this, I argue, is an example of her acquiring cultural capital. She knew how to show teachers that she cared about her studies. For example, she had a flawless attendance record, always did her homework, showed teachers drafts of projects and papers, and asked for help when she needed it. Obtaining this level of strategic competence in school was not a small accomplishment and it seems that Fadumo created/fashioned her own strategies, on her own terms. Fadumo forged a student identity along with behaviors that endeared her to her teachers. She remained immune to peer pressure and focused on her educational goals.[6]

Fadumo said that her biggest challenge in her junior year was passing the state-mandated graduation tests. After taking them 3 times, she passed them the summer before her senior year. Fadumo said that her biggest challenges presented to her in her senior year were knowing how to apply for college, take the SATs, and fill out financial aid forms. Her academic literacy skills were not well developed, despite having obtained a very high grade point average. In fact, her reading and writing skills upon graduation from high school were still quite low, something that Fadumo did not seem to identify as a potential problem for her future education. I was concerned that her dream of becoming a nurse would be limited by her secondary education experiences and an inflated vision of her academic skills. In the end, Fadumo needed to spend a couple of years at a community college working on her English skills and then she was able to enroll in a program for ultrasound technicians. I continue to be bothered by the question of whether Fadumo's high school education failed her. Should she have stayed in high school longer? Did she need a different type of schooling experience to acquire the literacy skills needed for a career in health care?

Conclusion

It is important to theorize about Fadumo's experiences carefully. There is always a risk that we present her, and others like her, solely as victims or heroes of poverty, war, or displacement. Fadumo is a person who migrated within a set of circumstances and resettled in a state with another set of circumstances. Clearly, she is a remarkable person, but she is also able to define and redefine herself within the social and cultural capital she has available to her in Minnesota. She accomplished a great deal in her four years of education with the help of her family and her Somali community. Could Fadumo's high school have prepared her better? Should her high school experience have been extended beyond four years, given the fact that this was her *first and only*

---

6. It is possible that being Muslim will help girls like Fadumo survive high school. One study about adolescent alcohol abstainers in Oslo found that Muslim immigrant girls are the biggest group of abstainers (Pedersen & Kolstad, 2000). Could being Muslim be a form of cultural capital because by following Islamic law keep Muslim girls from beings exposed to the risks involved with, for example, drinking alcohol or dating?

formal schooling experience? These questions cause me to wish to revise what should be defined as "success" in high school for Fadumo and other adolescents like her. It seems that it is entirely reasonable to envision secondary programs for students like Fadumo that are better tailored to their needs and take longer to complete. This would give them time to develop better academic literacy skills needed to pursue the goals students like Fadumo envision for themselves. Fadumo has the desire and support to persevere, but may have been better served with a stronger high school background. Furthermore, she needed different kinds of support as she moved through high school. Her most urgent need toward the end of her high school years was guidance in choosing and taking her next steps after high school.

Perhaps Somali community members who are experts on certain topics could partner with teachers to discuss difficult concepts with Somali youth.[7] Knowing that she does not know how to reach logistically her post-secondary goals is essential. Schools need to take on the role of helping students like Fadumo do such things as find out about jobs students can do, apply for scholarships, fill out college applications and financial aid forms, meet deadlines for registering for the SAT, get recommendation letters, write personal statements and visit campuses. If this does not occur, students like Fadumo may discover that while they have much social capital, they cannot leverage it because of lack of this crucial body of cultural capital. It is important to recognize the powerful assets of Fadumo's life, particularly her family and her community. At the same time it is essential to see where her family and community leave off and where the school must continue. Educators must problematize this issue. As Lubienski (2003) argues, "Because our current ideologies cannot help but define what we consider a "problem," the restrictions against discussing "problems" that diverse groups can have can bias research conducted on diverse students' experiences in classrooms" (p. 35). It is essential that we all engage in recognizing "problems" in order to raise expectations of all marginalized youth and equitably education all students.

Fadumo, and students like her, are more dependent on schools for knowledge about what it takes to get into and succeed in college than their peers who have this cultural capital. Teachers need to be able to build cultural capital in order to harness the social capital many refugee youth bring to school. Failure to do so represents missed opportunities for immigrant youth at a time when a college diploma is an essential credential for economic survival.

---

7. It is important that parents do not have asymmetrical alliances with schools or teachers where "one component is defining and limiting the role of its counterpart" (González, 2005, p. 42).

This analysis of social and cultural capital points to the need to reconcile how funds of knowledge fit into this a framework for how to identify and characterize the assets Fadumo has. Her social capital consists of people she knows, but many of these people speak Somali. To unlock her Somali social capital, Fadumo needs to maintain her Somali language skills. But Somali is not the language of the dominant society, so it cannot be categorized as cultural capital. Likewise, so many of the things that Fadumo's mother knows are not the knowledge of the dominant society in Minnesota. In fact, much of what she knows may seem at odds with what a mother from the dominant society might think or do.

For this reason, it is important to retain the concept of "funds of knowledge" (González, 2005) to be able to name Fadumo's assets – her Somali language skills, her mother's ways of interacting with school systems and educators. Funds of knowledge research should be part and parcel of any analysis that looks at social and cultural capital in order to challenge deficit framings and views of immigrant and refugee-background youth.

Discussion Questions[8]

1. Do you think Fadumo's teachers failed her by rewarding her with good grades without providing adequate support to develop the literacy skills she needed for her educational and career aspirations? Why or why not?

2. How can schools and educators help students like Fadumo leverage her family's funds of knowledge as well as acquire more cultural and social capital?

3. How does Fadumo's story complicate the narrative of the American dream? In other words, how does her story inform the relationship between hard work and success in the United States?

4. How can you, or a teacher you know, systematically incorporate students' funds of knowledge into classroom learning?

5. How do you make a deposit into a student's cultural capital without making a withdrawal from their funds of knowledge?

6. How can we problematize the goal of finishing high school in four years for newcomers with limited formal schooling? How do we disassociate an extra year or two in high school from negative stigma of being "held back" for failing or seeming unintelligent?

---

8. Many thanks to the Second Language Education Postbacs of 2018–2019 for helping me write these questions and trying them out with me.

7. Where do students get social and cultural capital that they can use to succeed in school if they have do not get it from teachers? Can you imagine systems that offer access to people and knowledge that leads to jobs, out-of-school learning opportunities, and educational opportunities?

Note

This chapter was published in an earlier form in this outlet:

Bigelow, M. (2007). Social and cultural capital at school: The case of a Somali teenage girl with limited formal schooling. In N. R. Faux (Ed.), *Low-educated adult second language and literacy acquisition proceedings of symposium* (pp. 7–22). Richmond, VA: Literacy Institute at Virginia Commonwealth University.

References

Bourdieu, P., & Passeron, J.-C. (1977). *Reproduction in education, society, culture*. Beverly Hills, CA: Sage.

Coleman, J. S. (1990). *Foundations of social theory*. Cambridge: The Belknap Press of Harvard University Press.

Cummins, J. (1981). The role of primary language development in promoting educational success for language minority students. In California State Department of Education (Ed.), *Schooling and language minority students: A theoretical framework* (pp. 3–49). Los Angeles, CA: National Dissemination and Assessment Center.

Datnow, A., & Cooper, R. (1997). Peer networks of African American students in independent schools: Affirming academic success and racial identity. *The Journal of Negro Education, 66*(1), 56–72. doi:10.2307/2967251

Dinovitzer, R., Hagan, J., & Parker, P. (2003). Choice and circumstance: Social capital and planful competence in the attainments of immigrant youth. *Canadian Journal of Sociology/Caiers canadiens de sociologie, 28*(4), 463–488.

Faulstich Orellana, M. (2003). Responsibilities of children in Latino immigrant homes. *New Direction for Student Leadership: Understanding the Social Worlds of Immigrant Youth, 100*, 25–39.

Gibson, M. A. (1988). *Accommodation without assimilation: Punjabi Sikh immigrants in American high schools and community*. Ithaca, NY: Cornell University Press.

Gonzales, R. (2003, May 14). Kid translators. *Morning Edition, National Public Radio*. Available at http://www.npr.org/templates/story/story.php?storyId=1262985.

González, N. (2005). Beyond culture: The hybridity of funds of knowledge. In N. González, L. Moll, & C. Amanti (Eds.), *Fund of knowledge* (pp. 29–46). Mahwah, NJ: Lawrence Erlbaum Associates, Publishers.

Heller, M. (1987). The role of language in the formation of ethnic identity. In J. Phinney & M. Rotheram (Eds.), *Children's ethnic socialization* (pp. 180–200). Newbury Park, CA: Sage.

Ibrahim, A. (2010). "Hey, whadap homeboy?" Identification, desire & consumption: Hip-Hop, performativity, and the politics of becoming black. In S. Steinberg & L. Cornish (Eds.), *Taboo: Essays on culture and education* (pp. 117–137). New York, NY: Peter Lang.

Ibrahim, A. (2014) Research as an act of love: Ethics, émigrés, and the praxis of becoming human. *Diaspora, Indigenous, and Minority Education, 8*(1), 7–20.

Lincoln, Y., & Guba, E. G. (1985). *Naturalistic inquiry.* Beverly Hills, CA: Sage.

Lubienski, S. T. (2003). Celebrating diversity and denying disparities: A critical assessment. *Educational Researcher, 32*(8), 30–38.

Lopez, G. R. (2001). The value of hard work: Lessons on parent involvement from an (im)migrant household. *Harvard Educational Review, 71*(3), 416–437.

Lopez, N. (2003). *Hopeful girls, troubled boys: Race and gender disparity in urban education.* New York, NY: Routledge.

Olsen, L. (1997). *Made in America: Immigrant students in our public schools.* New York, NY: The New Press.

Pedersen, W., & Kolstad, A. (2000). Adolescent alcohol abstainers: Traditional patterns in new groups. *ACTA Sociologica, 43,* 219–233.

Portes, A. (1998). Social capital: Its origins and applications in modern society. *Annual Review of Sociology, 24,* 1–24.

Portes, A., & MacLeod, D. (1996). Educational progress of children of immigrants: The roles of class, ethnicity, and school context. *Sociology of Education, 69,* 255–275.

Portes, A., & Rumbaut, R. G. (1996). *Immigrant America: A portrait.* Berkeley: University of California Press.

Portes, A., & Zhou, M. (1993). The new second generation: Segmented assimilation and its variants. *Annals of the American Academy of Political and Social Science, 530,* 74–96.

Rymes, B. (2001). *Conversational borderlands: Language and identity in an alternative urban high school.* New York, NY: Teachers College Press.

Trueba, H. T. (2002). Multiple ethnic, racial and cultural identities in action: From marginality to a new cultural capital in modern society. *Journal of Latinos and Education, 1*(1), 7–28.

Valenzuela, A. (1999). *Subtractive schooling: U.S.-Mexican youth and the politics of caring.* Albany: State University of New York Press.

White, M. J., & Glick, J. E. (2000). Generation status, social capital, and the routes out of high school. *Sociological Forum, 15*(4), 671–691.

White, M. J., & Kaufman, G. (1997). Language usage, social capital, and school completion among immigrants and native-born ethnic groups. *Social Science Quarterly, 78*(2), 385–398.

Willis, P. (1977). *Learning to labour: How working class kids get working class jobs.* London, UK: Saxon House.

Zhou, M., & Bankston, C. L., III. (1994). Social capital and the adaptation of Vietnamese youth in New Orleans. *International Migration Review, 28,* 821–845.

7 Taking Control of the Narrative: Empowering Black Immigrants through an African-Centered Approach

BABATUNJI IFARINU
DeKalb County School District

Introduction

A common precept in education is that teachers are the most important determining factor of student success (Tucker & Stronge, 2005). This statement holds some ramifications that must be critically examined. This idea affirms that teachers hold a great amount of power over what students will learn, how they conceptualize themselves, and ultimately, who they are. As Woodson (1933/1998) stated:

> When you control a man's thinking you do not have to worry about his actions. You do not have to tell him not to stand here or go yonder. He will find his "proper place" and will stay in it. You do not need to send him to the back door. He will go without being told. In fact, if there is no back door, he will cut one for his special benefit. His education makes it necessary (p. xi).

The educational system in the United States lacks diversity. This is a long-standing issue. To this point, the student population in US schools is becoming more diverse, while the teaching force shows slight changes in terms of diversity (de Brey, Musu, McFarland, Wilkinson-Flicker, Diliberti, Zhang, Branstetter, & Wang, 2019). Because of this issue, it is even more important a culturally responsive pedagogy becomes the norm in the Education system. By using a culturally responsive pedagogy, the teacher has the ability to create a learning environment that is relevant and effective for ethnically diverse students. As an outcome, the culturally responsive educator recognizes the importance of racial and cultural diversity and learning and uses it to empower ethnically diverse students (Gay, 2000).

There are very few research studies that affirm the importance of African centered pedagogy. I argue that the need for culturally responsive pedagogy is of utmost importance for Black immigrant students for two reasons. First, as a group that has experienced a history of oppression by dominant groups, I argue that a culturally responsive pedagogy is necessary to not only enhance the cultural competency of educators but also disrupt the hegemonic systems that perpetuate problems experienced by Black immigrant students in US school systems. Second, I argue that culturally responsive pedagogy which is African-centered will enable Black immigrant students to develop self-efficacy and to take control of the narrative as it relates to curriculum standards. Writing about African centered pedagogy is limited and refers mostly to African Americans. There is a need for more research on this topic and an expansion of the scope to include students throughout the African diaspora. To understand both the scope of this challenge and the historical dynamics of oppressive groups and the oppressed, I first describe the geographical and historical characteristics of Black immigrants as members of the Black student population.

For this chapter, I define three subgroups of individuals of African descent that collectively make up the Black student population. The first subgroup, Continental African immigrants, those born on the African continent, and have immigrated to the United States are from different regions of Africa. Continental African immigrants represent one of the largest groups of immigrants moving to the United States (Bryan, Cooper, & Ifarinu, 2019). The second subgroup is immigrants of African descent are those who come from the Caribbean and Latin America as well as other regions of the world (Bryan, Cooper, & Ifarinu, 2019). Both the first and second subgroups share similarities in that some immigrated to the United States voluntarily while others came as refugees.

Additionally, both subgroups possess unique cultures and histories. For consistency purposes, I refer to this first and second group collectively as Black immigrants. African Americans are the third subgroup of Black students, those born in the continental United States. This third subgroup, with its own influential and rich culture, is connected to the other two subgroups by its shared heritage of African ancestry. When I use the terms, "African" and "African people," I am referring to the convergence of all three subgroups through a shared history of African ancestry, minority status in the US regardless of the land of birth. When I use the terms, "Black" and "Black student population," I am referring to the convergence of all three subgroups as it relates to their needs for culturally responsive pedagogy. Within this chapter, I am focusing on the particular experiences and culturally responsive pedagogic needs of Black immigrant students.

Despite the experiences and culturally responsive pedagogic needs of the Black immigrant population, the US school system has not been successful at educating students of African descent. This is illustrated by the disproportionate number of Black immigrant children in special education programs as well as those who receive suspensions (Hale-Benson, 1982). Black immigrant children must have a culturally responsive educational system that recognizes their strengths, their abilities, and their culture. In addition, a culturally responsive education would incorporate these attributes into the learning process (Hale-Benson, 1982). As a result, an African-centered pedagogy is essential for the holistic education of Black immigrant students. From much of the information about African-centered pedagogy, there is an exclusive focus on African American students. However, with an increasing number of Black immigrants entering US public schools, an African-centered pedagogy is essential to recognize as well as similarities between the cultural and educational needs of African American students and those of Black immigrant students. I argue that designing an African-centered pedagogy that targets Black immigrant students is necessary to shift the US school system from disproportionately neglecting the needs of Black immigrant students to one that successfully educates them.

A critical step for educators to create a culturally responsive education system for Black immigrant students is to recognize that both oppression and degradation of African people are embedded in American ideology, culture, and schooling (Murrell, 2002). The African-centered educator is not only aware of this but endeavors to create a learning environment that challenges white superiority. The goal is to increase the self-efficacy of Black immigrant students so that their innate ability to achieve is released. An educator who becomes African-centered in his or her thinking not only deconstructs assumptions about the social paradigm that validates European-centered hegemony but also reconstructs the social reality of African people (Shujaa, 1993).

When discussing African-centered education, Shujaa (1993) recommends more emphasis should be placed on pedagogy than on curriculum. He argues that pedagogy conveys the importance of the educator to the education process while curriculum is too often reduced to documentation (Shujaa, 1993). This means that the responsibility for providing a culturally responsive educational experience for Black immigrant students belongs to the educator. Ideally, this should happen despite the curriculum that is being used (Shujaa, 1993).

To engage students through an African-centered pedagogy, educators would need to go beyond their initial training and certification programs. To this end, educators would need to be lifelong learners. Instruction would need to be based upon the cultural needs of their students. Educators should be educated about the cultural experiences of their students. This is especially difficult because professional learning for educators with a focus on cultural competency is not readily available nor required. In most cases, acquiring cultural competency is an endeavor that educators must embark on independently.

An approach to creating an African-centered pedagogy requires educators to conduct constant research and self-analysis. Educators will need to know the background and history of Black immigrant students in their classrooms. Constant research means being in constant communication with their students and intentional about building relationships with them. Regarding self-analysis, educators will need to recognize their ignorance and biases that may interfere with the instruction of Black immigrant students. In summary, the best environment for creating an African-centered pedagogy is one in which educators learn from their students as much as the students learn from them.

Recognizing Your Connection to the Brave Hunter

While conducting a professional learning session on empowering Black English language learners to a white majority audience, I showed pictures of a hunter, a pair of deer, a dead deer, and a deer attacking a hunter. I asked them to view the pictures and tell the story from the perspective of the deer. The audience was reluctant to participate. However, one female educator stood up and said, "I'll try." Her first remark was that the hunter reminded her of her uncle. Next, she began to tell a story, mostly describing the personality and intentions of her uncle as the hunter. Finally, she remarked that the deer had attacked the hunter because the hunter had killed the deer's companion. Despite my instruction to tell the story from the perspective of the deer, instead, we received a story that portrayed the hunter as the victim. I drew a parallel between the inability or unwillingness of the educator to tell a story from the perspective of the deer to the inability or unwillingness of educators to be culturally responsive and aware of the needs of Black immigrant students.

There is a longstanding structure to US school systems by which an oppressive group narrates (teaches) while the oppressed group listens (learns) (Freire, 1972). This structure, the narrator, or educator, expounds on topics that are alien to the experience of the listeners, or the students. The goal is to deposit information into the minds of the students without consideration of the content or how the content affects the students. Freire refers to this as "banking concept of education" in which information is deposited into the minds of students (Freire, 1972). One consequence of this banking approach is that the educator, as a representative of the oppressive group, systematically devalues the experiences and ultimately diminishes the self-efficacy of the students, the oppressed group. The goal of African-centered pedagogy is to systematically interrogate the ideologies of repression (Murrell, 2002). This is a distinct contradiction to the banking concept of education.

African-centered educators must be continuously self-reflective to assure that they are not practicing the banking concept of education. Using this approach, educators must analyze how living in a hegemonic society has affected their worldview and, subsequently, how their worldview imparts an oppressive pedagogy on students. In short, an educator's relationship with the dominant group in a hegemonic society influences how he or she thinks about themselves and their students.

Jane Elliot, an American educator, illustrated the influence of hegemonic systems in schools in 1968 when she conducted an exercise in her third-grade classroom. She informed the brown-eyed students in her class that they were superior to the blue-eyed students, and they were to act as such. This experiment was a very short exercise. However, in the course of 15 minutes, Elliot witnessed her brown-eyed students transform from nice and accommodating to viciously discriminating students. At the same time, she witnessed her confident blue-eyed students become timid, frightened, angry, and unable to learn. Elliot began to conduct this exercise on people of different ages throughout the country to demonstrate how a system of inequity affects achievement and self-worth. After witnessing these behaviors happening within a short period in her classroom, Elliot questioned how these behaviors affect people who experience inequitable conditions over a lifetime. She conducted this exercise for more than 50 years with the same results. In a 2017 NBC news report, Elliot discussed the experiment and stated that she feels that her exercise is currently being reenacted on a national level in the United States (Anti-Racism Educator, 2017). What Elliot has demonstrated is that systems of oppression play out in schools wherever there is an opportunity for members of a dominant group to exploit an oppressed group.

With the "Brave Hunter and the Deer" exercise, I purposely referred to the hunter as "the Brave Hunter." This example illustrates how lessons in school curriculums are presented to students of African descent. For example, colonization is referred to as conquering. Enslaved Africans are simply referred to as slaves, which minimizes them as humans. Educators who are not cognizant of their relationship to dominant oppressive groups may unintentionally yet routinely assign slave identities to their African students. The educator who identified with the hunter is expected to tell the story from the perspective of the deer regardless of her identification with the hunter. In a sense, the educator, if she attempts to tell the story from the perspective of the deer, is brave because she is taking a position that is counter to her relationship with the dominant group (i.e., the hunter). In this situation, educators often feel guilt or express denial when addressing issues of oppression and inequity in society and within the curriculum. These types of responses not only interfere with the educators' ability to adequately critique content but also to respectfully engage Black immigrant students. To develop a learning environment that promotes self-efficacy for Black immigrant students, educators who have ancestral connections (i.e., people of European descent) with those who have colonized African people must be educated as to how to best instruct those whose ancestors were colonized or enslaved (i.e., people of African descent).

In 2015 the *Washington Post* reported that school officials in Texas changed the state guidelines for teaching American history so that it did not mention the Ku Klux Klan or Jim Crow laws (Brown, 2015). Also, slavery was deliberately written as a secondary issue of the Civil War. This change affected at least five million public school students in Texas and has influenced textbooks across the country. This push to exclude information that challenges the American and European hegemonic system illustrates the danger of privilege and the power to control the narrative.

The Privilege and Power of Perspective

> To manipulate history is to manipulate consciousness; to manipulate consciousness is to manipulate possibilities, and to manipulate possibilities is to manipulate power.
>
> Amos Wilson (2014)

In the 1940s, psychologists Kenneth and Mamie Clarke designed an experiment to study the effects of segregation on Black children. The experiment, which was called the doll test, presented children with dolls identical in physical features except for skin color. The children were asked which doll they felt was nice and pretty versus ugly and bad. The majority of the children attributed positive characteristics (i.e., nice and pretty) to the white doll. In 2016 the American Association of University Women (AAUW) reported that this experiment has been replicated over the last 80 years and has yielded similar results (Gould, 2016). Although de jure segregation was outlawed by Civil Rights legislation, the results of this experiment are frequently attributed to the persistence of a de facto segregated society.

The narrative of African people worldwide is being controlled by Eurasian people who have historically oppressed African people. This oppressive narrative shapes the consciousness and psychology of both the oppressed and the oppressor. The oppressed internalizes the oppression to the point in which they believe the narrative written about them. They act out the narrative by behaving in subordinate ways which further perpetuates the oppressive narrative. The doll test illustrates this internalization. As a result, the oppressive system is legitimated, and the imbalance of power is maintained in favor of the oppressor (Wilson, 2002). When using an African-centered pedagogy, educators and students are encouraged to be critical of the Eurasian narrative promoted in the schooling environment and society as a whole. In other words, instead of telling the story from the hunter's perspective (or the oppressor), the goal is to tell the story from the perspective of the deer (or the oppressed).

Recognizing the Narrative in Curriculum

There are consequences to the historical narrative of African people being written and interpreted by the oppressor. The creation and shaping of a subordinate and inferior African consciousness and psychology is one consequence. Through the Eurocentric version of history, African people are stripped of their valuable resources, including their knowledge of truth and reality of self (Wilson, 1993). Being aware of the Eurocentric version of history and adequately creating an opportunity for the critical analysis of it is an essential aspect of African-centered pedagogy. The following is a high school Social Studies lesson based on the Georgia Performance Standards.

Standard SSUSH11: The student will describe the economic, social, and geographic impact of the growth of big business and technological innovations after Reconstruction.

a. Describe the inventions of Thomas Edison. Include the electric light bulb, motion pictures, and the phonograph, and their impact on American life. This is an example of identifying and addressing Eurocentric historiography. During class, my students and I were analyzing the Georgia Performance Standard above. I asked my students, "After reading the standard for today, what is missing from the standard?" Amidst a flurry of answers, one student yelled out, "The Black man who helped." He didn't know his name, but he knew from Black History Month that a Black man had something to do with the creation of the light bulb. We discussed the contribution of this Black inventor, Lewis Latimer. I later asked the students why they think Latimer was left out of the state standard although the invention of the light bulb would not have been possible without him. To encourage a response to my question, I instructed the students to write a statement from Latimer's perspective about the creation of the light bulb and how it impacted American life. After writing statements, I asked the students to conclude this exercise by explaining how they, as Black students, felt about being omitted from the state standard from Latimer's perspective.

As my example of state standards and the omission of Latimer's contribution to technological innovation has shown, African-centered pedagogy requires that educators know historical information beyond the state curriculum. Also, educators must be able to critically analyze the curriculum and, at the same time, cover the assigned information so students will be successful. The educator must be vigilant about the intentional exclusion of African people in the curriculum and the effects this has on African people, and ultimately all students. As students realize that the curriculum is not designed for the self-efficacy of all students, they become aware of the effects of being taught a curriculum that excludes the achievements of non-Europeans. It is this awareness that enables students to recognize the importance of taking control of the narrative.

Voices of Black Immigrants

Before transferring to a school made up of a significant population of Black immigrant refugee students, I taught in schools that were predominately Black. However, I've always had students from different regions of Africa. In my last four years as a classroom teacher, I taught Black immigrant students, most of whom had immigrated to the US
as refugees. Many of these students were continental Africans, mostly from central and east Africa. I taught Social Studies to classes made up of students in the English to Speakers of Other Languages (ESOL) program. I taught World Regional Geography and American Civics. I was charged with increasing the students' proficiency in English while simultaneously teaching state Social Studies standards. The students, including the continental Africans, had never been exposed to African-centered pedagogy.
The following statements were written by former students of mine who were English learners. They were asked about their experience in an African-centered classroom setting, and how it affected them as students and as an individual.

Yared (pseudonym) is an Eritrean student, born and raised in the Atlanta metro area. He was a senior in my Psychology class at a predominantly Black high school. Currently, he is a student at the University of Georgia pursuing a second undergraduate degree in Environmental Engineering after completing a degree in Biology. He has attended predominantly Black schools since the third grade. He has had continental African teachers in the past who had talked to him about recognizing his African heritage. However, he had never experienced an African-centered pedagogy.

Before entering Mr. Ifarinu's psychology class in the spring of 2010, I had never experienced a class setting where exploring our identities as "Africans" was revered. As a first-generation American, I was reminded daily at home of my African roots. From childhood, I was constantly [and] repeatedly told my identity as an Eritrean took precedence to being American. But like most kids, even wise advice from parents can go through one ear and out the other. And while I will admit, I had experience with several teachers in grade school who made it a point to preach pride in being black (which goes without question); these same teachers never had much to say about our history pre-slavery. That all changed this particular semester when Ifarinu took it a step further in anchoring our attention to where it all started: Africa.

Looking back now I can see reasons why it was so easily overlooked. My African American teachers in grade school were just that: African Americans. Meaning they were (as many of their preceding family of the last century) born in the United States. Having never breathed the air or walked the land of our ancestors, it can be intimidating to claim the continent so recreationally scrutinized and disrespected. Having attended all-black schools up until this point, I had seen classmates who were asked about their African ties give off looks insinuating their mothers were just insulted. Weirdly enough, their reaction, while misguided, was also in fact genuine. In school, entertainment, and everywhere else I was predisposed to the point that being African was considered second-class (if even that high) relative to being an American. But then here comes this unapologetic teacher, referring to my classmates and myself as "Africans" and ruffling up feathers left and right. Mr. Ifarinu made it a point that our connection to Africa wouldn't be patronized in his classroom as simply, "the continent where my ancestors are from but not me" but instead to inquire, "Why was there an effort to disconnect us with our homeland? Why wasn't the retention of our names, languages, religions, and other aspects of our culture respected in our transition to this foreign land we were uprooted to come to?" He shared his personal story of exploring Nigeria where he even adopted a name and spirituality that were more closely related to what his ancestors followed than what most of us had ever known. Stepping into his class was truly a breath of fresh air every time because you were never quite sure what was being discussed that day. One thing I always knew, however, was that I would be challenged to reflect on, "How do I feel about this and why?" He used to talk about how the world surrounding us has worked so hard to condition us in an effort (explicitly and covertly) to strip us of our real names, languages, and culture. And by us shutting our eyes and covering our ears to this message, we unknowingly perpetuate in this toxic cycle of being lost and become participators in our own oppression which is called cultural hegemony (one of the first terms I learned in Ifarinu's class.)

African-centered teaching, I believe, is essential to fostering young people mental maturity by giving them a foundation that keeps them from wavering at the sight of something else. Upon graduating, I attended a predominantly white institution which proved to be a hurdle before I even stepped into the classroom. However, leaving high school after interactions with Mr. Ifarinu better equipped me to not be intimidated even as a minority. The identity that I had at the time compared to now was still in its infancy. However, my sense of security anchored me so that I would never be swayed to adopt another's culture just to avoid momentary discomfort or insecurity.

An important concept in African-centered pedagogy is critiquing the narrative of self-identity that has been largely accepted. I often hear my fellow educators refer to continental Africans as "the Africans" thus separating themselves. In his statement, Yared mentioned his experience with self-identity and the identity of African people in America. I was very intentional about creating an environment where it was understood that we are African people. This pan-African approach to identity set up the learning environment for using an African-centered pedagogy.

Another point to discuss from Yared's statement is the empowering effect that an African-centered pedagogy has on students. The common narrative that I have heard from many parents and professionals is that African students must experience a more diverse (White) setting in order to be prepared for the "real world." This narrative is especially dangerous, especially since White children are not being told that they must be around people of color to be successful. As a result, an African-centered pedagogy, and not a high population of White students, is what is needed to instill confidence in African students.

Muyombo (pseudonym) is a student from the Congo. He was a freshman taking a sheltered instruction World Regional Geography course. At that time, he had been in the US for three years. Currently, he is a junior at Georgia State University pursuing a Computer Science degree.

As opposed to other American schools I attended previous to attending Mister Ifarinu's class, I had realized that Mister Ifarinu's teaching style was different. Anywhere else, history is told from the perspective of the so-called "conquerors" who are in reality viewed as the oppressors by those who they "conquered" and enslaved for the so-called purpose of "civilizing" them. In-class discussions increased the level of enthusiasm in the students instead of the boring teaching methods which imposed the use of books and nothing else to convey a one-sided perspective (usually the one telling history as imperialists saw it). One day, I remember vividly Mister Ifarinu asking: "What or who did the first explorers take from Africa to the Americas by the millions?" And the class as a whole shouted in response: "slaves!" Because that is how we were taught to think. Then, after a long moment of silence, Mister Ifarinu answered by saying that "Humans ... they got humans! People like you and I were deported and enslaved." Also, we learned about the history of African people—the Bantu of central and southern Africa for example. Many history classes spend a lot of time mentioning Europeans accomplishments. Not that it is terrible, however, it becomes bad when the first time that Africans are ever mentioned in our history classes is when they are bound to captivity, enslaved, and deported to the Americas as though they had not contributed to history. In reality, grand monuments and structures such as the great ones in Zimbabwe and Egypt were thought of and realized by Africans. Mansa Musa, the king of Mali, was the wealthiest man to ever walk this earth as he would be worth around 400 billion USD today because of the gold his kingdom possessed. The man was probably one of the most influential the world has never known as by his simple pilgrimage to Mecca, through Cairo, he caused massive inflation by giving away so much gold that gold became worthless. But who talks about all that today? Well, we did in Mister Ifarinu's class. Finally, attending mister Ifarinu's class was very beneficial to me as I learned to view certain events in history through completely different lenses.

It should be noted that Muyombo had attended school in his native country. Despite being in a schooling environment on the continent of Africa, he was not exposed to an African-centered pedagogy. Attention should also be placed on the question about "... Who or what was taken from Africa?" mentioned in his writing. The fact that this was impactful after more than six years demonstrates the importance of intentional critical analysis of the Eurocentric narrative and historiography. Word choice plays a role in the process of dehumanization and within an African-centered context, it is critically analyzed.

Conclusion

In the context of an increasingly Black immigrant student populations and the achievement gap between White students and students of African descent, an African-centered pedagogy is essential for the academic and social development of African students in the US African students in the US are a very diverse population and educators must be involved in continuous self-development to effectively address the needs of these students.

The Eurocentric narrative of African people throughout the world has psychological, economic, academic, and social consequences (Wilson, 1993). A pedagogy that links the political, the cultural, and the social with identity is needed to instruct Black immigrant students successfully (Ibrahim, 1999). African-centered pedagogy requires both teacher and student to be critical of Eurocentric versions of African identity (Murrell, 2002).

Discussion Questions

1. What aspects of your life and upbringing affect your perspective of race, privilege, and power?
2. What is your connection to the story of the "Brave Hunter"? How are the narratives of the hunter and the deer related to how curriculum is written and taught?
3. How much do you know about your students beyond demographic information?
4. Who is responsible for providing information to you about your students?
5. How much do you know about current politics in certain African countries and how those issues are related to Black immigrants in the US who come from those countries?
6. Do you know the origins of the turmoil in African countries and the effects of colonization and the enslavement of African people?
7. How do you empower African students, or other traditionally marginalized student populations, and support their academic development and overall self-efficacy?

References

Anti-racism educator Jane Elliot: 'There's only one race. The human race' [Video file]. (2017, September 29). Retrieved from https://www.nbcnews.com/video/anti-racism-educator-jane-elliott-there-s-only-one-race-the-human-race-1058048579664

Brown, E. "Texas Officials: Schools Should Teach That Slavery Was 'Side Issue' to Civil War." The Washington Post, 5 July 2015, https://www.washingtonpost.com/local/education/150-years-later-schools-are-still-a-battlefield-for-interpreting-civil-war/2015/07/05/e8fbd57e-2001-11e5-bf41-c23f5d3face1_story.html.

Bryan, K., Cooper, A., & Ifarinu, B. (2019). From majority to minority advocating for English learners from the African Diaspora. In H. Linville & J. Whiting (Eds.), *Advocacy in English language teaching and learning* (pp. 190–201). New York, NY: Routledge.

de Brey, C., Musu, L., McFarland, J., Wilkinson-Flicker, S., Diliberti, M., Zhang, A., Branstetter, C., & Wang, X. (2019). Status and Trends in the Education of Racial and Ethnic Groups 2018 (NCES 2019-038). U.S. Department of Education. Washington, DC: National Center for Education Statistics. Retrieved [date] from https://nces.ed.gov/ pubsearch/.

Freire, P. (1972). *Pedagogy of the oppressed*. New York, NY: Herder and Herder.

Gay, G. (2000). *Culturally responsive teaching: Theory, research, and practice*. New York, NY: Teachers College Press.

Gould, S. (2016, February 10). Why we're still talking about the doll racism test. Retrieved from https://www.aauw.org/2016/02/10/doll-racism-test-today/

Hale-Benson, J. (1982). *Black children: their roots, culture, and learning styles*. Provo, UT: Brigham Young University Press.

Ibrahim, A. (1999). Becoming black: Rap and hip-hop, race, gender, identity, and the politics of ESL learning. *TESOL Quarterly, 33*(3), 349.

Murrell, P. C. (2002). *African-centered pedagogy: Developing schools of achievement for African American children*. Albany, NY: State University of New York Press.

Shujaa, M. J. (1993). *Too much schooling, too little education: A paradox of black life in white society*. Trenton, NJ: Africa World Press.

Tucker, P. D., & Stronge, J. H. (2005). *Linking teacher evaluation and student learning*. Alexandria, VA: Association for Supervision and Curriculum Development.

Wilson, A. N. (1993). *The falsification of Afrikan consciousness: Eurocentric history, psychiatry and the politics of white supremacy* (1st ed.). New York, NY: Afrikan World InfoSystems.

Wilson, A. N. (2002). Blueprint for black power [Audiobook]. Retrieved from https:// www.worldcat.org/title/blueprint-for-black-power-part-1–2/oclc/52961300

Wilson, A. N. (2014). *The developmental psychology of the black child* (2nd ed.). New York, NY: Afrikan World InfoSystems.

Woodson, C. G. (1998). *The Mis-education of the Negro*. Trenton, NJ: Africa World Press. (Original work published in 1933)

8 #BlackImmigrantsMatter: Preparing Teachers to Center Black Immigrant Youths' Intersectional Identities through Activism and Education

KISHA BRYAN
Tennessee State University

Introduction

The Black immigrant population is one of the fastest-growing segments of U.S. society, increasing by about 200% during the 1980s and 1990s and by 100% during the 2000s (Capps, McCabe, & Fix, 2012). In the past 10 to 15 years, the population grew from 2.4 to 3.8 million, indicating a 56% increase (Anderson, 2015). Just less than half—48 percent—of all black immigrants come from the Caribbean, 43 percent from African countries, and 3.6 percent from South America. The largest individual home countries of black immigrants in the United States today are Jamaica (693,000), Haiti (654,000), Nigeria (304,000), Ethiopia (237,000), and Trinidad and Tobago (171,000). In addition, Black immigrants make up more than one-quarter of all Black residents of the Boston, Miami, Minneapolis, New York, and Seattle metropolitan areas (Svajlenka, 2018; OELA & WHIEEAA, 2015).

In 2015, the White House Initiative on Educational Excellence for African Americans (WHIEEAA) and the U.S. Department of Education Office of English Language Acquisition (OELA) released data which showed that Maine has the highest concentration of Black English Learners (ELs) (48.6%), and Minnesota has the greatest percentage of Black ELs (19.9%). While 11 to 20% of the EL student population in New York and Florida is Black, Washington D.C., Maryland, and Texas report 6 to 10% of their EL populations as Black. Thirty one percent of Black ELs are first generation immigrants and Igbo, Yoruba, Bantu, Amharic, and Swahili are among the top 15 languages spoken by Black ELs. Hernandez's (2012) research suggests that 12% of all U.S. Black children from birth to age 10 have at least one foreign-born parent. At the post-secondary level, approximately 13% of all Black undergraduates are immigrants, a percentage that doubles and triples at the most selective colleges (Massey, Mooney, Torres, & Charles, 2007).

While Black immigrants, particularly from Africa and the Caribbean, share some of the racialized experiences of native-born Black Americans, they also have distinctive cultural contexts and identities. The U.S. education system presents an ideal environment to investigate these dynamics and experiences, as immigrants have the fastest growing child population, and these children are increasingly entering the U.S. education pipeline (Mwangi & English, 2017; Portes & Fernandez-Kelly, 2009). As Black immigrants' representation increases in U.S. education, likewise scholarship is seeing an increase of research published on their educational experiences. Yet, traditional Black identity development models and studies regarding the experiences of Black students often fail to identify how intersections of race, ethnicity, and immigration status impact students who are both Black and immigrant (Mwangi, 2014; Mwangi & English, 2017).

In this chapter, I argue that teachers and teacher educators must acknowledge and consider implications of the intersections of race and language while imagining the ways in which schools and teacher preparation program can use the Black Live Matters movement to affirm Black immigrant youth identities and provide culturally sustaining pedagogies. I share a few culturally sustaining strategies that I have utilized in a ESL teacher preparation program at a mid-size HBCU in the mid-South region of the United States.

Conceptualizing Black Immigrant Identities

Rong and Brown (2002) published a review of scholarship on Black immigrants covering the period 1982–2002. The authors examined how racial socialization intersects with identity and sociocultural factors, such as class and social norms, to impact the educational approaches of Black immigrants. They suggested that in the context of the United States, "immigration has played an essential role in shaping and reshaping the dialogues of many social situations" (p. 249) to include equality and equity in schooling, racial/ethnic identities in affirmative action, racial poverty, social mobility and language, culture, and traditions. Rong and Brown (2002) further suggests that for Black immigrants, the ambivalence that America has had toward immigration and immigrants may be compounded due to the legacy of racism, discrimination, and xenophobia. Rong and Brown's declaration of a decade and a half

Figure 8.1: Newsweek December 2017

ago are personified in the current president of the United States who sparked and uproar when he made incendiary and racially charged comments about immigration. In December 2017, it leaked that President Trump had reportedly made inflammatory about Nigerian immigrants not wanting to "go back to their huts" and that Haitian immigrants "all have AIDS," drawing widespread rebukes, including from the Haitian ambassador to the United States (See Figure 8.1).

In January 2018, Trump referred to Haitian and African immigrants—among others—as coming from "shithole countries" (See Figure 8.2).

Adding to the work of Rong and Brown (2002), Mwangi and English (2017) conducted a critical and systematic review of contemporary research of the experiences of Black immigrant youth in the U.S. P-20 education pipeline. Using a framework based on Chimamanda Ngozi Adichie's (2009) TED Talk about the "danger of a single story," Mwangi and English argues that a "universal Black experience" or the homogenous single story of Black youth that is portrayed in some contemporary research is "marginalizing and runs counter to the rhetoric of diversity, inclusion, and multiculturalism presented within the field of education" (p. 101).

In their advocacy framework for Black immigrant youth and ELs from the African diaspora, Bryan, Cooper, and Ifarinu (2019) utilized an intersectional approach (Crenshaw, 1991; McCall, 2005) to highlight discriminatory actions or inequitable practices that we otherwise might not recognize with

Figure 8.2: The Washington Post January 2018

regard to this population. While intersectionality was initially conceived as a way to present a simple reality that seemed to be hidden by conventional thinking about discrimination and exclusion, disadvantage or exclusion can be based on the interaction of multiple identities rather than just one. For Black immigrant youth, race, English proficiency (or lack thereof), religion, and/or immigration status is often consequential. Research has pointed out the ways in which dominant institutions, such as schools, play a legitimizing role in identity construction as they condone particular cultural, religious, and/or linguistic practices while ignoring others (DeCuir & Dixson, 2004; Kanno, 2003; Villenas & Foley, 2002). In addition, policies become synonymous with individuals based on their identities, to the exclusion of others. For example, when considering the DREAM Act or Deferred Action for Childhood Arrivals (DACA), the majority of Americans conjure images of Latinx youth and young adults. Svajlenka (2018) suggests, however, that nearly 11,000 DACA recipients are from countries where more than half of the nations' immigrants to the United States are Black. Additionally, the Migration Policy Institute estimates that roughly 3 percent, or 36,000 African immigrants, would have been eligible for DACA, meaning that the population of Black Dreamers is potentially much higher than those currently protected by DACA.

Black Immigrant Youth and #Black Lives Matter

Since 2016, Black Lives Matter (BLM) has also been fighting for Black immigrant populations. BLM regularly holds protests speaking out against police killings of black people, and broader issues such as racial profiling, police brutality, and racial inequality in the United States criminal justice system (Friedersdorf, 2017). On its webpage, BLM describes its mission to:

> Affirm the lives of Black queer and Trans folks, disabled folks, undocumented folks, folks with [criminal] records, women, and all Black lives along the gender spectrum. Our network centers those who have been marginalized within Black liberation movements. We are working for a world where Black lives are no longer systematically targeted for demise. We affirm our humanity, our contributions to this society, and our resilience in the face of deadly oppression (BLM, 2018).

They conclude by stating that "The call for Black lives to matter is a rallying cry for ALL Black lives striving for liberation" (BLM, 2018). Their mission includes the protections of Black immigrant populations.

In 2016, the BLM movement announced it has adopted a 10-point platform that includes a call to end all deportations. It adopted a more comprehensive platform developed by the Movement for Black Lives, which has a list of demands, including a call for an "end to the war on Black immigrants" (Rivas, 2016). The group has specifically called for an end to immigration raids, a halt to deportations and assurances that all immigrants have access to an attorney before going before an immigration judge. Carl Lipscombe, who was involved in drafting the platform as a member of the Black Alliance for Just Immigration (BAJI), a racial justice and immigrant rights organization stated that "The issues impacting immigrants are the exact same issues that impact black people in the United States" (Rivas, 2016). Black immigrants are nearly three times more likely to be detained and deported as a result of an alleged criminal offense, according to the Movement for Black Lives. Nevertheless, the fight for immigrant rights still has a Latino face in this country. When Rivas interviewed Lipscombe for his article, he asked him how often were there stories about black immigrants in national newspapers or news channels? Lipscombe laughed and said "Absolutely never." By advocating for the rights of Black immigrants, Black Lives Matter is targeting the same system that detains and deports all immigrant and marginalized groups.

Preparing Teachers to Support Black Immigrant Youth through Activism and Education

Most teacher education programs require pre-service teachers to write teaching philosophies. These philosophies are often sterile, color-blind attempts to connect theory to practice in linear ways that view classrooms and students as monolithic. Hardly ever do we ask pre-service teachers to include their experiences in the K–12 system or consider students' intersectional identities, or the sociopolitical environments that impact them, the education system, and the families of the children who they will be teaching as they philosophize the ways in which they will plan, instruct, and assist. I wanted to change the colorblind, non-critical practices of my teacher preparation program, and I figured that there was no better place to start than in the TESOL program in which I am a faculty member and coordinator of the program. While I cannot control what my colleagues do and how they teach, I am committed to evaluating my teaching practices and changing them based on the sociopolitical environment, the changing student demographics, and my commitment to criticality in literacy and language teaching. Hence, my research questions were: 1) In what ways do I, as a teacher educator, center the experiences of Black immigrants in the context of U.S. society and school? and 2) In what ways do I provide pre-service educators opportunities to understand and contribute to activism on behalf of Black immigrants?

I must also acknowledge that I am situated at a historically Black college/ university (HBCU) in the mid-south, which provides a level of comfort that may not exist at a predominately White institution in the same geographical area. Although my university is classified as a HBCU, more than half of the elementary education majors are White and female. While this demographic may be surprising in the context of an HBCU, it should be of no surprise because the majority of the K–12 teaching work force is reflective of our elementary education population – female and white (USDOE, 2016).

Methodology

Because this research was self-reflective in nature, I opted to use an autoethnographic approach. Autoethnography is a useful qualitative research method used to analyze people's lives, a tool that Ellis and Bochner (2000) define autoethnography as "… a genre of writing that displays multiple layers of consciousness, connecting the personal to the cultural" (p. 739). There are different uses of the term and it varies according to the relations between the researcher's personal experience and the phenomenon under investigation (Foster et al., 2006). Autoethnography can range from research about personal experiences of a research process to parallel exploration of the researcher's and the participants' experiences and about the experience of the researcher while conducting a specific piece of research (Ellis & Bochner, 2000; Maso, 2001).

McIlveen (2008) states that the core feature of autoethnography "… entails the scientist or practitioner performing narrative analysis pertaining to himself or herself as intimately related to a particular phenomenon" (p. 3). Thus, it is not just writing about oneself, it is about being critical about personal experiences in the development of the research being undertaken, or about experiences of the topic being investigated. Although autoethnography can be approached with I would like to adhere to the description given by Ellis (2007), who states: "Doing autoethnography involves a back-and-forth movement between experiencing and examining a vulnerable self and observing and revealing the broader context of that experience" (p. 14).

During the 2017–2018 academic year, I taught two Teaching English to Speakers of Other Languages (TESOL) graduate courses: *Introduction to TESOL and Second Language Acquisition* and *Methods of TESOL*. I collected materials, documents, and journaled about assignments and my perceptions regarding the students' utilization of these materials. I also reflected on the assignments and opportunities that were provided for these students to understand and contribute to activism on behalf of Black (and) immigrant youth. The section below outlines strategies, assignments, and materials used in both courses.

Findings

My goal was to find ways to strengthen the TESOL curriculum at my university so that it is inclusive of the experiences of Black immigrant students within the context of the U.S. school system. I felt this to be necessary for two reasons: (1) This population is often at the margins of the TESOL profession and society in general. They are often labeled the "other" Blacks and are provided a lack of regard for their various experiences, the identity struggles, and the racism and/or discrimination that they often encounter as they "become Black" (Ibrahim, 1999); and (2) these students are often (knowingly or unknowingly) the target of anti-immigrant, anti-Black, anti-Muslim sentiments by the current administration and its supporters – to include those who occupy the role of "educator." As I outline my efforts to diversify the TESOL curriculum (see Table 8.1), I acknowledge that there is so much more to be done and so many more resources that could be included. This is only the beginning.

Academic Texts

For both courses, I intentionally assigned academic texts that focused on the Black immigrant population. In the *Intro to TESOL & SLA* course, students read all of the assigned articles and were asked to submit literature reviews based on the readings, the corresponding course lecture, and discussions. The lecture and discussions were based on a newly implemented Race and Language module, which is framed by the ideas presented in Alim, Rickford, and Ball's (2016) edited book entitled *Raciolinguistics: How Language Shapes Our Ideas About Race*. In the *Methods of TESOL* course, students were required to read two of the provided academic articles regarding Black immigrants. Those articles were the basis of classroom conversations and were discussed as we sought to understand the contexts for teaching and learning with regard to the various student populations in the local school district.

Non-academic, informative texts also supported the information presented in the courses. Information from the Migration Policy Institute, Office of English Language Acquisition, and the White House Initiative on Educational Excellence for African Americans provided the majority of demographic and quantitative information that I presented regarding the Black immigrant population. I also provided recent news articles for our

Table 8.1: Efforts to diversify curriculum to include Black immigrants

	Intro to TESOL & SLA	Methods of TESOL
Academic Texts	Mwangi, C. A. G., & English, S. (2017). *Being Black (and) immigrant students: when race, ethnicity, and nativity collide.*	Nero, S. (2014). *Classroom encounters with Caribbean Creole English: Language identities, pedagogy.*
	Ibrahim, A. E. K. M. (2005). *"Whassup, homeboy?" Joining the African diaspora: Black English as a symbolic site of identification and language learning.*	Ibrahim, A. E. K. M. (1999). *Becoming black: Rap and hip-hop, race, gender, identity, and the politics of ESL learning.*
	Diette, T. & Oyelere, R. (2017). *Gender and Racial Differences in Peer Effects of Limited English Students: A Story of Language or Ethnicity?*	Rong, X. L., & Brown, F. (2002). *Socialization, culture, and identities of Black immigrant children: What educators need to know and do.*
Non-academic Texts	Capps, Randy, Kristen McCabe & Michael Fix. (2012). *Diverse streams: Black African migration to the United States.*	X
	OELA & WHIEEAA. (2015). *English Learners who are Black.*	
	Rivas, J. (2016). *Black Lives Matter is joining the fight against deportations—and it could be a game changer.*	
Children Books	X	*Mama's Nightingale: A Story of Immigration and Separation* by Edwidge Danticat
		I'm New Here by Anne Sibley O'Brien
		My Name is Sangoel by Karen Williams and Khadra Mohammed
		Brothers in Hope: The Story of the Lost Boys of Sudan by Mary Luana Williams
		Islandborn by Junot Diaz

Table 8.1: Continued

	Intro to TESOL & SLA	Methods of TESOL
Assignments	Review and critique two of the articles on Black immigrant students. What are the implications for K–12 education and/or language education policy. Watch the 2018 blockbuster movie 'Black Panther'. Respond to the following questions: 1. What did you notice about language use in "Black Panther"? Be specific with your examples. 2. What did you notice about cultural, linguistic, and gender diversity in this movie? 3. How could this movie be an aspect of a culturally relevant pedagogy in a classroom with African immigrants or Africans in the diaspora? 4. In what ways do you think Black Panther can help to change stereotypical beliefs about the peoples and cultures of Africa? 5. In what ways does Black Panther reinforce stereotypical beliefs about the peoples and cultures of Africa? 6. In what ways does Black Panther reinforce some of the tenets of the Black Lives Matter movement? 7. How could (specific scenes from) this movie be used in the elementary, middle, or high school classroom to address issues of language/cultural diversity or language use? Identify the subject, the age group, and the general standards that might be met.	Using one of the focal texts and the lesson plan template provided, create a lesson plan that addresses a language skill for English language learners at the beginning, intermediate, and advanced proficiency levels. Consider the following: • Who are your students and what is the context for teaching & learning? • What is the central focus of the lesson? • What are the state standards? • What are that content & language objectives? • How will you use the focal text? • In what ways do you differentiate? • In what ways do you provide comprehensible input? • In what ways do you increase thinking skills? • In what ways do you increase interaction amongst interaction and with students? • Are your assessments valid and reliable based on the content and student proficiencies?

Continued

Table 8.1: Continued

	Intro to TESOL & SLA	Methods of TESOL
		In groups of 4, choose one of the following EL populations represented in _____ school district. Based on your in-depth research about this student population, create a handout or pamphlet to distribute to teachers in your district that addresses the following:
		• General information about your chosen student population (no stereotypes or essentialization) • How to assist these students academically • How to support these students socially • How to make parents feel welcome and supported • Community organizations that can assist students' families
		Native American Sudanese Somalian Kurdish Caribbean (Anglophone or Francophone) Other population with permission
Organizations	BAJI (Black Alliance for Just Immigration) BELPaF (Black English Language Professionals & Friends) Adult Literacy Coalition Catholic Charities Black Lives Matter	Same as Intro to TESOL & SLA

think-pair-share sessions. Two of the articles that generated great discussion were Svanjlenka's (2018) article, *The Top 3 Things You Need to Know About Black Immigrants in the United States in 2018*, and Rivas's (2016) article, *Black Lives Matter is joining the fight against deportations—and it could be a game changer*. The readings provided helped to reinforced my lectures and set the stage for these student teachers to be inclusive in their thinking, planning, and activism.

Course Assignments and Products

I believe that pedagogies should not only be culturally relevant, but they should be culturally sustaining. Paris and Alim (2017) suggest that schooling should be a site for sustaining the cultural practices of communities of color rather than eradicating them. My goal is for my students to demonstrate teaching that perpetuates and fosters linguistic, literate, and cultural pluralism for positive transformation. During the *Intro to TESOL & SLA* course, students were not only required to provide literature reviews where they critique articles, but I thought it was the perfect opportunity to have students consider the linguistic principles that were taught and apply them to the 2018 Marvel blockbuster *Black Panther*. Students discussed the cultural, linguistic, and gender diversity in the movie. They were able to connect the movie to the BLM movement and they acknowledged ways in which the movie (although inaccurate in some sense) could be a tool for empowerment in society and in classrooms. In the *Methods of TESOL* course, students were required to create ESL lesson plans with using children's books with characters who are immigrant and phenotypically Black (e.g. *Islandborn*, *Mama's Nightingale*, and *My Name is Sangoel*). This assignment was especially important because in order for pedagogy to be culturally sustaining, children must see themselves in the curriculum. The characters represented in the texts are from the same countries as a significant portion of our local immigrant population.

Pre-service teachers also conducted in-depth research on racial minoritized immigrant populations and created handouts and pamphlets that provided general information about the student population as well as advice regarding academic and social support for the student and their families. Pre-service teachers also had the opportunity to share local resources and community organizations whose mission it is to help immigrant students and their families. The goal for this assignment was for these graduate students to become familiar with this population and local resources and to be able to produce documents that could assist their future colleagues in teaching and advocacy.

Conclusion

The texts and assignments added to my courses are not exhaustive. I also do not claim that they are the best assignments or texts for the purpose of understanding the experiences of Black immigrant students and acknowledging that Black immigrants matter. I know that there is more that can be done. However, I argue that it is a much- needed start that has provided my students, directly and indirectly, exposure to a population of students that are often not highlighted in textbooks, academic articles, or the media. As an educator, I subscribe to Baldwin's (1979) quote that "… A child cannot be taught by anyone who despises him, and a child cannot afford to be fooled. A child cannot be taught by anyone whose demand, essentially, is that the child repudiate his experience, and all that gives him sustenance …" In that spirit, I challenge all teacher education programs to highlight the experiences of populations of students who have been made invisible. I challenge TESOL programs to highlight intersectional identities, theories of "becoming," and the central role that language plays in shaping ideas of race as well as the role that race plays in shaping ideologies regarding immigration and language acquisition. We can only expect teachers to do what we have taught them to do. If we want them to be inclusive, we need to show inclusivity in our curriculum. If our desire is for them to be advocates for all students, we need to demonstrate advocacy and activism in the work that we do in higher education.

Discussion Questions

1. What are the dangers of having an identity-neutral teacher education curriculum? In what ways do you include issues of race, gender, religion, and sexuality in your ESL teacher preparation curriculum?
2. What are some other materials and/or resources that you can bring into your classroom (higher education or K–12) to discuss the intersectional identities of ELs from the African diaspora?

References

Adichie, C. (2009). The danger of a single story [Video file]. Retrieved from https://www.ted.com/talks/chimamanda_adichie_the_danger_of_a_single_story?language=en

Alim, H. S., Rickford, J. R., & Ball, A. F. (2016). Introducing raciolinguistics. In *Raciolinguistics: How language shapes our ideas about race* (pp. 1–30). New York, NY: Oxford University Press.

Anderson, M. (2015). *A rising share of the U.S. Black population is foreign born*. Washington, DC: Pew Research Center

Baldwin, J. (1979, July 29). If black English isn't a language, then tell me, what is? *New York Times*. https://archive.nytimes.com/www.nytimes.com/books/98/03/29/specials/baldwin-english.html?_r=1

Black Lives Matter. (2018). https://blacklivesmatter.com/

Bryan, K., Cooper, A., Ifarinu, B. (2019). From majority to minority: Advocating for English Learners from the African Diaspora. In H. Linville & J. Whiting (Eds.), *Advocacy in English language teaching and learning* (pp. 190–202). New York, NY: Routledge.

Capps, R., McCabe, K., & Fix, M. (2012). *Diverse streams: Black African migration to the United States*. Washington, DC: Migration Policy Institute.

Crenshaw, K. (1991). Mapping the margins: Intersectionality, identity politics, and violence against women of Color. *Stanford Law Review, 43*(6), 1241–1299.

DeCuir, J. T., & Dixson, A. D. (2004). "So when it comes out, they aren't that surprised that it is there": Using critical race theory as a tool of analysis of race and racism in education. *Educational Researcher, 33*(5), 26–31.

Ellis, C. (2007). Telling secrets, revealing lives: Relational ethics in research with intimate others. *Qualitative Inquiry, 13*, 3–29.

Ellis, C., & Bochner, A. P. (2000). Autoethnography, personal narrative, reflexivity: Researcher as subject. In N. K. Denzin & Y. S. Lincoln (Eds.), *Handbook of qualitative research* (pp. 733–768). London, UK: Sage.

Foster, K., McAllister, M., & O'Brien, L. (2006). Extending the boundaries: Autoethnography as an emergent method in mental health nursing research. *International Journal of Mental Health, 15*, 44–53.

Friedersdorf, C. (2017, August 31). How to distinguish between Antifa, white supremacists, and black lives matter. *The Atlantic*.

Hernandez, D. J. (2012). *Changing demography and circumstances for Black children in African and Caribbean families*. Washington, DC: Migration Policy Institute.

Ibrahim, A. E. K. M. (1999). Becoming black: Rap and hip-hop, race, gender, identity, and the politics of ESL learning. *TESOL quarterly, 33*(3), 349–369.

Ibrahim, A. E. K. M. (2005). "Whassup, homeboy?" Joining the African diaspora: Black English as a symbolic site of identification and language learning. In *Black linguistics* (pp. 181–197). New York, NY: Routledge.

Kanno, Y. (2003). *Negotiating bilingual and bicultural identities: Japanese returnees betwixt two worlds*. New York, NY: Routledge.

Maso, L. (2001). Phenomenology and ethnography. In P. Atkinson, A. Coffey, S. Delamont, J. Lofland, & L. Lofland (Eds.), *Handbook of ethnography* (pp. 136–144). Thousand Oaks, CA: Sage.

Massey, D. S., Mooney, M., Torres, K. C., & Charles, C. Z. (2007). Black immigrant and Black natives attending selective colleges and universities in the United States. *American Journal of Education, 113*(2), 243–271.

McCall, L. (2005). The complexity of intersectionality. *Journal of Women, Culture, & Society, 30*(3), 1771–1800.

McIlveen, P. (2008). Autoethnography as a method for reflexive research and practice in vocational psychology. *Australian Journal of Career Development, 17*, 13–20.

Mwangi, C. A. G. (2014). Complicating blackness: Black immigrants & racial positioning in US higher education. *Journal of Critical Thought and Praxis, 3*(2), 3.

Mwangi, C. A. G., & English, S. (2017). Being Black (and) immigrant students: when race, ethnicity, and nativity collide. *International Journal of Multicultural Education, 19*(2), 100–130.

Nero, S. (2014). Classroom encounters with Caribbean Creole English: Language identities, pedagogy. In A. Mahboob & L. Barratt (Eds.), *Englishes in multilingual contexts. Multilingual education* (Vol. 10). Dordrecht: Springer.

OELA & WHIEEAA. (2015). English learners who are black. Retrieved from https://ncela.ed.gov/files/fast_facts/Combined_Black_ELs_Brochure.pdf

Paris, D., & Alim, H. S. (Eds.). (2017). *Culturally sustaining pedagogies: Teaching and learning for justice in a changing world.* Teachers College Press.

Portes, A., Fernández-Kelly, P., & Haller, W. (2009). The adaptation of the immigrant second generation in America: A theoretical overview and recent evidence. *Journal of Ethnic and Migration Studies, 35*(7), 1077–1104.

Rivas, J. (2016). Black Lives Matter is joining the fight against deportations—and it could be a game changer. *Splinter News.* Retrieved from https://splinternews.com/black-lives-matter-is-joining-the-fight-against-deporta-1793860869

Rong, X. L., & Brown, F. (2002). Socialization, culture, and identities of Black immigrant children: What educators need to know and do. *Education and Urban Society, 34*(2), 247–273.

Svanjlenka, N. (2018). The top 3 things you need to know about black immigrants in the United States in 2018. Retrieved from https://www.americanprogress.org/issues/immigration/news/2018/01/12/445015/top-3-things-need-know-black-immigrants-united-states-2018/

U.S. Department of Education. (2016). The state of racial diversity in the educator workforce. Retrieved from https://www2.ed.gov/rschstat/eval/highered/racial-diversity/state-racial-diversity-workforce.pdf

Villenas, S., & Foley, D. E. (2002). Chicano/Latino critical ethnography of education: Cultural productions from la frontera. In *Chicano school failure and success: Past, present, and future* (Vol. 2, pp. 195–226). New York, NY: Routledge Falmer.

9 Documenting Blackness: Representations of the Haitian Community at the U.S.-Mexico Border

EBONY BAILEY
Universidad Nacional Autónoma de México

Introduction

I first met the Haitian community in Tijuana through a computer screen. While reading about migration in Mexico in the online newspaper *La Jornada,* I saw a photo of dozens of Black people crowded at the U.S.-Mexico border. I thought to myself, "more people who look like me in Mexico?" I was eager to learn more about this community that I immediately felt a bond to upon seeing their photos.

Since 2016, thousands of Haitian migrants have arrived at various cities along the northern Mexican border in order to seek refuge in the United States, with a large concentration in Tijuana. Because of a change in U.S. policy toward Haitian refugees, many ended up stranded in Mexico. As Blackness is not normally seen as a common site in Mexico, their arrival piqued the interest of journalists, photographers, and documentarians. I was personally interested in exploring how the intersection of race and migration play a role in the greater social and cultural context of Mexico, so in December of 2016, I traveled to Tijuana and filmed material for the short documentary *Life Between Borders: Black Migrants in Mexico.* I consider *Life Between Borders* to be a visual ethnography of the Haitian community in Tijuana, as well as a commentary on the greater issue of Black invisibility in Mexico.

Visual ethnography is based on traditional methods of written ethnography, but applied to mediums such as visual art, photography, and film. In this sense, the medium itself is converted into a research method. Due to the amplitude and the singularity of the ethnographic method, it is at times difficult to determine if a visual work is "purely ethnographic." Sarah Pink (2013) points out, "there is no simple answer or definition of what it is that makes an image, text, idea or piece of knowledge ethnographic … but these will be defined as such through interpretation and context" (p. 35). When a researcher tries to distinguish visual ethnography from photojournalism, documentary film, and among other genres, they will often find the line more blurred than it initially seemed.

This chapter is a reflection of my research and production process in the making of *Life Between Borders.* The chapter first addresses the general phenomenon of Haitian migration at the U.S.-Mexican border as well as the context of Blackness in Mexico. Following those sections, I discuss the origins of visual ethnography and its role as a perpetrator for the colonial gaze. Then, through a reflection of my ethnography process in *Life Between Borders*, I propose strategies on how visual ethnography can emancipate from that gaze. Specifically, I consider the role of diaspora and decoloniality in the representation of other Black bodies in Mexico.

I chose to address this topic in the form of visual ethnography so that this information could be accessed by populations outside of higher learning academia. A visual representation of this topic also contributes to diverse forms of learning. Documentaries can be used in the classroom as resources for learning in social sciences and humanities, or in community screenings as parting points for race and migration advocacy. Blackness in Mexico has been erased from the "official" discourse in Mexican history. This erasure affects current Afro populations in Mexico as well as the relationship between Black and Latinx populations that reside in the United States. By addressing this topic in a documentary that can be accessed freely online, I aim for *Life Between Borders* to be used as a point of reflection on race and migration in many different learning environments. Furthermore, it can be used as a point of comparison to see how race, migration, and cultural identity in the United States intersect with other countries, specifically our neighbors south of the border.

Haitian Migration at the U.S.-Mexico Border

While the numbers are not precise, it is estimated that about 3,000 Haitian migrants are currently residing in Tijuana (Solis, 2018). In 2016, a flux of Black migrants arrived at the northern Mexican border with hopes of crossing to the United States. While some of these migrants were from Africa, the majority were Haitian. "The Haitians and Africans should start to see

Figure 9.1: U.S.-Mexico border from Tijuana from *Life Between Borders: Black Migrants in Mexico* (Bailey, 2017)

Mexico as a country to reside, as a nation that they can take refuge in because their places of origin are in crisis[1]" (Gomez, 2016, p. 1). Haitian migration in Mexico is, thus, related to Haitian migration to the United States – it is a consequence of the search that thousands of migrants embark on for the "American Dream." Their migration, along with the migration of Central Americans, is contributing to the conversion of Mexico into not only as a sending and transit country, but as a receiving country as well (Roldán, 2018).

The causes for the Haitian community's arrival in Tijuana can be attributed to a number of reasons: the 2010 Haiti earthquake, Brazil-Haiti relations, U.S.-Haiti relations, and the geopolitical context of the U.S.-Mexican border. The majority of the Haitians residing in Tijuana made their way there from Brazil. The 2010 earthquake forced thousands of Haitians to migrate from their home country, but the causes of Haitian migration run deeper than the earthquake. Political instability, lack of infrastructure, Western intervention, and the legacy of French colonialism[2] have all contributed to Haiti's status as the poorest, least developed country Latin America. When all of these factors collapse together in an earthquake, the bodies affected by disaster are

1. All translations from Spanish to English are done by the author.
2. When Haiti gained independence, it was forced to pay France the estimated equivalent of $21 billion in today's U.S. dollars, a tax that France called "reparations" (Alcenat, 2017). It has been argued that this debt has hindered the long-term economic development of Haiti.

left with scarce options, one of them being to leave their home territories in search for a more dignified life. In "Dispatches from the Apocalypse," Junot Díaz (2011) calls on us to reflect on the social and political implications of natural disasters. "We must refuse the old stories that tell us to interpret social disasters as natural disasters" (Díaz, para. 40).

Brazil offered a number of humanitarian visas to Haitians, although many other Haitians were living there were undocumented, arriving there through the jungle (Millan, 2018, p. 37). Furthermore, Brazil's participation in the 2014 World Cup and the 2016 Summer Olympics opened up a number of opportunities for Haitians to work in construction. However, since 2015, Brazil was hit with a political and economic crisis, with the unemployment rate hitting 11.9% by the last quarter of 2016 (Millan, 2018, p. 43). Because of this, the Haitian community in Brazil began to consider residing else-where in the search for a better life, with many looking toward the United States; thus, beginning their cross-continental journey toward the North. They traversed the continent by land – bus, taxi – foot – traveling through eight countries and even crossing the Darien Gap by foot. In his memoir *Survivors: Citizens of the World,* Haitian migrant Ustin Dubuisson recounts his journey through each of the countries, calling the Darien Gap "the most horrible part of the game":

> We were all afraid to start this journey, however, we used that fear that ran through our bodies to defend ourselves and continue on despite everything. Our struggles didn't stop us from dreaming of reaching our end goal, independently of what our situation was (p. 34).

Upon arriving to the northern Mexican border, the Haitian community was left on standby, waiting several months in shelters for their appointment with U.S. immigration authorities. In December of 2016, when I filmed for *Life Between Borders,* there were twenty-eight migrant shelters in Tijuana, up from the eight that existed in May of that same year.

After the 2010 earthquake, the United States granted Temporary Protection Status (TPS) to thousands undocumented Haitians living in the United States. Additionally, many Haitians who arrived in the United States were granted a humanitarian parole that allowed them to stay temporarily in the country (Paik, 2019). This is what initially attracted many of the Haitians in Brazil to seek asylum in the United States. But in September of 2016, under the Obama administration, the United States put that policy to a halt. Then, with the election of Donald Trump, harsh immigration rhetoric deterred many Haitians from attempting to cross from the United States. Once in office, the Trump administration decided to officially terminate TPS. This left several Haitians with the decision to stay in Tijuana instead of attempting to

Figure 9.2: Haitian man at a migrant shelter from *Life Between Borders: Black Migrants in Mexico* (Bailey, 2017)

cross to the United States, for fear of being deported back to Haiti by United States authorities.

Since then, the Haitian community has strived to make Tijuana its home. A number of Haitians who were staying in other cities on the U.S.-Mexico border have moved to Tijuana. In a matter of months, many Haitians have learned conversational to fluent-level Spanish. Several have signed up for university, while others have had children with Mexican partners. Haitian barber shops and restaurants have popped up in Tijuana's city center, particularly on la *calle Negrete*. In addition, civil society and organizations have provided relief support for the Haitians. In fact, some Haitians actively collaborate with these organizations in order to pay it forward to other migrant communities in Tijuana. The presence of the Haitian community in Tijuana allows us to consider the social and cultural outcomes of a new era of Blackness in Mexico.

While filming my documentary *Life Between Borders*, I was curious about the reaction from local Tijuana residents of the newly arrived Haitian community. When I asked migration activist Paulina Olvera Cañez, she said "I think that although Tijuana is a city of migrants, we have never had migrants from Africa or Haiti" (Bailey, 2017, scene 2). The abundant number of Black bodies occupying space in Tijuana was unseen before, causing a mixture of curiously, hostility but also solidarity among the *Tijuanense*[3] community.

---

3. The Spanish term "Tijuanense" refers to someone from Tijuana.

The Context Blackness in Mexico

In order to understand the context of the Haitian community in Tijuana, it is important to address the history of the African presence in Mexico. Even though Black populations have existed in Mexico since the colonial era, Blackness has been rendered invisible and problematic. This is due to a construction of a national identity in Mexico, *the mestizaje,* that is built around colorblind myth of "racial harmony."

Africans – principally from the eastern and central parts of the continent – were brought to New Spain as enslaved people. Fifty years after the conquest of Tenochtitlan (what is now called Mexico City), the African population in this area surpassed the Spanish population. By the year 1640, the Spanish imported approximately 275,000 Africans to New Spain. Since then, Africa has contributed to Mexico in a variety of ways – through food, language, music, among other things – but the contribution has been largely invisible to the majority of the Mexican population. "The history of the formation of Afro-Mexican culture, especially among the free, languishes in a tradition of neglect and indifference" (Bennett, 2009, p. 7). This neglect and indifference for the Afro heritage in Mexico has continued to exist to this day: Black populations are still not recognized as an ethnic group in the National Constitution in Mexico.

Mexico is a country whose national identity is centered around the *mestizaje*. In the colonial era, "mestizo" was *casta* (caste) that meant to categorize someone of Spanish and Indigenous heritage. *El mestizaje* is an ideology adapted from this "mestizo" casta that gained momentum in the early 20th century after former Mexican Secretary of Public Education Jose Vasconcelos (1925) wrote the essay, *La Raza Cósmica*. In the text, he described that Latin America was on a "ethnic mission" to push the region into modernity (p. 10). In this construction of *mestizaje,* Blackness has been rendered invisible in the category of Mexican national belonging. Because of this, reference to Blackness in Mexican popular culture often characterize Afro populations as foreign and problematic. We can see this in the popular Mexican comic, Memín Pinguín. Memín, the protagonist, is characterized in the image of the Little Black Sambo. His mom embodies the stereotypical trope of the Mammy. The classic Mexican movie *Angelitos Negros* (1948) features characters in Blackface as well as portrayals of the Mammy. These educational and cultural references to race in Mexico – the stereotypes of Blackness in popular Mexican culture along the erasure of the Afro-Mexican population – has affected the perceptions of the Haitian migrants from the Mexican public. In his memoir, Ustin Dubuisson (2018) recounts his experiences with the local

Tijuana community upon first arriving to the border: "The looks towards us from the first *Tijuanenses* we encountered were looks of displeasure, discontent and discrimination. It looked like that they had never seen a Black person before" (p. 135).

Ethnography and the History of the Colonial Gaze

It is important to think of how the concept of representation has historically been expressed in ethnography. With what right or privilege does an investigator choose to represent a certain community? How does a researcher's own background influence the way in which their subjects are perceived? To answer these questions, we must consider the origins of visual ethnography and the role it has had on shaping our perceptions of racially marginalized populations.

Visual ethnography can be seen as a practice that has historically worked to perpetuate the colonial gaze. In its beginning, ethnography was distinguished as a social science camp that studied communities as "disappearing," "primitive," or "uncontaminated" (Tobing Rony, 1996, p. 196). In other words, the study of the Other. Many initial anthropological and ethnographic practices were intimately linked with colonial economic interests. Fatimah Tobing Romy discusses ethnography's role in constructing the "Savage" and the "Primitive," describing early ethnographic cinema as "voyeuristic" in the sense that it was assumed that the communities filmed were "ignorant of technology ... in need of interrogation" (p. 11). In addition, she states that indigenous and non-Western communities were seen as having a more "authentic" humanity (p. 12). Early ethnographers searched for a type of "nostalgia" of the human experience in their study of the Other.

This search for nostalgia is particularly noted in *Nanook of the North* (1922), known to be the first-ever example of ethnographic filmmaking. The film paints itself as an ethnographic portrait of the Inuit community in Canada. In the film, community members are assigned certain roles predetermined by the director, Robert J. Flaherty. For example, he obligated community members to engage in practices that they no longer did, such as hunting walruses with spears, doing this in an attempt to revive an exotic "nostalgica" of the human experience. In reflecting on *Nanook*, Tobing Rony (1996) describes the portrayal of the protagonist as a "kind of archetypal 'natural' and Primitive Everyman" (p. 11). The film, in an attempt to visualize the Inuit population, actually works to otherize them, propping this community on the big screen as a spectacle for the Western gaze.

Just as mainstream Hollywood cinema depicts Western peoples in obviously scripted narrative films, the Primitive is constructed in a genre of film akin to the nature film … many anthropologists, although acknowledging particular ethnocentric biases of the filmmakers, still do not dispute the status of the ethnographic film as an empirical record. (Tobing Rony, 1996, p. 11)

It is in this light that we should consider the colonial notions of the visual ethnography and ethnographic film. Fatimah Tobing Rony (1996) describes ethnographic cinema as a matrix of films that racializes indigenous peoples and situates them in a "displaced temporal realm" (p. 8). Visual structures of representation have worked to otherize, exoticize, and racialized non-occidental bodies, essentially displacing them from a sense of belonging within humanity. How have these structures worked to represent the Haitian community?

After the 2010 earthquake, many representations of Haitians were portrayed through the lens of "poverty porn" – the visual exploitation of their vulnerability and suffering as a way to reach the masses. There was a specific interest in representing the "vulnerable Haitian child." Hoffman (2012) points out that representations, such as the images below, "enable a critique of the Haitian culture and nation itself as fundamentally flawed and in need of saving through the interventions of the international order" (p. 155).

There is no disputing that the earthquake in Haiti was a tragedy. But this victimization of the Haitian community paints them as a people who have no self-determination of their own. As Díaz (2011) stated, "we must refuse the familiar scripts of victims and rescuers that focus our energies solely on charity instead of systemic change" (para. 40). Haitians' Blackness has also played a role in this victimization and dehumanization. Filmmaker Harun Farocki (2013) comments on this, stating, "when the earthquake happened in Haiti, German public television showed an image of a 16-year-old naked girl. That would not have happened if the girl had not been Black" (p. 289). Indeed, Black bodies have been particularly subject to objectification in visual anthropology. Brenda Farnell (2011) discusses the role in anthropology in portraying the racialized body as a "cultural object":

"It" it is observed, classified, written about and represented visually … from the earliest description of exotic others, and prior to the discipline's inception, we find representations and studies of the often racialized bodies of non-Western Others, viewed as cultural objects. (p. 4–5)

These representations of the Haitian community perfectly illustrate this assumption by Farnell. As racialized bodies, Black Haitians are being painted as an "it" whose trauma can be freely consumed and observed by the Western eye. When displayed in this manner, Black people are stripped from their autonomy – their right to choose how they want to be represented.

Decolonial Methodology of Visual Ethnography

Throughout the 20th century, visual ethnography has continued as a matrix for the colonial gaze. However, in the 90s, anthropologists and ethnographers started to question these paradigms. Postcolonial and decolonial theory began to move away from the dominant discourses in ethnography, which were seen as anchored in the old systems of thought of European imperialism (Clair, 2003, p. 18). Instead, they sought to re-consider ethnography in ways that would unveil the complexities of colonialism while also suit the cultural practices of the colonized: "Ethnography is taking a turn from expressing a one-sided view of the Other to expressing its own possibilities as a language of resistance and emancipation" (Clair, 2003, p. 19).

In *Life Between Borders,* I aim to embrace these possibilities of resistance and emancipation by proposing a decolonial approach in my visual ethnography of the Haitian community at the U.S.-Mexico border. A colonial approach to ethnography imagines "human relations in terms of categories and procedures," whereas a more decolonial approach involves embracing "the messiness of ethnography" (James, 2016, p. 6). That is, moving away from the "dehumanising neatness" that is found in traditional ethnographic methodology (James, 2016, p. 6). This messiness involves acknowledging the limitations of a decolonial approach and the potential for an ethnography to continue on after the initial project is completed.

Limitations of Decoloniality: The Camera as a Colonial Tool

There is a level of coloniality from simply using a camera to document marginalized populations. The presence of a camera in any given space involves an inherent power dynamic between the representer and the represented. The camera has been historically associated with documenting the raw "truths" of society, further heightening this power dynamic by naming the representers intentions as "objective." "During colonialism photographs portrayed explicit cultural ideas, justified colonization, advertised empire and represented different peoples and cultures, and fed into a racial discourse of European superiority" (Mabry, 2014, p. 6).

Given this history of photography in Othering marginalized populations, I had to be conscious of what my presence with a camera could imply for the Haitian community. As mentioned before, because their arrival was seen as a "new" phenomenon, several documentarians and photojournalists were interested in documenting their experience. This left Haitian bodies to be subject to the flash of the camera shutter every day, something potentially taxing for a community whose main objective is simply to seek a better life. In my case, if someone did not want to be filmed, they would give me an unhappy glare or simply say "no photos." These moments forced me to reflect on my position as the representer. How could I share the stories of this community without reproducing these colonial dynamics? I thought about our shared experiences. Although we have different nationalities, the Haitian community and I have a shared history in that we are part of the greater African Diaspora. With this in mind, I began to think of the role that diaspora could play in framing my ethnology.

Diaspora as a decolonial method Malcolm James (2016) discusses the role of diaspora as a decolonial method of ethnography:

> Whereas colonial methodologies are concerned with the categorisation and ordering of human life, in relation to race and nation, decolonial methodologies have been concerned with poetic and dialogic forms of being and knowledge. Poetics in this work is used to denote the motifs, relations, spaces, ambiguities, partialities, errantries, ruptures and allegories of everyday life. (p. 4)

Within this mode of thinking comes diaspora. "Diaspora" in the traditional sense implies categorization of the displacement and disbursement of ethnic groups from their homeland. But in decolonial ethnography, diaspora is more concerned with attending to displacement and culture ways that challenge traditional notions of race and nation. It is this mode of thinking that I apply to my study of the Haitian community in Tijuana. In documenting this community through the lens of diaspora, I interpret poetics in the way in which I observed and represented the different ways that the Haitian community in Tijuana has performed self-determination – whether through community work, cooking or personal testimony – and the way Haitian history takes a role in their current situation.

My first approach was recognizing what I call a spiritual and cosmic connection between the Haitian community and the greater Afro community in Mexico. Haitian resistance from French colonialism led to the founding of the first Black independent nation in the western hemisphere. In Mexico, a slave rebellion in Veracruz led by the African slave Yanga led to the founding of the first free Black town in the Americas. The spirit of *cimarronaje*[4] lives within both of these communities. With this in mind, I made the decision in my documentary to connect the stories of the Haitian community with the stories of other Afro communities in Mexico. I interviewed Amadou Gueye, a migrant

---

4. *Cimarronaje* (or marronage) refers to the legacy of resistance and rebellion among colonized populations. It was originally employed by Europeans in the colonial era to criminalize Black people who escaped from slavery, but has been re-appropriated by Afro populations to promote the spirit of resistance.

Figure 9.3: Seynabou Diehdiou working at her food stand in Mexico City, from *Life Between Borders: Black Migrants in Mexico* (Bailey, 2017)

from Senegal who arrived to Mexico City as part of a scholarship program between the Mexican and Senegalese governments. I also interviewed Koulsy Lamko, a refugee from Chad who became director of La Casa Hankili Africa in Mexico City. Additionally, I spoke to Seynabou Diedhiou, a Black Mexican born in Mexico City to a Senegalese father and an indigenous mother from Puebla. When filming the Haitian community in Tijuana, I was always conscious of how I would connect Haitians' stories with the people I interviewed in Mexico City, of how I could interlace these experiences through diaspora. Toward the end of the documentary, Seynabou makes a statement that relates her experience with the experience of the newly arrived Haitian migrants:

> I would tell all of the Black people coming here to Mexico to not give up hope. That the literal problem that exists is that we are Black. Because European immigration does not bring discomfort. It is welcome. White migration is welcome. It's not a problem. Black migration will always be one. So don't lose hope. Don't put down your head. Work hard. (Bailey, 2017, scene 5).

A second approach is involving myself personally in the ethnography. In a traditional sense, ethnographers are meant to be objective observers, so involving myself in the process is part of my objective to challenge traditional notions of ethnography. I am not a migrant, but as a Blaxican woman currently living in Mexico, I feel a shared experience with the Haitian community just from the simple fact of being a Black body that occupies space in this national territory. Fatimah Tobing Rony (1996) discusses how people of color use "the third eye" to deal with the way racialized bodies are represented in film:

> For a person of color growing up in the United States, the experience of viewing oneself as an object is profoundly formative … we turn movies to movies to find images of ourselves and find ourselves reflected in the eyes of other. (p. 4)

With *Life Between Borders,* I aim to twist this narrative, becoming the representer and the represented. Although I do not appear explicitly in the documentary, my voice shines through with cut in the montage. I do not wish to hide behind the lens of objectivity. My experiences are transmitted through the testimonies of the people interviewed. Additionally, I involved myself directly with the relief support efforts in Tijuana, be it helping to pack up donations or smaller acts such as cooking with the Haitians. This allowed me to explicitly share my solidarity with the Haitian community beyond the camera, with many of them confusing me as one of their own.

My ethnography of this community has not stopped with *Life Between Borders.* Since filming this documentary in December of 2016, I have gone back to Tijuana multiple times to conduct field research on the integration of the Haitian community in Tijuana. In this process, I have met Ustin Dubuisson, Michelle Coulange Ilocee, and Stebenson Richemond, three Haitian migrants who have become community organizers with the non-profit Espacio Migrante. I have filmed the buildings of "Little Haiti," a neighborhood in the outskirts of Tijuana that was built by Haitian migrants and leaders of the Embajadores Church. I attended and shot footage of an all-Creole church service at the Primera Iglesia Bautista de Tijuana (First Baptist Church of Tijuana) which has now served the Haitian community for nearly two years. Additionally, as more Haitians learn Spanish, I am able to communicate verbally with more members of this community. One limitation I had in my initial ethnography was being limited to speak the few Haitians who spoke Spanish, as I do not speak French nor Haitian Creole.

I have become acquainted with Haitian soccer teams and jazz bands in the city, and have tried food at the many Haitian restaurants that have popped up on *la calle Negrete* in the city center. I have also had the pleasure of meeting Andre Dubuisson, Ustin's son, who was born in Tijuana as a half-Haitian, half-Mexican *HaiTijuanense*, representing a new generation of Mexican-born Haitians in this border city. In this light I am interested in exploring the way the Haitian community can further contribute to the overall legacy of Black heritage in Mexico.

In this ethnography, I will continue to connect the experience of the Haitian community with the experience of other Black communities in Mexico. I have conducted interviews and visual documentation of Afro communities in Mexico City, La Costa Chica of Oaxaca and Veracruz. The final result will be a documentary film that tells the story of the Afro experience in Mexico to baby Andre, as a sort of "passing of knowledge" for the next generation of Blackness in Mexico.

Figure 9.4: Haitian woman walking in the Mercado Hidalgo in Tijuana from *Life Between Borders: Black Migrants in Mexico* (Bailey, 2017)

Conclusion

Visual ethnography can be a powerful tool for giving us a glimpse into the ways of life of other cultures. Historically, it has been used in categorizing and racializing populations that did not fit into Western standards of "civilization," often painting them as "primitive" or "savage." In documenting Black migration, such as the Haitian community in Tijuana, a different strategy of ethnography is required in order to avoid the colonial dynamics of visualizing the Other. I propose a strategy of reclaiming diaspora in order to document the experiences of this community in the short documentary *Life Between Borders: Black Migrants in Mexico.*

The arrival of Haitian migrants at the northern Mexican border has been described as a new phenomenon by local residents and activists. This abundance of Black bodies in a country where there are supposedly "no Black people" has sparked curiosity and interest from journalists, photographers, and documentarians alike. With this in mind, I filmed this community fully aware of the violence that my camera could impose, but also with the goal of amplifying their agency and self-determination. By placing the Haitian community in Tijuana within the larger context of Blackness in Mexico, I did so in hopes of constructing a diasporic solidarity among these different populations and promoting the resilience of the Haitian community.

Discussion Questions

1. How will Haitian migration contribute to the overall question of Black identity in Mexico? Furthermore, could this possibly have an impact on Black and Latinx relations in the United States?
2. In what ways does Haitian migration in Mexico intersect with migration patterns in the United States?
3. How can we document historically marginalized populations without falling into the lens of poverty porn?

References

Alcenat, W. (2017, January 14). The case for Haitian reparations. *Jacobin*. Retrieved from https://www.jacobinmag.com/2017/01/haiti-reparations-france-slavery-colonialism-debt/

Bailey, E. [Ebony Bailey]. (2017, February 9). *Life between borders: Black migrants in Mexico* [Video file]. Retrieved from https://vimeo.com/203384382

Bennett, H. L. (2009). *Blacks in the diaspora: Colonial blackness: A history of Afro-Mexico*. Bloomington: Indiana University Press. Retrieved from http://www.ebrary.com

Clair, R. P. (2003). *Expressions of ethnography: Novel approaches to qualitative methods*. New York, NY: State University of New York Press.

Díaz, J. (2011). Dispatches from the APOCALYPSE. *Utne, 167*, 50–55. Retrieved from http://search.proquest.com/docview/888056368/

Dubuisson, U.P. (2018). *Sobrevivientes: Ciudadanos del Mundo*. Tijuana: ILCSA Ediciones.

Farocki, H. (2013). *Desconfiar de las imágenes*. Buenos Aires, Argentina: Caja Negra Editora.

Farnell, B. (2011). *Theorizing 'the body' in visual culture* (pp. 136–158). Chicago, IL/London, UK: Chicago University Press.

Gomez Sanchez, L. (2016, November 30). Trump propicia asilo de haitianos en México. *El Mexicano*. Retrieved from http://www.el-mexicano.com.mx/informacion/noticias/1/3/estatal/2016/11/30/1004135/trump-propicia-asilo-de-haitianos-en-mexico

Hoffman, D. (2012). Saving children, saving Haiti? Child vulnerability and narratives of the nation. *Childhood: A Global Journal of Child Research, 19*(2), 155–168. https://doi.org/10.1177/0907568211415297

James, M., Harries, B., Hollingworth, S., & James, M. (2016). Diaspora as an ethnographic method: Decolonial reflections on researching urban multi-culture in outer East London. *Young, 24*(3), 222–237. https://doi.org/10.1177/1103308815618138

Mabry, H. (2014). Photography, colonialism and racism. *International Affairs Review, 3*. Retrieved from https://www.usfca.edu/sites/default/files/arts_and_sciences/

international_studies/photography_colonialism_and_racism_-_university_of_san_francisco_usf.pdf

Millan, B., Yarris, K., Joya, A., & Olivos, E. (2018). *Contemporary displacement patterns and responses: Haitians at the U.S.-Mexico border.* ProQuest Dissertations Publishing. Retrieved from http://search.proquest.com/docview/2088973121/

Paik, A. N. (2019). Between rights and rightlessness: Haitian migrants and the elusive promises of humanitarianism. *emisférica, 14*(1). Retrieved from https://hemisphericinstitute.org/en/emisferica-14-1-expulsion.html

Pink, S. (2013). *Doing visual ethnography* (3rd ed.). Los Angeles, CA: SAGE.

Rony, F. (1996). *The third eye : Race, cinema, and ethnographic spectacle.* Durham, NC: Duke University Press.

Roldán, M. (2018, June 8). "Mexico has become a receiving country," says UN representative. *El Universal.* Retrieved from https://www.eluniversal.com.mx/english/mexico-has-become-receiving-country-says-un-representative

Solis, G. (2018, December 8). Tijuana's Haitian immigrants seen as model for other newcomers. *Los Angeles Times.* Retrieved from https://www.latimes.com/world/mexico-americas/la-fg-haitians-tijuana-mexico-20181208-story.html

10 Trapped on the Island: The Politics of Race and Belonging in Jazirat al-Maghrib

ISABELLA ALEXANDER-NATHANI
Emory University

Introduction

My recent fieldwork in Morocco was bookended by murder.[1] On August 12, 2013, months after beginning a large-scale ethnographic research project on the new migratory patterns re-shaping North Africa's sociopolitical landscapes, a Moroccan man stabbed a young Senegalese man to death on a public bus. As news of this violent murder spread through the capital city, reactions to it signaled a country divided into two camps on the issues of immigration and border control. One side condemned the tragedy, calling out *"Murderer!"* and demanding that the basic human rights of Morocco's rapidly expanding population of migrants, refugees, and asylum seekers be upheld.[2] The other side chanted approval, even encouraging others to *"Protect our country!"* and *"Send them [the migrants] home!"* I had arrived to a nation taut with tension between citizens and migrants, Arabs and Blacks, Moroccans and "Africans." There appeared to be a dividing line between those who defined themselves by their placement in the northwest corner of the Maghrib, an island distinct from the larger continent, and those who were instead defined by their "African-ness" and all that it has come to represent in the Maghribi imagination (El Hamel, 2002, 2014). When a similar story made headlines twelve months later, reactions had changed. Silent were the voices demanding social change and emboldened were those calling out for political change – for stricter immigration policies and tighter border controls. A Moroccan police officer slit the throat of another young Senegalese man, leaving him to bleed to death on a public street, and for the first time,

I began hearing an open discourse about Morocco's "black problem" – "*le peril noir.*"

As Europe strengthens its own border controls in response to record numbers of immigration, Spain has quietly been investing in making Morocco a final destination country for those seeking passage across the Strait of Gibraltar or over the fences protecting the Spanish enclaves of Ceuta and Melilla in northern Morocco (de Haas, 2005, 2012).[3] The result is a growing population of migrants who find themselves trapped between their home countries in West and Central Africa and their intended destinations. Just beyond Europe's southernmost borders, this population is confronting the Moroccan state with a host of new political challenges, and also giving rise to a new marginalized identity that conflates presumed markers of race and non-citizen status within popular imagination (El Hamel, 2002, 2014; Hall, 1997, 2011). This article dives into the lived experiences of two well-established minority identities in Morocco – working-class Moroccan citizens who identify as "black" and upper-class foreign exchange students who identify as "African." I will explore how the informal economies that have long provided income for Morocco's working-class are becoming spaces increasingly identified with migrant labor, and how this is impacting all, but especially the racial minority Moroccans, who work there. Secondly, I will examine how Morocco's role as the first university exchange program for African students continues to bring a diverse community to Rabat every year, and how the increasing racism against blacks in public spaces is impacting the experiences of Africans from all socioeconomic backgrounds in Morocco. In both cases, markers of culture and class emerge as critical tools for asserting belonging in places where racial identity is now linked to social and political inclusion or exclusion.

Foundational to my early research questions was the idea that border regions, located at the geographical and cultural intersection of nation-states, offer an ideal site for studying new and contested notions of individual, group, and national identities. Morocco is situated at one of our world's most critical borders, first serving as a point of departure for those enslaved and conscripted to serve in foreign homes and armies and now as contemporary one for those seeking political refuge and economic opportunities in the European Union (Baldwin-Edwards, 2006; Ennaji, 1994; Phillips, 1985).[4] Despite the Maghrib's role as a crossroads between Europe and Africa, it has maintained its cultural distinction from surrounding regions – a fact been best evidenced to me by the terms that Moroccans use to describe their own identity in contrast to the other, or those who fall beyond the island, *Jazirat al-Maghrib.*[5]

An Island Surrounded by Land

New patterns of movement and detention are serving to solidify the Maghrib as an island, rather than diversify it, and applying the trope of "island-ness" provides a lens into why this may be the case (Baldacchino, 2004). In my first months of research, I noted the ubiquity with which the terms "Moroccan" and "Arab" were used interchangeably by Moroccan respondents, often in direct opposition to "sub-Saharan" or "African." The term "sub-Saharan" – one that is commonly used by Moroccan citizens and non-citizens to group together those whose journeys began in West or Central Africa – brings a number of issues to the surface. The UN Development Program currently lists 46 of Africa's 54 recognized countries as "sub-Saharan," excluding only Algeria, Djibouti, Egypt, Libya, Morocco, Somalia, Sudan, and Tunisia.[6] If this term were truly meant to divide the continent based on one geographic feature – the Sahara Desert – then Mauritania, the majority of which is located in the Sahara, would not be considered a part of the sub-Saharan region. In fact, four of the countries excluded from the sub-Saharan are in the Sahara, and Eritrea is deemed "sub," while its southern neighbor Djibouti is not. It seems inescapable that in this sense, "sub" connotes not only below, but lesser than. The lexical trick of dividing Africa into what is "sub" and "above" an imagined line is rooted in a division of the continent based on race and not geography. It has become, as Tatenda Chinondidyachii Mashanda claims, "a way of saying 'Black Africa' and talking about 'black Africans' without sounding overtly racist" (de Haldevang, 2016).

With the implementation of "sub-Saharan" as the nouveau "Black Africa," the Maghrib remains a space just white enough to be distinct from the continent, but not white enough to be European. It navigates between the two worlds, aiding in the detention and movement of those traveling the well-worn paths north (Ceuppens & Geschiere, 2005; Geschiere, 2009). But in both regions, "sub" and "above" the racial divide, there has been a failure to recognize the degree of variation present. One is glossed over as "sub-Saharan" and the other as a sub-set of the Middle East North Africa (MENA) block, regardless of the vast differences between countries like South Africa and the Sudan, Morocco, and Iran. This failure is most glaring in the "sub" region, where thousands of distinct languages and cultural heritages are found. After reflection, I have chosen to group Morocco's population of foreign students and workers under the common term "sub-Saharan" in my analysis, in order to reflect the ways in which both groups consistently identified themselves to me and identified in Morocco's public sphere. Although there were more than one dozen nationalities represented in the group of foreign students involved in my research, and are even more represented among migrant workers, the lack of space allowed for either to establish an identity beyond their race – to acknowledge, for instance, the importance of nationality, ethnicity, or class in shaping their identity – highlighting the role that blackness has long played in distinguishing the Maghrib from the African continent (El Hamel, 2002, 2014; Khatibi, 1983, Laroui, 1983, Lewis, 1979).

While "island-ness" is often theorized in terms of isolation, Brunhes (1920) encouraged it be thought of in terms of *location* and *identity* instead. "An island's signature is its obvious optic: it is a geographically finite, total, discrete, sharply precise physical entity which accentuates clear and holistic notions of location and identity" (Brunhes, 1920, p. 160 in Baldacchino, 2004, p. 272). He describes an island that exists naturally with a clearly defined boundary around its physical space and an equally clear understanding of who belongs as a citizen of that space. Morocco, a crossroads of human migration, does not exist as a natural island. Rather, it has constructed its "island-ness" in spite of its location, requiring an even stricter boundary to be drawn and policed around identity. As the population of sub-Saharans living in the Maghrib grows and diversifies, this Moroccan identity is challenged. I argue that the same ideology used to group the sub-Saharan region on a macro level is operating on a micro scale within the Moroccan state, where race is determining lines of belonging. Drawing on my close following of popular media and interviews with citizens, migrants, and governmental officials between 2013 and 2015, I shine a light on the treatment of a newly racialized migrant subject, asking: What happens when all who are assumed to be migrants are black, and all who are black are assumed to be migrants?

Every Story Has Two Sides

> "I'll tell you how it happened. A young man boarded a bus from Rabat to Fes. He told the woman who was sitting in his seat that she was in the wrong seat. She refused to move. She pretended that she didn't hear him. She refused to let him sit in the open seat beside her. She pretended that she didn't see him, and she moved her bags to the open seat. The husband of the woman boarded the bus and confronted the young man – 'Why are you speaking to my wife?' A fight broke out between them, the husband pulled out a knife, and he killed the young man right there on the crowded bus. No one tried to stop him. He was a military man. The young man was a migrant."
> - Chidiki, M, 22, Nigerian migrant[7]

My two respondents both told me, *"His name was Ismaila Faye."*

"You let a migrant tell you the story? He won't tell you right. It's not about race.

You know, there's a section of the Qur'an that tells us color makes no difference. It's what lies in the heart of a man that matters. There's no racism in Morocco, because the Prophet, Salla Allah Alaihi wa Salaam (peace be upon him), *told us that every man – white, black, red, yellow – every man is made the same.*

It's not about race, it's about culture.

Africans have a different language, a different religion, different customs, so you wouldn't want them living in your neighborhood or marrying your children. I'm not a racist. I have black friends. I even have a black girl who's a friend, but I can't imagine having a black girlfriend. It's not about race. I wouldn't want someone who was obese or wore a hijab everyday as my girlfriend either. Would you judge me if I said I didn't want someone who was misshapen or blind? To me, it's just not attractive. And can you imagine, I would have a black child! I just can't imagine having a black child. In Morocco, the lighter your skin is, the more attractive you are. Everyone would question why a lighter-skinned Moroccan married a darker-skinned Moroccan. They would think I had lost my mind if I married someone black.

It's not about race, it's about history.

You know, blacks have been in Morocco for a long time, but they started here as slaves, and it's difficult for them to escape their history. It's the same for Moroccans in Spain. No one wants a Muslim as their neighbor there. They worry for the safety of their children. The Spanish don't look down on us because of race. They look down on us because we're different. To them, we look dangerous and poor, like people who should clean their streets. They think we're all coming up to steal their jobs from them. They think we're all terrorists.

It's not about race, it's about work.

I have a friend who runs a construction company, and he pays Africans 20 dirhams an hour and Moroccans 10 dirhams an hour, because he knows that Africans work twice as hard. Africans are hard working. If Moroccans worked harder, he would pay them more. They're going to takes all of our jobs from us soon.

It's not about race, it's about money.

If you hear someone say they don't want an African to live in their apartment, it's not really to protect their neighborhood. Why would I rent my apartment to someone when I'm not sure if they're going to be able to pay me rent next month?

You know, I lived in the same building as a Congolese man when I was in school, and our neighbor always called him a goat. The boys from the building would throw rocks at him sometimes when he passed them on the street. He always paid his rent early. He smiled at me when I passed him. At first, I thought there was no racism in Morocco. But when I reflect on it, I start to remember little things like this."

\- Amine, M, 22, Moroccan

My two respondents both told me, *"Allahu Akbar! Thanks be to God."*

The racism in Morocco is really harsh. It's a way of life. Africans are only Muslim brothers inside of the mosque. Outside of it, they are blacks. Why did no one on that bus call Ismaila Faye his brother?

\- Chidiki, M, 23, Nigerian migrant

The competing accounts told to me by Chidiki, a Nigerian migrant, and Amine, a Moroccan university student of the same age, revealed deeper tensions in each man's understanding of himself in relation to the other. Their stories were not simply about the state of rising aggression between Moroccans and Africans. Subsequent interviews with each revealed that their stories were also about how they made sense of themselves in the changing times. Amine asserted that hierarchies of racial difference are no different from those of regional difference and that just as many "*Rabatis*" would protest their daughter marrying a "*Marrakechi*," any Moroccan man would protest his daughter's marriage to an "African." However, this language of cultural difference seems to cloak his obsession with blackness, highlighting the deep-rooted racisms born, in part, as he says, out of Morocco's own long history of slavery (El Hamel, 2002, 2014; Lewis, 1979). I could not help but notice the parallels that Amine drew between the treatment of Moroccans in Spain – where, as "darker" and presumably "dangerous" Muslims, he believed they are feared for stealing jobs and demoralizing communities – and the treatment of sub-Saharans in Morocco – where they, too, are often feared for the presumed economic and social threats that they present (McMurray, 2000).

As the population of young men like Chidiki and Faye continues to grow, Moroccan media is more frequently addressing the perils and problems of migrant-populated settlements around Rabat, Tangier, and other urban centers and the growing presence of migrant workers in these city's outdoor marketplaces. In recent years, they have linked sub-Saharans to the "mounting racism of Moroccan nationals" (*L'Economiste*), the "spread of disease, drugs, and prostitution" (*Telquel*), and a "growing humanitarian crisis concurrently produced and ignored by the E.U." (*Al Massae*). All of this followed the popular Moroccan news magazine, *MarocHebdo*, which international critique when it ran its cover story titled, "*Le Peril Noir*," or "The Black Problem," along with a closely cropped image of a young black man's (and assumed migrant's) face in 2012 (Boukhari, 2012).

My fieldwork at this time was rooted in Taquadoum, which is one the most heavily migrant-populated suburbs of Rabat.[8] It is the representative of the other suburbs that have shifted from lower-income Moroccan communities into mixed settlements of Moroccan citizens and sub-Saharan residents over the past decade. The time that I spent living there highlighted the kinds of prejudice that racial minorities face on a daily basis in Morocco, ranging from the racial slurs called out to them on the street to their difficulty finding landlords who would rent to them, or charged much higher monthly rents when they did (Alexander, 2016). It also revealed to me a mounting sense of fear among all who might be racially identified as migrants in the public

Figure 10.1: "The Black Problem."

sphere. As the boundaries of *Jazirat al-Maghrib* and its distinct communities were being challenged, contested notions of belonging were beginning to impact the identities of black Moroccans who "look like," "work like," or "live where" migrants are expected to, in what I termed new "spaces of illegality."[9] The following two case studies explore how the conflation of race and belonging is shaping the contemporary experiences of those who identify as black but not "illegal."[10]

Moroccans Working in Migrant Spaces

I developed many close friendships over the course of my time in Morocco, but one family grew to feel more like an extension of my own than any other. Adil, a 36-year-old Moroccan man born in one of the poorer corners of Salé (Rabat's neighboring city), had been recruited by the Moroccan national soccer team at a young age and relocated to "the barracks" with other promising young athletes. It had been decades since Adil last wore his uniform, but he was still recognized by former fans, who would often stop him on the street to ask, "Barihsina?" " *Na'am*," he would reply " *'ana* Adil Barihsina." Adil maintains the physique of an athlete, but he now sports dreadlocks down to his waist and is hardly recognizable from the old photographs that I had seen of him with his team. He might argue that these fan sightings were rooted in his memorable scoring record alone, but I would content that his race – as one of the few black Moroccans to play for a recognized team – also contributed to the city's lasting memory of him.

Despite Adil's years of employment on the field, he is no better off than his family. They live in an old building, which like most of the other buildings in Sidi Moussa, looks eternally under construction. The walls are cinder block, many of the doors and windows are missing, and the electricity is spotty at best. Together with his maternal grandmother, parents, two brothers, four sisters, two brothers-in-law, four nieces and nephews, and two cousins, he calls the small kitchen, living room, and bathroom home. But unless it is raining, Adil prefers to sleep on the roof. It was on the roof, with clotheslines and clucking chickens around us, that I had some of my most insightful conversations with him and his extended family network about the effects of Morocco's growing migrant community on perceptions of race and belonging.

Lacking official data, Adil and I estimated that his surrounding blocks included approximately 75% who he identified to me as "Moroccan," 25% who he identified as "black Moroccan," and no sub-Saharans. Adil and his family all considered themselves to be part of the sub-set that was both phenotypically black and Moroccan, but when asked about experiences of racism in their community, they could cite none. Having known them for many years, I, too, was at a loss to recall any experiences of overt racism against them in their neighborhood. But race was ever present within their home. I often spoke with his two younger sisters – a few years younger than me – about their friends' love lives and their own prospects for marriage, and I could not remember a single conversation in which markers of phenotypic variation were not central. "He's too dark for you!" Hanan would say to Najia. "She's so beautiful – she has such straight hair!" "She's the lightest one in her family, so she'll marry first." I remember them writing to me years later to tell me that their younger cousin had in fact married a "very handsome" and "very light" man from one of the newer, middle class housing developments outside of Rabat just before her 18th birthday.

Race was most central though in conversations with their youngest sibling, Simohammed, who is notably darker skinned than the rest of the family. Many of our dinners together ended in eruptions of laughter as the children taunted their mother, Rafika. "Where did Simo come from, Mama?" "Simo is from the Sudan!" "Was there a *special* cousin we don't know about, Mama?" Adil would ask, shaking his finger in Rafika's direction, as she rolled over in a fit of laughter. Their father, always a man of few words, wore a smile on his face as the scene unfolded. "We don't know why Simo is so dark," he would sometimes say to me, as if to offer finality to the conversation. But this conversation unfolded again and again, almost word for word, as Simo grew older. It was never mean-spirited, yet Simo was certainly becoming aware of how race was linked to beauty by his sisters, and I wondered when he would become aware of how it was also being linked to marginalized political status outside the walls of his home.

The family's jokes about Simo being "from the Sudan" reminded me of the insults I occasionally heard shouted at one of the Moroccan boys who sold orange juice in the marketplace by my apartment. Abdul-Aziz had worked at his father's fruit stand since he was old enough to count change, and he told me about the frequent tormenting by his peers in school. "They'll say things like, '*He only speaks Wolof now*' or '*Show us your papers, Aziz!*'" Shifting migratory trajectories were clearly transforming what had been a space associated with lower-class Moroccan labor to one that is increasingly associated with a state of political vulnerability. Abdul-Aziz is what Adil would classify as "Moroccan," not black Moroccan, and even so, his work in Morocco's informal economy had pushed him into a new space of "illegality." How, then, was this shift in social categories of belonging effecting black Moroccans who occupied the same space?

Adil's experiences of racism indicated that his family's limited accounts of it were linked more to the small orbit of their lives around Sidi Moussa and less to the changing sociopolitical climate. They lived in a home that their paternal grandfather had built, their daily routines rarely took them more than a few blocks from it, and they were respected in their community. Adil was more aware of changing perceptions of blackness in Morocco, because he had been selling used shoes in Rabat's main *souk*—the same marketplace where Abdul-Aziz worked—for more than a decade. Spreading his goods out on a blue plastic tarp in the middle of the main thoroughfare every day, he sells socks for as little as 1 *dirham* and shoes for as much as 20 (approximately 2 USD). If he makes enough to cover the cost of his trip to the city and back, he considers it a success. Adil had seen the dramatic transformation of this space since the time that migrants first began selling alongside him. "Every day," he explained, "it seems like there's one more migrant hawking here. There's one less Moroccan." The majority of sub-Saharan migrants living in Rabat now scrape together a living by "hawking" everything from fresh fruit to counterfeit goods. The ambulatory nature of the work allows them to quickly move from one corner to another when routinely hassled by Moroccan police.

Adil never had the chance to finish high school, but he had devoted much of his adult life to learning, and most important to him was mastering the English language. Speaking English was one of the multiple tools he used to present himself as distinct from migrant men in the marketplace. Adil credits his love of foreign (mostly American) films for his American accent and frequent use of colloquialisms. He can be heard calling out in English, "Twenty bucks!" "Hot deal!" We wear his hair in a non-traditional style that links him more to Rastafarian than Muslim culture and hand-selects stylish pieces of clothing from the piles of second-hand goods around him. He speaks freely about these being his "tactics." His mission? To appear non-migrant. But rather than striving to appear like a citizen, a Moroccan, his goal of belonging in the space was actually realized through appearing non-African altogether. "I try to look cool, American, you know, like Michael Jackson or Bob Marley," he told me one night, standing beside his tarp in his signature second-hand Nikes, tight gray jeans, foreign-logo tee-shirt, and black fedora. "I'm not African, like 'I walked here from the Congo' African, but if I don't act foreign, then everyone will think I'm Congolese!"

I could tell Adil was growing concerned about his younger brother when he started coaching him on how he, too, could "act cool." "When I was a soccer player," he recounted to me in a Skype conversation in the spring of 2016, "I wasn't the black one. I was Adil. I was the one with the fast feet. None of us worried about race. But I hear the things they shout at Simo on the field now." Unlike Adil, who played in the late-nineties, Simo was constantly singled out for his race. By coaches, fellow players, cheering fans and opponents alike, he was defined by his blackness and not only his skill. "Last week, they were all shouting at him, 'The African!' 'Pass it to the African!' No one would have called me the African when I played." For someone born on the African continent, why was this an insult that Adil so deeply feared? I wondered if he ever thought about the treatment of migrant men in Morocco, about the brutal treatment of some, and worried that his brother was coming of age in a distinctly different country than he had less than two decades before?

African Students Finding Home on the Island

Ousmane had been living in Rabat for four years when I first met him, but he still called Dakar home, and he returned there to visit his friends and family when his classes were on break. Of course, not all sub-Saharans travel the same route to Morocco, and not all have a boat crossing or fence scaling in mind when they arrive. The nation is also home to an expanding population of students like Ousmane who migrate from Senegal and other West African countries under Morocco's university exchange program. Rabat's "University Village" was first developed in the 1980s when The United Nations Educational, Scientific, and Cultural Organization (UNESCO) created the first university exchange program for African students in Africa. The program's current director explained to me how they choose Morocco because it was seen as both politically stable and in need of financial aid (lacking in oil) at the time. Although UNESCO has since cut funds for the program, Morocco continues to offer scholarships to a large number of Senegalese students in exchange for generous taxation and importation policies, and they have expanded the program to include students from other West African nations and former French colonies in the Caribbean in recent years.[11] This makes "The Village," as the students call it, a unique space, home to a diverse population similarly marked by their blackness and upper-class status relative to migrant workers in Morocco. My engagement with this population helped to disentangle how factors of race and class distinctly and simultaneously impact the experiences of all sub-Saharan migrants – students and workers – in Morocco.

Because the majority of sub-Saharans work in the informal economy, it did not take Ousmane long to realize that his race was linked to a presumed economic marginalization and political vulnerability in the public sphere. Like Adil, he started carrying carefully constructed markers or class and culture around with him, using dress and speech, "little things like always carrying this briefcase or always responding to people in English, even though English isn't my language!" in an attempt to distance himself from Morocco's migrant workers (Hall, 1997). It was again through performances of foreign-ness that I saw a racial minority asserting his right to belong in Morocco. Ousmane explained that it was only within the walls of The Village that he felt comfortable "being African" in the Maghrib.

The Village reminded me more of military barracks than an island of safety, surrounded on all sides by high concrete walls. "No one visits us here. None of us has any family in Morocco. We don't have any friends who don't live here [in the Village] with us. The University thinks it's only drug-dealers or prostitutes who visit us here. I guess you don't look like a drug dealer," he joked in reference to the many hours I had spent under questioning by the two Moroccan guards on duty that night. But Ousmane's comment echoed something I frequently heard in my interviews with Moroccans – a familiar cry against *"drugs and prostitution!"* whenever the subject of immigration was broached.

I returned to University Village several times in the months following our first interview to continue my conversations with other students, and on later visits, I was finally granted access to the premise. Ousmane explained that Buildings A and B are female dormitories, C and D are male, and E is reserved for students from the Caribbean. The courtyard that links them is a dusty patch of land with concrete benches. A basketball goal with no net stands at one end, and a building that serves as the cafeteria and recreational room is at the other. I arrived early one evening, and the "house," as they call it, was beaming with life. There were students crowded around a soccer game on the television screen and others placing bets over two miniature pool tables. They were laughing, flirting and cheering. It was not until that moment that I realized the complete lack of leisure in my other spaces of observation throughout Morocco – in the squalid apartments and marketplaces where most sub-Saharan migrants' daily lives were playing out. Ousmane and his peers were not like the population of migrant workers that I spent the majority of my days with. Both were young, male-dominated groups from West and Central African countries, but within the walls of the Village, I recognized that they had carved out an uncommon space that allowed them to be seen and heard.

Ousmane had grown up in a "nice home," he and his brothers had all attended "good private schools," and his family had "never worried over change." In fact, he said it was not until he moved to Morocco that he truly appreciated the depth of poverty that existed in his own country. But like

Chidiki, Faye, and the tens of thousands of others who cross through Morocco with the dream of reaching foreign labor markets every year, Ousmane hoped to someday reach European soil. "We all dream of finding good job abroad – in Europe or even in America." Ousmane's roommate, also from Senegal, explained, "No one wants to stay here. In Morocco, you're always the black. You'll always be stuck at the bottom of the ladder. In my country, at least I have the chance to move up with hard work." Ousmane and his room-mate's desire to leave Morocco in search of social and economic mobility echoed that of Morocco's migrant workers. The primary difference was that Ousmane's eventual return to Senegal was not contingent on his success. "My parents want to tell their neighbors that I live in Europe, that I have a good job, that I drive a nice car. They want this because it gives them pride, they don't need this because it puts food on their table." His future success (or failure) would be weighed for the social value it held – for its ability to uplift his family's standing in the community – but he knew that he would never carry the weight of physically lifting his family from poverty. He would try to reach Europe, and if he failed, he would return home. This was a lux-ury not afforded to those whose community had supported their journey to Morocco – those like 16-year-old Mamadou, who told me, "You can't go home unless you make it all the way. I'll make it to Europe, or I'll die trying." The experience of Morocco as an island holds the most truth for those whose footsteps cannot be retraced without money in hand.

Students like Oumane argued that their embodied experiences of mar-ginalization in Morocco were even more difficult because they were moving from elite positions in their sending countries. Yet, workers like Mamadou countered this assertion. The boys and men who make the long journey to Morocco have often been chosen by their families for a reason. In the stories that other migrants shared with me, I heard common refrains of past suc-cesses and a sending community's high hopes – often deemed "the smart-est" in the schoolhouse or "the hardest working" in the family business. It takes many people pooling their resources to afford the high fees demanded by smugglers, and communities are thoughtful about this investment.[12] The students and workers who find themselves grouped together under the com-mon category of "sub-Saharan" in Morocco have more in common than they might at first think, coming from similarly elite social standings within their sending communities, despite vast differences in economic status.

It was outside the Village gates, as had been true for Adil outside the orbit of Sidi Moussa, that race marked Ousmane and his peers as not belong-ing. Education and higher economic status provided Ousmane with more opportunities to manipulate his identity in the, using clothing and language to continually assert his belonging in spite of his blackness (Bourdieu, 1999; Hall, 1997). But he still moved through public with an awareness that he, too, could be subject to the violence that had been witnessed against Faye – another young Senegalese man. "Is Morocco not in Africa?' Ousmane asked me one night walking home from the *souk*. "But here, I'm the African, and here, it's a bad thing. In Morocco, Africa is associated with sex and AIDS, with drugs and alcohol, with a loosening of moral values and a twisting of Islamic tradition. It's never thought, what could a migrant contribute to my country? Migrants are always thought of in terms of their African-ness." When asked what this meant to him, he replied, "African-ness is always bad."

Is It a Crime?

Chidiki and Amine had told me conflicting narratives of the same murder, but there are a few facts that I know to be true. I know that Ismaila Faye, a 31-year-old migrant from Senegal, was stabbed to death with a knife. I know that he was awaiting departure from Rabat's central bus station, where I traveled to and from on most days. I know that the man who murdered him (whose name was never released, for his own protection) remains uncharged for the crime. It is still debated whether Faye asked a Moroccan man's wife to move from the seat that was assigned to him, or whether, as some Moroccan sources claim, Faye was already seated and was asked by the man's wife to move, so that she did not have to sit beside him. It is also debated whether Faye was a student or a worker. However, both sides agree that the altercation ensued when the man boarded the bus and saw Faye speaking to his wife (al Makhfi, 2013). He was stabbed multiple times. In the weeks that followed, public attention turned to a collective of European non-governmental organizations that had begun organizing a series of protests in Rabat for the regularization of migrants ("*Papiers pour tous*") and launched an anti-racism media campaign that went viral in late 2014 ("*Masmiytich Azzi*," or "My Name is not Nigger").

"Is it a crime now, being black? Is it punishable by death? Will there be no retribution?" asked Eric Williams, a sub-Saharan migrant, when interviewed for a local news report on Faye's murder (al Makhfi, 2013). This particular question, "Is it a crime now, being black?" stuck a cord with the public, being repeated again and again in various media clips on the story. Parliamentary member Mehdi Bensaïd, from Morocco's Authenticity and Modernity Party (PAM), was the first Moroccan to publicly declare Faye's murder "racist." He added that "when faced with immigration, [Moroccans] behave like members the *Front National* in France," making reference to the European party's

Figure 10.2: "My Name Is Not Nigger."

staunch anti-immigration policies (Bachelet, 2014).[13] Despite his statements, the legislative draft for Morocco's first anti-racism law, which was put forward by PAM in the following year, still sits on the parliamentary shelves to this day. It was only twelve months after Faye's death, with public attention so recently turned to rising racism in Morocco and international human rights campaigns still attracting a growing audience, that another young man was murdered – this time, at the hands of a police officer. The headlines were all too familiar. On August 29, 2014, Charles Ndour, a 25-year-old migrant from Senegal, was found on the outskirts of Tangier. The Moroccan who murdered him (name unreleased) remains uncharged.

> According to eyewitnesses, some Moroccans stormed into the apartment where Charles Ndour lived with seven other migrants in Tangier's peripheral neighborhood of Boukhalef. They led the women to the back of the apartment and asked all the men but Charles to stand outside, "as if they wanted to make an example out of him, as if they wanted to show us what they were capable of, really terrorize us," [said one.] They slit Charles' throat open with a knife and pushed him outside to die on the street. He was found face-down in a pool of his own blood. The mishandling of this affair by Moroccan authorities has sparked outrage in Senegalese and Moroccan communities who protest the conditions surrounding his death (Bachelet, 2014).

In contrast to the protests and anti-racism campaigns launched in Rabat in the wake of Faye's murder, Boukhalef saw a series of xenophobic demonstrations and the organization of a militia calling themselves the "*Syndicat des racistes*," or "Trade Union of Racists" (Bachelet, 2014). There were many in support of the eventual finding that Ndour's death was the result of an "altercation" between sub-Saharans and Moroccans and that no one could be blamed. In the months that followed, reports of murder continued to surface. Moussa Seck, a 19-year-old migrant from Senegal, and Cédric Bété, a 23-year-old migrant from Cameroon, were the next to make headlines. The first young man "fell" from the window in his fourth-floor apartment building in Boukhalef during a police raid, and the second was chased onto the roof of his four-story building by raiding police officers before also "falling" to his death. Both were deemed "highly suspicious conditions," but no arrests were made following the investigations (Bachelet, 2014).

"Can you imagine the fear that we walk down the street with every-day?" Ousmane asked. He told me that his friends, like him, were concerned about the violent tide of racism against blacks in Morocco, but that when he tried to explain the situation to his parents, they brushed it off. "I think it's hard for them to imagine that something like that would ever happen to me—because I'm from a good family. They don't understand that here, everyone black is a migrant." When speaking to Adil about the latest murders, he expressed a similar fear. "It's harder and harder for me to fit in." Adil argued that as a lower-class Moroccan, he had even less tools to draw on when trying to manipulate his identity than an upper-class student like Ousmane would have. "I can't always afford the right clothes. My siblings can't afford to study English." To both, belonging remained rooted in foreign-ness. In his research on identity making, Hall notes the significance of "material and symbolic resources," which are required if one aims to maintain control over their identification (1997, p. 17, Bourdieu, 1999). Most importantly for this research, his work underscores how those individuals already inhabiting positions of racial or ethnic privilege are the ones most likely to possess the resources needed to remain in control of their identification. I would further contend that positions of privilege can be used to sustain the marginalized subject position of the other, as is seen through the police violence against Morocco's sub-Saharan population.

Boubker el-Khamlichi of *l'Association Marocaine des Droits Humains* (The Moroccan Association for Human Rights), publicly condemned the treatment of sub-Saharan migrants by Moroccan police as "savage" and charged that recent murders were part of a deliberate plan, constructed and backed by the E.U., to deter any more migrants from attempting to make crossings (Rippingale, 2014). He was among the first to publicly make this connection between the treatment of sub-Saharan migrants in Morocco and the investment of the E.U in its southernmost borders. No longer drawing on the historic construction of blacks as slaves in the Maghribi imagination, he suggested that blacks have become inextricably linked to the fear of and desire to control the migrant subject (El Hamel, 2002, 2014; Fikes, 2009). When I interviewed el-Khamlichi at his office in Casablanca one month later, he expanded on his claim. "It's a policy really. It's a way of pressuring migrants to leave our country voluntarily before they make it any further north. You had better believe that Europe is giving money to Morocco to play the role of their policeman." The blame, therefore, lies not only with the state, but with the neoliberal arm that has been reaching south of its own borders to construct a new class of marginalized subjects in the Maghrib.

Tangier's police chief, Abdellah Belahfid, declined to offer me any response on the deaths of Moussa or Cédric, but he did publicly deny that his force was bowing to any European pressure to stop the flow of migrants traveling north (Rippingale, 2014). "These raids are a part of our routine police operations," he claimed in our later interview. It was a routine established "to fight the migrants responsible for the trafficking of hard drugs" and "to protect our local communities." The unspoken link between sub-Saharans and the political status they were assumed to occupy as undocumented migrants by way of their blackness was clothed in his racially charged dialogue. He linked race to an (assumed) origin in sub-Saharan Africa and, in turn, linked sub-Saharan Africans to an (assumed) political vulnerability. Yet, he was able to navigate his description of the Moroccan police force's routinized brutality against blacks without the mention of race. It had become not a question of blackness, but a question of rightful belonging.

Conclusion

Studies of migration raise two simple questions: Who has the right to move across space and who has the right to occupy space? The treatment of sub-Saharan migrants in Morocco indicates that while there is a long history of migration through the country, their right to occupy space as fixed subjects in *Jazirat al-Maghrib* remains highly contested. Rather than conceiving of identity in the traditional sense, I draw on Hall's conception of identification as "the marking of difference and exclusion," and what is left outside the symbolic boundary constitutes the identity of what is permitted inside (2000, p. 17). The creation of new categories of political exclusion therefore requires a restructuring of categories of inclusivity or belonging. Even as "the most inclusive category," the citizen requires a boundary (1997, Gledhill, 2003, p. 209). The Moroccan, can be seen to exist only in relation to the

African – the citizen, only in relation to the migrant – and the island, only in relation to its borders.

Europe's third-party political agreements with Morocco have impacted migratory flows into the E.U. as anticipated, but in doing so, they have established a new population trapped in North Africa between their sending countries and desired destinations (Natter, 2013). Despite representing the full range of identities found across the sub-Saharan region, this population is identified through their status as racial minorities, effecting even sub-Saharans from upper-class backgrounds like Ousmane. As the murders of Faye and Ndour reveal, the human rights violations against this population in Morocco's public sphere is not unique to political status or economic standing, but to race alone. I contend that as the political and economic entanglements between Morocco and its surrounding regions have proliferated, so too has the desire for Moroccans to distinguish themselves from the other, ensuring the continuation of the Maghrib as an artificial island.

As the lines between categories of political inclusion and race become blurred, Moroccans feel their own rights to belonging challenged, and Adil's case highlights how racial minority and lower-class Moroccans are most likely to find themselves marginalized in emergent spaces of "illegality" (De Genova, 2005; Fikes, 2009; Geschiere, 2009). They grasp for markers of foreign-ness and not Moroccan-ness, sub-Saharan students and minority Moroccan citizens alike, drawing on language and dress to assert their belonging. Though performances of class and culture, the two groups struggle to place their roots beyond the island, and their belonging within *Jazirat al-Maghrib* ultimately depends on their ability to have placed their roots above and not below the imagined line that splits the continent, sub and above the racial divide.

Discussion Questions

1. In the US, are there assumptions commonly made about an individual's class or legal status based on their race? If so, what are the assumptions and how do they shape the experiences of citizens and non-citizens living in the US?
2. Are there other contexts around the world in which a conflation of categories of race, class, or legal status might be shaping human experience in new ways? How do these experiences compare to those of minorities in the US?
3. How have changing patterns of migration (both forced and voluntary) in the US historically impacted categories of racial identification? Are

there recent shifts in immigration policy that have introduced new categories of identity?
4. What is the role of individual narrative in exploring broader socio-political shifts? Can comparisons be made between the contemporary experiences of minoritized populations in different world regions, and if so, what is the benefit of cross-cultural comparisons in social science research?

Notes

1. During my fieldwork period, I divided my time between: Rabat (approximately 12 months), Tangier (approximately 6 months), Oujda (approximately 3 months), Ceuta and Melilla (approximately 2 months), Nador (approximately 3 months), and other locations throughout the country (approximately 4 months). The main sites of ethnographic engagement within these cities included: detention centers and border camps (Oujda, Ceuta, Melilla, and Nador), Spanish, French, and Moroccan-run migrant aid organizations (Rabat, Casablanca, and Tangiers), migrant-populated slums (Rabat and Tangier), and the marketplaces where smugglers seek clients and many migrants work in the informal economy (Rabat and Tangier). My methodology can be broken down into six distinct phases, although the latter phases were often carried out in tandem with one another: (1) A demographic survey phase in heavily migrant-populated neighborhoods, (2) A combined interview/participant observation phase with core participants, (3) A life history phase with select participants, (4) Ongoing participant observation as a resident in heavily migrant-populated neighborhoods and a volunteer caseworker at one of the largest migrant aid organizations (5) Ongoing review of Moroccan media centered on issues of migration and EU-Moroccan relations, and (6) A final "visual life history" phase with select participants.
2. Unless referring specifically to immigration law, I use the term "migrant," regardless of documented or undocumented legal status. Unlike the terms "emigrant" or "immigrant," "migrant" retains a sense of movement, or what de Genova calls the "consequent irresolution of social processes of migration" (2005, p. 3). From this point forward, I will include the category of "asylum seeker" under the term "migrant," as well, to underscore their similar treatment and marginalization in political and social spheres in Morocco.
3. Over the past decade, the E.U. has taken significant steps to intensify its control over migrants (Moroccan and sub-Saharan) attempting to cross into Europe. In the early 2000s, Spain erected a new ring of fences around Ceuta and Melilla, and they recently installed an underwater radar detection system at the Strait of Gibraltar. Spain has also exerted pressure on Morocco to strengthen its own border controls, amend its new immigration policies, and sign repatriation agreements leading to the deportation of tens of thousands sub-Saharan Africans with burned papers to Morocco every year (de Haas, 2012). In exchange, Morocco is offered financial support in the name of "development aid," military equipment, and a small number work permits for highly skilled Moroccan emigrants (*ibid*).
4. The Arab Slave Trade, which began in 650 and was not officially abolished until 1970, predates the European Slave Trade by over 700 years. Estimates of the slave

population differ widely, with historians believing that between 8 million (Luiz Felipe de Alencastro) and 25 million (Paul Bairoch) sub-Saharan African slaves were taken across the Red Sea, Indian Ocean, and Sahara Desert to serve as soldiers, servants, laborers, concubines, and eunuchs throughout the Muslim world, which stretched over three continents at its peak (Bairoch, 1994). Those settling in Morocco were concentrated in wealthier, urban enclaves and came primarily from East Africa (Nubians and Zanj). Scholars have since drawn on art, journals, and legal documents to examine how notions of racial identity and racialized stratification were shaped by the large numbers of slaves living in Morocco at the height of the trade (el Hamel 2002; Khatibi 1983; Laroui 1983; Lewis, 1979).

5. *Jazirat al-Maghrib* can be translated to "North Africa as an island."

6. The UN Development Program's categorizations of African countries can be reviewed in greater detail at: //www.africa.undp.org/content/rba/en/home/regioninfo. html

7. Some names and other identifying details have been changed to protect the privacy of my research respondents.

8. Taquadoum is located east of *centre ville* in the Youssoufia region, which is considered a lower-income bedroom community and is home to a majority of Rabat's growing sub-Saharan migrant population.

9. Past research on racialization has illustrated how just as legality is "stamped" on migrants at the physical border (Fikes, 2009), race can be "written" on subjects and is contingent on not only their physical characteristics, but also on the social spaces that they inhabit (Hall, 1997). I argue that in "borderlands" like Morocco (Anzaldúa, 1999), one individual may be alternately labeled as "Arab" *and* "black," "Moroccan" *and* "African," "citizen" *and* "migrant" in the course of one day, depending on factors such as their dress, speech, or the particular spaces that are occupied by or denied to them.

10. Any terms referencing "illegality" are placed in quotations in order to problematize the notion of the individual as an "illegal" subject and raise questions about the conditions under which such "il"/legalizations are constructed.

11. Morocco and Senegal have a long-standing relationship "founded on values rooted in the soil of faith and culture" (Sall) and strengthened through trade agreements and multilateral regional investments by Senegalese president Macky Sall and King Mohammed VI in recent years (*BBC 2014*). As of 2014, Senegal was Morocco's leading African trade partner with a volume estimated at 122 million USD.

12. Migrants making the Congo-Morocco journey (one of the longer journeys that sub-Saharan migrants to Morocco make) are required to pay their "camels," or smuggling services, an average of 5,000 USD in one lump sum upfront.

13. The National Front is a socially conservative and nationalist far-right political party in France, known for their opposition of the European Union.

References

Alexander, I. (2016, August 17). The crossing. *Global Post.*

al Makhfi, J. (2013, September 6). Morocco's African immigrants fear rising racism tide. *AFP.*

Anzaldúa, G. (1999). *Borderlands: The New Mestiza = La Frontera*. New York, NY: Aunt Lute Books.

Bachelet, S. (2014, September 23). Murder of Senegalese migrant overshadows "radically new" politics of migration in Morocco. *All Africa*.

Baldacchino, G. (2004). The coming of age of island studies. *Journal of Economic and Social Geography*, *95*(3), 272–283.

Baldwin-Edwards, M. (2006). Between a rock and a hard place: North Africa as a region of emigration, immigration and transit migration. *Review of African Political Economy*, *108*, 311–324.

Boukhari, K. (2012, September 11). Pourquoi le "péril noir" de Maroc Hebdo provoque l'indignation. *Courrier International*.

Bourdieu, P. (1999). *Language and symbolic power*. Cambridge, MA: Harvard University Press.

Brunhes, J. (1920). *Human geography*. London, UK: Metheun.

Ceuppens, B., & Geschiere, P. (2005). Autochthony: Local or global? New modes in the struggle over citizenship and belonging in Africa and Europe. *Annual Review of Anthropology*, 34, 385–407.

De Genova, N. (2005). *Working the boundaries: Race, space and "illegality" in Mexican Chicago*. Durham, NC: Duke University Press.

De Haas, H. (2005). Morocco's migration transition: Trends, determinants and future scenarios. *Global Migration Perspectives*, 28, 1–38.

De Haas, H. (2012). Trans-Saharan migration to North Africa and the EU: Historical roots and current trends. *The Migration Information* Source [digital version].

De Haldevang, M. "Why Do We Still Use the Term 'Sub-Saharan Africa'?" *Quartz Africa*, 1 Sept. 2016, qz.com/africa/770350/why-do-we-still-say-subsaharan-africa/.

El Hamel, C. (2002). 'Race,' slavery and Islam in Maghribi Mediterranean thought: The question of the Haratin in Morocco. *The Journal of North African Studies*, *7*(3), 29–52.

El Hamel, C. (2014). *Black Morocco: A history of slavery, race, and Islam*. London, UK: Cambridge University Press.

Ennaji, M. (1994). *Soldats, domestiques et concubines. L'esclavage au Maroc au XIXe Siècle*. Casablanca: Editions Eddif.

Fikes, K. (2009). *Managing African Portugal: The citizen-migrant distinction*. Durham, NC: Duke University Press.

Geschiere, P. (2009). *The perils of belonging: Autochthony, citizenship, and exclusion in Africa and Europe*. Chicago, IL: University of Chicago Press.

Gledhill, J. (2003). Rights and the poor. In R. Wilson & J. Mitchell (Eds.), *Human rights in global perspective: Anthropological perspectives on rights, claims and entitlements*. London, UK: Routledge.

Hall, B. (2011). *A history of race in Muslim West Africa, 1600–1960*. Cambridge, UK: Cambridge University Press.

Hall, S. (1997). *Representation: Cultural representations and signifying practices*. New York, NY: Sage.

Hall, S. (2000). "Who needs 'identity'?" In P. du Gay, J. Evans, & P. Redman (Eds.), *Identity: A reader* (pp. 15–30). New York, NY: Sage.

Khatibi, A. (1983). *Maghreb Pluriel.* Paris: Denoel.

Laroui, A. (1983). *The history of the Maghrib: An interpretive essay.* Princeton, NJ: Princeton University Press.

Lewis, B. (1979). *Race and color in Islam.* New York, NY: Octagon Books.

Mamdani, M. (1996). *Citizen and subject: Contemporary Africa and the legacy of late colonialism.* Princeton, NJ: Princeton University Press.

McMurray, D. (2000). *In and out of Morocco: Smuggling and migration in a Frontier Boomtown.* Minneapolis: University of Minnesota Press.

Natter, K. (2013). The formation of Morocco's policy towards irregular migration (2000–2007): Political rationale and policy processes. *International Migration, 5,* 15–28.

Phillips, W. (1985). *Slavery from Roman times to the early transatlantic trade.* Manchester, UK: Manchester University Press.

Rippingale, J. (2014, November 22). Are Moroccan gangsters being paid to beat up sub-Saharan migrants? *Vice.*

11 Organizations that Support Black Immigrants in the United States

AYANNA COOPER
A Cooper Consulting

This chapter serves as a resource list of organizations that support Black immigrants and refugee populations. This list is not exhaustive but rather highlights specific national, local, and professional organizations. This chapter also serves to provide information about the vision, mission, and contact information for these organizations. The ultimate goal is to inform readers, connect those in need, and to encourage those in positions to advocate for the voices of Black immigrants and refugees.

National Organizations

African Communities Together

http://www.africans.us

African Communities Together (ACT), a non-profit organization since 2013, has been advocating for immigrant families, especially those of African descent. ACT's mission statement affirms:

> African Communities Together is an organization of African immigrants fighting for civil rights, opportunity, and a better life for our families here in the U.S. and worldwide. ACT empowers African immigrants to integrate socially, get ahead economically, and engage civically. We connect African immigrants to critical services, help Africans develop as leaders, and organize our communities on the issues that matter. (ACT, 2019)

ACT believes it is necessary to increase the visibility of African immigrants so that the government is inclusive of all immigrant populations when funding opportunities are available and when policies are drafted. In the New York office, staff members are from seven different countries: Senegal, Gambia,

Ivory Coast, Ghana, Ethiopia, Nigeria, and Yemen. They speak a total of six-teen languages: Afemi, Agni, Akan, Amharic, Arabic, Djola, French, Fulani, Hausa, Krio, Mandingo, Mandinka, Oromo, Twi, Wolof, and Yoruba. The program manager, Maimouna Dieye states, "Our staff reflects the population we serve. We want to make sure that anyone who walks through our doors feels welcomed and at home by either connecting with a staff member from their country or who speaks their language" (Dieve, 2019). Table 11.1 shows some of the advocacy projects ACT has sponsored in recent years.

In a recent victory, ACT advocates led national campaigns that defended immigration policies that benefited African immigrants with Temporary Protected Status (TPS). Immigrants from the following countries were at risk for deportation if those programs were not granted extensions: Somalia, Sudan, South Sudan, Guinea, Liberia, and Sierra Leone. Because of those wins, thousands of immigrants with TPS were able to maintain legal status and work permits (ACT, 2019). ACT's goals for the next five years include leadership development; expanding into other metropolitan areas such as Minneapolis-St. Paul, MN; increasing their financial resources; strengthening their financial, administrative, technological, and governance infrastructure; and expanding their leadership role in state and federal African immigrant policy legislation.

Table 11.1: African communities together, summary by the numbers 2013–2018

Number	Accomplishment
$5m	Estimated increase in wages as a result of the successful campaign for the DC Airports Wage Policy
244.6K	Total number of Temporary Protected Status (TPS) holders benefiting from the injunction
95K	Minimum estimate of New Yorkers who benefited from increased language access
1.5K	Community members and allies mobilized for 2018 World Refugee Day
1.2K	The number of community members reached over the past year through community education - "know your rights sessions"
1.04K	Number of Sudanese TPS holders who benefit from injunction to block termination of TPS
500	Number of community members and allies mobilized for 2017 World Refugee Day
30	Number of African immigrant community members who attended ACT's first Membership Meeting in 2013

(selected information adapted from ACT annual report, 2018)

African Law Center, Inc.

http://africanlawcenter.org/

Founded in 2013 by Africans living in the United States, the African Law Center services clients throughout the U.S. by appointment only. Their mission states:

> African Law Center's mission is to defend the rights of African refugees and immigrants within countries where they seek refuge and opportunities. We achieve our mission by providing culturally appropriate and linguistically accessible services through direct legal aid, community legal empowerment, case management, strategic litigation, and policy advocacy.
>
> (African Law Center, 2019)

The African Law Center helps clients with issues such as combating derogatory stereotypes, discrimination, housing, employment, and access to healthcare. The legal assistance they provide includes legal counsel for refugee and asylee processes, citizenship through naturalization, applying for a green card, K–1 fiancé(e) visas, removal of Conditions, applying for extreme hardship waivers and applying under the Violence Against Women Act (VAWA). Potential clients can complete in-take forms and receive updates on their case(s) via an online portal.

Five tools used to help African immigrants navigate their lives in the U.S. include:

1. Individualized Legal Counsel and Representation
2. Community Legal Empowerment
3. Case Management
4. Strategic Litigation
5. Policy Advocacy

Black Alliance for Just Immigration

https://baji.org/

Black Alliance for Just Immigration (BAJI) was founded in 2006 due to the opposition and repressive immigrant bill under consideration at that time. This national organization currently has offices in New York, NY, Los Angeles, CA, Oakland, CA, Atlanta, GA, and Miami, FL. BAJI serves to educate, advocate, and collaborate with those in support of racial, social and economic justice.

Their mission:

The Black Alliance for Just Immigration (BAJI) is a racial justice and migrant rights organization which engages in education, advocacy, and cross-cultural alliance-building in order to strengthen a national movement to end racism, criminalization, and economic disenfranchisement in African American and Black immigrant communities.

(Guidestar, 2019)

BAJI also hosts a Black Immigrant Network (BIN) that serves as a national network of people and organizations serving Black immigrant and African American communities who are focused on supporting fair and just immigration (baji.org/black-immigration-network/). BAJI provides a number of resources available on its website such as reports, webinars, fact sheets, tool kits, and other related resources. A list of BAJI's programs and activities include:

1. BAJI Organizing Committees (BOCs)
2. The Black Immigration Network (BIN)
3. Technical Assistance and Training (TAT) Program
4. The Communications And Media Education on Race in America (CAMERA) Program
5. Advocacy STAND (Solidarity and Taking Action for New Directions) Program
6. The Faith Advocacy for Immigrants and Refugees (FAIR) Project
7. African Diaspora Dialogues (ADD) and African-American-Immigrant Dialogues (AAID)
8. The State of Black Immigrants Research Institute
9. BAJI CLINIC (Cultural and Legal Immigration Navigation for Interdependent Communities)

The State of Black Immigrants Research Institute, a partnership and initiative of BAJI, publishes reports, fact sheets and research briefs that offer information about select black immigrant groups such as *The State of Black Immigrants in California*, *The State of Black Immigrants*, and *Black Lives at the Border*.

Black LGBTQIA + Migrant Project

https://transgenderlawcenter.org/programs/blmp

The Black Lesbian, Gay, Bisexual, Transgender, Queer, Intersex, and Asexual (LGBTQIA) + Migrant Project (BLMP) is headquartered at the Transgender Law Center in Oakland, CA. The organization encourages leadership development, capacity building, and organizing community building

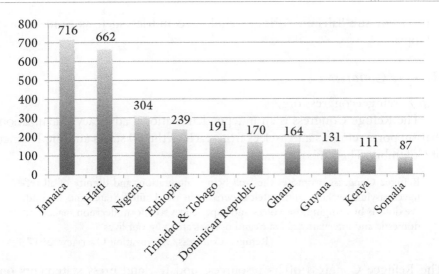

Figure 11.1: Total foreign-born Black populations in the United States, in thousands, 2016

events to reduce isolation of Black LGBTQIA members. BLMP also hosts nationwide events, assists in providing access to legal services for those in need, and conducts research studies about the experiences of the Black LGBTQIA. Their website also offers resource pages in Spanish.

Council on American-Islamic Relations

https://www.cair.com/about_us

Established in 1994, the Council on American-Islamic Relations (CAIR) is a grassroots civil rights and advocacy organization that works to promote Muslim-Americans and Islam in a positive light. With headquarters in Washington, D.C. and regional offices nationwide. CAIR's vision and mission states:

> CAIR's vision is to be a leading advocate for justice and mutual understanding. CAIR's mission is to enhance understanding of Islam, protect civil rights, promote justice, and empower American Muslims.(CAIR, 2018)

In addition to offering resources on their website, such as the Know Your Rights pocket guide, the Islamophobia pocket guide, and the Community Safety kit, CAIR also offer a portal to report incidents of religious discrimination. Black people in the United States (not including those of Hispanic descent or mixed race) make up 20% of the country's overall Muslim population, according to a 2017 Pew Research Center survey. Many black Muslims come from sub-Saharan Africa, including countries such as Somalia and Ethiopia.

Refugee Congress

http://refugeecongress.org/

The Refuge Congress is an independent national advocacy organization that supports refugees and asylees from each of the 50 states and the District of Columbia. Their mission states:

> Refugee Congress promotes the well-being, integration, and dignity of all refugees, asylum seekers, and stateless persons in the United States and beyond. We do this by bringing our voices and experiences to inform decision makers on domestic and international issues and policies affecting our lives.
>
> (Refugee Congress Organization Overview, 2017)

The Refugee Congress offers resources, updates, and press statements on their website as well as the contact information for delegates of all 50 states and the District of Columbia. Some of the delegates are representatives from the following countries: Bhutan, Brazil, Cuba, Congo, Eritrea, Ethiopia, Gambia, Liberia, Mozambique, Rwanda, Sierra Leone, and Somalia. The organization's website features an interactive map of resettlement agencies. The organization also offers a lesbian, gay, bisexual, transgender, queer, and intersex, (LGBTI) Caucus. This caucus, which comprises gay and lesbian refugees from around the world who are now settled in the United States, works to support LGBTI refugees. The mission of the LGBTI caucus states:

> Achieve the full enjoyment of human rights of LGBTI refugees, asylum seekers and stateless in the U.S. To serve as a resource for the Refugee Congress on LGBTI issues and working toward the elimination of hate –motivated violence, and the improved health and well being for refugees, asylum seekers and stateless persons regardless of sexual orientation or gender identity/expression.
>
> (Refugee Congress, 2019).

Goals of the LGBTI caucus include:

1. Improve information collection on LGBTI refugees for better resettlement outcomes.
2. Encourage the disclosure or self-identification of LGBTI refugees.
3. Cultural Competency for those dealing with LGBTI refugees is needed.
4. Bridging the LGBTI Refugees and the American LGBTI Community.

UndocuBlack Network

http://undocublack.org/
In January of 2016, 65 Black undocumented people participated in the first of its kind event, "The Undocumented and Black Convening." This event spearheaded the development of UndocuBlack Network, a national organization with regional chapters in Los Angeles, CA, New York City, and Washington DC. The organization's mission states:

> The UndocuBlack Network is a multi-generational network of currently and formerly undocumented Black people that fosters community, facilitates access to resources, and contributes to transforming the realities of our people, so we are thriving and living our fullest lives.(UndocuBlack, 2019)

There were 4.2 million Black immigrants living in the United States in 2016; in 2015, 619,000 of them were considered undocumented (Anderson & Lopez 2018). It is highly probable that the numbers are higher; in addition to an increase in people becoming undocumented because of termination of immigration protections and changes in policy, getting an accurate count of this population is difficult.

Challenges experienced by undocumented Black immigrants in the United States include being subjected to anti-Black racism, anti-immigrant rhetoric, ignorance, and misunderstandings regarding racial and immigrant justice. The lack of resources available to meet the needs of the undocumented Black immigrants are a direct result of the aforementioned experiences.

In a personal interview, Gabrielle, a therapist, clinical social worker, and founding member of UndocuBlack further explains the mission which also includes a focus on mental wellness:

> We must acknowledge the trauma experienced during pre- and post-migration and acculturation. Additionally, detention, incarceration, family separation, and deportations disproportionately affect the community, although Black undocumented immigrants make up a small portion of the 11.3 million estimate of undocumented immigrants. That means there is a lot of grief and loss to tackle. All of these experiences, in addition to but not limited to the experiences of rampant anti-Black racism and xenophobia, affect the community's mental health, and the ability to not just survive but thrive (G. Jackson, personal communication, May 9, 2019)

The Mental Wellness Initiative highlights the importance of expanding the dialogue and advocating for and facilitating access to mental health resources. This initiative also advocates for access to free or low-cost resources and supports ongoing professional learning and understanding around Black undocumented immigrants. In addition to professional learning some of the supports include access to free or low-cost resources, and therapists. Table 11.2 summarizes some of the considerations presented in UndocuBlack's Guide for Mental Health Wellness Specialists.

Other policies that UndocuBlack advocates for include: The Dream and Promise Act; protecting the Diversity Immigrant Visa Program (a program that encourages immigration for underrepresented countries); Temporary Protected Status (TPS); the Deferred Enforced Departure (DED); and the Public Charge policy. The following scenario outlines how these policies directly impact the situations Black undocumented immigrants face.

Scenario I: Mixed Status family

> A married couple from Jamaica with "mixed status" live in the northeastern region of the United States. One parent is a U.S. Citizen the other is not. They have two minor children who were both born in the U.S. and thus are U.S. citizens. Both parents are employed yet low-income. The children are eligible for and receive SNAP, TANF, and child care assistance benefits. The U.S. Government wants to consider the parent without U.S. citizenship a *public charge,* meaning the parent is "likely dependent on the government for subsistence," essentially making his or her ability to adjust their immigration status inadmissible. This label, *public charge*, puts the family at risk for separation, deportation, and other long-term negative impacts.

The family presented in Scenario I has to decide whether to apply for benefits they are eligible for or avoid revealing the undocumented parent's status. By understanding the proposed policies, their potential effects, and implications for Black undocumented immigrants and their families, advocates are better prepared to assist, advise, and support the communities they serve. It also allows for informed decision-making and potentially higher civic engagement.

The Federal Office of Refugee Resettlement

https://www.acf.hhs.gov/orr/resource/voluntary-agencies

The U.S. Department of Health and Human Services Office of Refugee Resettlement has a network of nine voluntary agencies that resettle all refugees coming to the United States. Each of the nine agencies has their own network of local affiliates across the United States. Regardless of their religious affiliation or title, all voluntary agencies resettle refugees from all over the world.

Table 11.2: Considerations for mental health services for undocumented Black immigrants

Considerations	Importance
Create a safe and supportive space	• Build a sense of trust and confidence in preparation for what might be difficult and sensitive conversations. • There may be distrust of engaging with professionals for fear of being reported to immigration/law enforcement. Use the physical space around them to identify support and allyship through posters, stickers, paintings, buttons, paper weights, etc. • Be clear in your statements of support.
Be present with an open mind	• Within the Black community, there is a stigma around engaging in mental health services. Be mindful of what the experience may be like for the person you are helping. • Some people may have preconceived notions about what their experience with a therapist will be like e.g., disconnected, judgmental, patronizing, and lack of confidentiality. • Be aware of how you are communicating, both verbally and nonverbally.
Educate yourself on the complexities of immigration as it relates to the African diaspora	• Develop a basic understanding of the immigration system and its processes, relevant legislation, and local and state immigration system and its processes. • Do not expect the Black undocumented client to educate you about immigration processes. This person is there to talk with you about their situation, needs, experiences, and coping difficulties. • Listen with intent, compassion, and non-judgement.
Discuss the availability of resources if the subject comes up, but do not assume that the person has not tried every avenue available so far.	• Focus on providing support vs. a "solution" to a person's immigration status. • Avoid presuming that Black undocumented people have not made attempts to rectify their immigrant status. • The process is long, the system is complex, restrictive, and costly.

Continued

Table 11.2: Continued

Considerations	Importance
Be conscious of your language and conversation.	• Avoid terminology, such as "illegal alien" and "illegal immigrant," because they are dehumanizing. • When referring to immigration status, "undocumented immigrant" is more appropriate. • Be mindful of how you react to your client's experiences. • Avoid phrases such as, "I didn't know you are undocumented" or "You don't look undocumented." • Get comfortable with hearing and using the words "Black," "Afro-Latinx," "Afro-Caribbean," "African."

(Information partially adapted from *UndocuBlack Guide for Mental Wellness Specialist, 2017.*)

Local Organizations

Ethiopian Community Development Council

https://www.ecdcus.org/

The Ethiopian Community Development Council was originally established to respond to the needs of the Ethiopian community in Washington, D.C. and throughout the United States. Today, although they offer programs and services to clients from diverse cultural backgrounds, one of the strengths of the Ethiopian Community Development Council is its service to African clients. To locate your local refugee resettlement agencies, visit the Refugee Processing Center website (http://www.wrapsnet.org/rp-agency-contacts) or contact your State Refugee Coordinator from this website (https://www.acf.hhs.gov/orr/resource/orr-funded-programs-key-contacts).

Association of Africans Living in Vermont (AALV)

https://www.aalv-vt.org/

This organization was initially established to help African immigrants who settled in Vermont. Since 2009 they have been a resource to all immigrant groups in their area such as Bhutanese, Burmese, and Iraqis. Some of the services they offer include; Interpreting & Translation, Legal Services, Workforce Development, Youth Development Programs, Agriculture, and Health & Behavior.

United African Organization

https://uniteafricans.org/

Located in Chicago, IL, United African Organization (UAO) is a coalition of community-based organizations that support African immigrant and refugees. They support social, and economic justice, civic participation, and empowerment. They also offer resources about the history of Africans in Chicago though an oral history project. Some additional resources they offer include websites, reports and videos about African Immigrant populations in Chicago and throughout the United States.

Additional State Specific Organizations

California: Congolese Family Support Organization http://www.congolese-refugees.org/

The Congolese Family Support Organization works to help Congolese families transition to life in the United States. They have a number of programs including one that focus on reducing domestic violence. Education services, newcomer orientation and a youth sports programs

Horn of Africa http://www.hornafrica.org/

Since 1995, the Horn of Africa has supported the social and emotion well-being of East African population is San Diego, California. Services offered include case management for asylum seekers, business development such as childcare training and a health and wellness initiative.

Illinois: Pan-African Association http://www.panafricanassociation.org

The Pan-African Association supports clients from over 20 countries including Bhutan, Burma, Burundi, Democratic Republic of Congo, Haiti, Rwanda, and Sudan. Some of the services they offer and initiatives support include workforce development, health and wellness, immigration and citizenship/civic education, and mentorship. One specific initiative is geared toward female entrepreneurship by offering and sponsoring, tuition-free cosmetology licensure.

Massachusetts: Congolese Development Center https://www.cd-c.org/

Located in Lynn, Massachusetts, the Congolese Development Center supports new immigrant and refugee populations from the Congo and other African countries. Assistance to newcomers, English language/translation services and legal services are some of the services they offer. They also support the Congolese increasing their capacity to become active members who are prepared to service within their communities.

Minnesota: Somali American Parent Association https://www.mnsapa. org/

The Somali American Parent Association (SAPA) serves to promote partnerships for Somali families and other Africans in communities around education, community engagement, and advocacy. Due to the large number of Somali and other East African in that area, reducing barriers to education and understanding cultural differences and socio-economic concerns are imperative in order to develop and sustain stronger home–school relationships. They also offer summer programs for students and community field trips.

Somali Parents Education Board https://speboard.org/

The Somali Parents Education Board serves to help parents navigate the K–12 education system including local, state, and federal policies. They offer workshops and foster positive relationships between families and their school communities with the primary goal of creating culturally responsive school communities. Through monthly sessions held on Saturdays, parents learn about sharing their vision for their children's education, addressing institutional racism, implicit bias, and authentic engagement between families and educators.

New York: African Services Committee http://www.africanservices. org/

Founded by Ethiopian refugees, since 1981 African Services Committee has been dedicated to serving immigrants and refugees of African descent. They provide services around housing, healthcare, legal services, and education. Their staff is multilingual, speaking over 25 languages and representing more than 20 countries. Based in Harlem, New York, they have expanded their services to include four HIV clinics in Ethiopia.

Washington State: Refugee Women's Alliance (ReWa) https://www. rewa.org/

Professional Organizations

National Council for Black Studies

Established in 1975, the National Council for Black Studies (NCBS) serves to expand and strengthen the academic community of scholars devoted to Africana/Black Studies diaspora. Their mission states:

> NCBS exists to promote academic excellence and social responsibility in the discipline of Africana/Black Studies through the production and dissemination of knowledge, professional development and training, and advocacy for social change and social justice.

Through membership to this organization, resources are offered such as a discounted conference registration, invitations and discounted fees to NCBS workshops and institutes a complimentary subscription to the International Journal of Africana Studies and Voice of Black Studies Newsletter Subscription as well as access to the NCBS Message Board and Job Postings (NCBS, 2019).

Black English Language Professionals and Friends of TESOL

https://sites.google.com/view/belpaf-2019/home

Black English Language Professional and Friends (BELPaF) of TESOL is a Professional Learning Network (PLN) of the TESOL International Association. Founded in the 1992 as an interest section, BELPaF was originally named the International Black Professionals and Friends. Years later it was reorganized into a TESOL Caucus then to its current format, a Professional Learning Network (PLN).

BELPaF's Statement of Purpose affirms:

> The Black English Language Professionals and Friends (BELPaF) exists to enhance the professional growth and development of Black English to Speakers of Other Languages (ESOL) professionals and supports the needs of Black ESOL students and their teachers. BELPaF is inclusive in nature and welcomes the participation of all who are committed to solving issues affecting Black students and teachers worldwide. BELPaF also serves as a resource for the TESOL community. BELPaF Goals include:
>
> 1. Ensure excellence in English language teaching by providing opportunities for networking and mentoring among Black professionals in the field of ESOL.
> 2. Provide support for teachers who teach ESOL students of African descent worldwide.
> 3. Increase the number of Black professionals in the field of ESOL.

4. Advocate for more racially and culturally diverse contributions to and representation in ESOL textbooks, materials, and literature.
5. Encourage research, publications, and convention proposals on issues related to varieties of English in their distinctive cultural, sociolinguistic, and educational contexts.
6. Oppose discriminatory hiring practices and stereotypes or negative images of people of African descent worldwide.

References

African Communities Together (ACT). (n.d.). Retrieved July 10, 2019 from http://www. africans.us

African Law Center. (n.d.). Retrieved July 10, 2019 from http://africanlawcenter.org/

Anderson, M., & Lopez, G. "Key Facts about Black Immigrants in the U.S." *Pew Research Center*, 24 Jan. 2018, www.pewresearch.org/fact-tank/2018/01/24/key-facts-about-black-immigrants-in-the-u-s/.

Association of Africans Living in Vermont. (2017). Retrieved July 10, 2019 from https://www.aalv-vt.org/

Black Alliance for Just Immigration (BAJI). (n.d.) Retrieved July 10, 2019 from https://baji.org/

Black English Language Professionals and Friends of TESOL (BELPaF). (n.d.). Retrieved July 10, 2019 from https://sites.google.com/view/belpaf-2019/home

Black LGBTQIA Migrant Project (BLMP). (n.d.). Retrieved July 6, 2019, from https://transgenderlawcenter.org/programs/blmp

Council on American-Islamic Relations. (2018). Retrieved July 10, 2019 from https://www.cair.com/about_us

Dieye, M. (2019, May 16). Understanding African Communities Together [Telephone interview].

Ethiopian Community Development Council. (2018). Retrieved July 6, 2019 from https://www.ecdcus.org/

Jackson, G. (2017). UndocuBlack Guide for Mental Wellness Specialist [Scholarly project]. In UndocuBlack. Retrieved July 10, 2019, fromhttps://undocublack.org/guide

Jackson, G. (2019, May 9). UndocuBlack [Telephone interview].

"National Council for Black Studies." National Council of Black Studies, http://ncbsonline.org/.

Refugee Congress. (2019). Retrieved July 6, 2019, from http://refugeecongress.org/

Refugee Congress [Organization Overview 2017]. (2017, July). Retrieved July 6, 2019, from https://docs.google.com/presentation/d/0B_n3P-u-mYbUbVVSODJ6d-VdhRWxqWGcwRG5zU0JDMDQ3anYw/edit#slide=id.p16

United African Organizations. (2019). Retrieved July 6, 2019 from https://uniteafricans. org/

U.S. Department of Health and Human Services Office of Refugee Resettlement. (2019, June 26). Retrieved July 6, 2019 from https://www.acf.hhs.gov/orr/resource/ voluntary-agencies

Afterword

We Still Can't Breathe! Teaching in a Time of Trauma, Pandemic and Riots

Awad Ibrahim & Ayanna Cooper

> But it is not enough for me to stand before you tonight and condemn riots. It would be morally irresponsible for me to do that without, at the same time, condemning the contingent, intolerable conditions that exist in our society. These conditions are the things that cause individuals to feel that they have no other alternative than to engage in violent rebellions to get attention. And I must say tonight that a riot is the language of the unheard. And what is it America has failed to hear? ... It has failed to hear that the promises of freedom and justice have not been met. And it has failed to hear that large segments of white society are more concerned about tranquility and the status quo than about justice, equality and humanity. (Martin Luther King, Jr, 1968)

How do we go on living and teaching after witnessing trauma and inhumanity? Both as teachers as well as students we are being traumatized in ways we are yet to fully understand. Not only that we can't breathe, but also thinking rationally seems like a luxury and an unnecessary (if not an absurd) act. We are angry in ways that language does no justice to, so we feel. In 2016, we attempted to put words to what left us speechless in our presentation at the TESOL International Association Convention, *All Lives Matter: The Language of Oppression, Resistance and Recovery*. This session was in direct response to the Baltimore, Maryland, riots that followed the death of Freddy Gray, a Black man who was killed while in police custody. History, it seems, continues to repeat itself.

George Floyd was just murdered in broad daylight, in front of our own eyes, hence the need for this Afterword, which was written a few days after his murder. His murder was a spectacle of horror that could have been out of a Middle Age barbarous textbook, but it was in America in 2020. The reason for his murder was an accusation of using counterfeit $20. He left too early; Mr. Floyd was only 46-year old.

A Black man who was pinned to the floor by a white police officer, Derek Chauvin. A very ugly one to be sure, but what a metaphor! Mr. Floyd does not just represent himself as a symbol, a gesture to the history of the pinning down, the oppression of the Black body by an absolute ugly figure of whiteness, but also represents so-many Black people who were killed by the police: Trayvon Martin, Tamir Rice, Michael Brown, Eric Garner, Philando Castile, Breonna Taylor, Ahmaud Arbery, Rayshard Brooks, to cite but a few.

Mr. Chauvin placed his left knee between Mr. Floyd's head and neck. "I can't breathe," Mr. Floyd said repeatedly, pleading for his mother who passed away two years before and begging "please, please, please." This was to continue for eight minutes and 46 seconds: Mr. Chauvin kept his knee on Mr. Floyd's neck. Still the cameras were rolling and in about six minutes into the video, Mr. Floyd became non-responsive. We the viewers were horrified and were shouting, 'take that knee from his neck!,' but Mr. Chauvin was clearly oblivious to our calls and continued on with his knee. We the viewers could also hear bystanders urging the officers to check his pulse. By the time one officer did, there was no pulse. Our trauma at this point was beyond anything we could describe because, first, we kept watching Mr. Chauvin placing his knee between Mr. Floyd's head and neck and, second, none of the three officers did anything. None talked to Mr. Chauvin to stop nor did they help Mr. Floyd. If lynching is defined as a killing committed by a mob, lynching is what those officers did with Mr. Floyd. Motionless, Mr. Floyd was rolled on to a gurney and taken to a hospital where he was pronounced dead about an hour later.

Not only traumatized, but this barbarous spectacle became a boiling point to so many: the largest uprising in the US since the Los Angeles Rodney King rebellion of 1992. Over 350 cities in the US marched, a global solidarity was for all to see (from Stockholm, to Accra, to Dublin, to Paris, to London, etc.), and with all unleashed anger, there was violence and explosive burst. America was not prepared for the latter despite the warning of Dr. King since the 1960s. Riots, argues Dr. King, are the entry point of the silenced and the oppressed into the political scene. The unheard, the unseen, and those who are systematically marginalized are now pulled into the center of power and can no longer be ignored or easily discarded. It is where a practice of freedom is possible, when even the police are afraid of the rowdy crowd.

What makes this whole scene more painful is that it is all happening in the midst of the COVID-19 pandemic. When the police are not murdering the Black body, the pandemic is affecting the Black community disproportionately. Black immigrants are not immune to this. We do not have statistics for it, but watching the TV news, one can see a good number of those who are working in meat processing plants who tested positive for COVID-19 are Black immigrants, of Somali origin in particular.

These two phenomena (the trauma of being murdered in public and the pandemic) call for a racial justice that "is forcing America to face all its interrelated flaws – racism, poverty, militarism, and materialism"; a justice that "is exposing the evils that are rooted deeply in the whole structure of our society"; and a justice that "reveals systemic rather than superficial flaws and suggests that radical reconstruction of society itself is the real issue to be faced" (King, cited in Taylor, 2020). Framing its resources within a similar call for social and racial justice, TESOL and the British Council have resources for language teachers, including English as a Second Language (ESL) teachers, that might start our journey into what might be called *racio-linguistic justice* (see especially Baker-Bell, 2020; Alim, Rickford, & Ball, 2016).

When situated within the field of TESOL, the *racio-linguistic journey* starts with an acknowledgment, an admission to the fact that the English language, its teachers and speakers are often times situated in and value whiteness. Romney's research on race, English language and native speakerism confirms, "…perceptions of a language generally influence perceptions of who its speakers are and who should teach it (2010, p. 19). As a profession, what is TESOL to do when it is and has been in a unique position to be allies to Black people while dismantling racist practices? As affirmed by Gerald,

> Many ELT professionals, though occasionally made aware of our field's white supremacy, cling to the perceived social good of our work to avoid considering the way our field centers and values whiteness above all else, even to the point that we are willing to begrudgingly accept forms of discrimination (e.g., linguistic imperialism, native speakerism, et al.,) so long as race itself is not the focus of the discussion. (2020, p. 47)

Recognizing that issues of race and language are inseparable is the next step in practicing a racio-linguistic justice. For some, this step, or mis-step can be one of the most difficult to take. Let us explain through two examples. The first example involved a potential white contributor whom we invited to write a chapter for this volume. They are from southern United States, an area that has a high population of K12 Haitian students who speak French/ Creole. We wanted to include their voices as part of this manuscript. The person declined our invitation in fear of naming race as a factor when teaching English. They were adamant that they did not focus on race but just on language when teaching ESL. When asked how, for example, they would help students communicate with police officers in their communities should they need to, there was no response. Silence has remained a form of passive agreement with oppressors. As Kubota (2002) argues,

> Discussing racism is often uncomfortable, particularly in TESOL and applied linguistics. The field of L2 education by nature attracts professionals who are willing to work with people across racial boundaries, and thus it is considered to be a "nice" field, reflecting liberal humanism. (p. 86)

The second example involved a session at the 2019 TESOL International Association Convention, which was held in Atlanta, Georgia, a pillar of the Civil Rights Movement. A white woman presented about the use of the "N-word" in a session that was framed as *the* Convention's session to shed light on social cultural discourse within the field of TESOL. Being white and presenting before an audience that was extremely qualified to speak to the topic were not enough, but to add insult to injure the session also included derogatory language associated with the LGBTQ community. Intentional or not, the session was so disturbing, insulting, and embarrassing that TESOL International Association issued a statement of apology to those "who were affected." (Dare we ask if white people were included in this category of those "who were affected"?) In the statement, they never named the session but committed to "do better." Nonetheless, the 2020 convention never revisited this session/issue and none of the featured or keynote sessions included speakers of African descent. How can a "nice" profession like TESOL do better when they are reluctant to name the problems they have? In order for TESOL and similar professions and organizations to do better, they must not only admit there is a problem but also commit to dismantling systems and structures that create an illusion of inclusion. Mission and vision statements alone will not suffice. Admit and commit! That is one of the premises of racio-linguistic justice, where the personal can be such a fertile ground for consciousness raising.

That is, as educators reckon with the brutality of anti-Black racism and attempt to create allyship with Black Lives Matter organizations, personal reexamination becomes extremely important. Critical educators must examine their own biases and prejudices and locate themselves in time and space and simultaneously question the adequacy of that location. Put otherwise, in addition to the necessary innerwork, evaluation of and objection to racist curriculum, materials, exclusionary research practices, and the like are imperative if we are to become the diverse and inclusive community we profess to be. For example, acknowledgment and celebration of Juneteenth, the day news of the Emancipation Proclamation reached enslaved people in Texas in 1865, two and half years *after* the official proclamation, was at an all-time high in June of 2020. The irony also lies in the fact that Juneteenth is just two weeks prior to America's widely known Independence Day celebration, July 4th. Corporations and non-profits declared Juneteenth as an official day of observance. In New York, Governor Cuomo signed an executive order for Juneteenth to be an official holiday for state employees. Cuomo stated, "although slavery ended over 150 years ago, there has still been rampant, systemic discrimination and injustice in this state and this nation, and we have been working to enact real reforms to address these inequalities" (Cuomo, 2020, n.p.). Cuomo also committed to advancing legislation to make it an official state holiday in the future. Here, for us, is a concrete example of an admit and commit action, a courageous act of redressing history and putting racial justice into practice, thus making the practice of racio-linguistic justice possible. Only then can we move together as a nation under one roof and indivisible (see also Costello, 2016).

We conclude by recasting our opening question: *how do we go on living and teaching after witnessing trauma and inhumanity?* As highlighted in this volume, this question calls for a racio-linguistic justice that is wide-awake to the history of racial injustice and the necessary transformation of the school so that it works for the communities it serves, be these communities immigrants or not. This manuscript is situated squarely within this wide-awake and racio-linguistic justice, which also calls for immediate action across all contexts, e.g., policy, education, healthcare, civil disobedience, and the like. If, as James Baldwin put it, "A writer is by definition a disturber of the peace," then we see our work in this collection as a form of organized protest. Here, we hope, Black immigrants and those who teach them will not be a silent subgroup! Only in materializing this hope can we all breathe.

References

Alim, S., Rickford, J., & Ball, A. (2016). *Raciolinguistics: How language shapes our ideas about language.* New York: Oxford University Press.

Baker-Bell, A. (2020). *Linguistic justice: Black language, literacy, identity, and pedagogy.* New York: Routledge.

Baldwin, J. (1969). "Disturber of the Peace – James Baldwin", in Standley and Pratt (eds.), *Conversations with James Baldwin*, p. 81.

Costello, M. B. (2016). *After election day: The Trump effect: The impact of the 2016 presidential election on our nation's schools.* Montgomery, AL: Southern Poverty Law Center.

Cuomo, A. (2020). Governor Cuomo issues executive order recognizing Juneteenth as a holiday for state employees. (2020, June 18). Available: https://www.governor.ny.gov/

news/governor-cuomo-issues-executive-order-recognizing-juneteenth-holiday-state-employees.

Gerald, J. (2020). Worth the risk: Towards decentring whiteness in English language teaching. *BC TEAL Journal, 5*(1), 44–54.

King, M. L. Jr. (1968). *The other America.* Available: https://www.gphistorical.org/mlk/mlkspeech/.

Kubota, R. (2002). The author responds: (Un) Raveling racism in a nice field like TESOL. *TESOL Quarterly, 36*(1), 84–92. doi:10.2307/358836.

Romney, M. (2010). The Colour of English. In Mahboob, A. (Ed.) *The NNEST Lens: Non native English speakers in TESOL* (pp.18–34). Tyne, UK: Cambridge Scholars Publishing.

Taylor, K-Y. (2020). How do we change America?: The quest to transform this country cannot be limited to challenging its brutal police. *The New Yorker.* Available: https://www.newyorker.com/news/our-columnists/how-do-we-change-america?

Contributors

Nimo Mohamed Abdi, Ph.D., is an Assistant Professor in the department of Curriculum and Instruction at the University of Minnesota. Her research focuses on immigrant and refugee education, particularly as it relates to cultural, racial, and religious diversity. Her primary methodological approaches are phenomenology, decolonization theory/methodologies, and discourse analysis. Her work examines Somali educational experiences in urban United States, United Kingdom, Sweden, and The Netherlands.

Melissa L. Alleyne, M.Phil., is a Planning Officer in the Office of Planning and Institutional Research for The University of the West Indies, Open Campus and a PhD student in Education at The University of the West Indies, Cave Hill Campus. Her research interests are in literacy, applied linguistics, online and distance education and institutional planning and development.

Ayanna R. Armstrong, Ph.D., originally from the Caribbean island of Barbados, Dr. Armstrong received her Bachelor of Arts in economics from Spelman College, an MBA with a concentration in Marketing and a Doctor of Philosophy, both from Clark Atlanta University. Especially interested in Research Methods, Statistics and Immigration Policy. In her personal time she enjoys cooking and spending time with her husband Amin and son Zaire.

Ebony Bailey, B.A., a filmmaker and researcher from Central California. As a self-described "Blaxican," she is interested in exploring issues such as race, gender, cultural intersections, and diaspora. Her work has been published in NPR, LA Times and Remezcla. Her documentaries have been screened at film festivals and forums in the US, Mexico and Europe. She studied

journalism at the University of Southern California and is currently pursuing her Masters degree in documentary film at the National Autonomous
University of Mexico.

Martha Bigelow, Ph.D., is a Professor in Second Language Education at the
University of Minnesota, USA. Her research focuses on equity in language
teaching and learning in the U.S. and abroad with particular emphasis on contexts with immigrant and refugee-background youth. Her newest book with
Doris Warriner is entitled Critical reflections on research methods: Power and
equity in complex multilingual contexts (Multilingual Matters).

Kisha C. Bryan, Ph.D., is an Assistant Professor of Education in the
Department of Teaching and Learning at Tennessee State University. She is
an advocate for ELs and other linguistically diverse populations. Her research
focuses on identity construction among Black and immigrant adolescents,
language acquisition in urban contexts, and teacher preparation.

Ayanna Cooper, Ed.D., is an author, advocate, keynote speaker, and owner
of ACooper Consulting. Her projects involve providing technical assistance
to state departments of education, school districts and organizations with
students identified as English Learners. In addition to building the capacity
of educators to support students who are learning English, she also emphasizes protecting their civil rights. She is the co-author of Evaluating ALL
Teachers of English Learners and Students with Disabilities: Supporting
Great Teaching (with Staehr Fenner & Kozik).

Awad Ibrahim, Ph.D., is an award-winning author and a Professor at the
Faculty of Education, University of Ottawa, Canada. He is a Curriculum
Theorist with special interest in cultural studies, applied linguistics, Hip-Hop,
youth and Black popular culture, philosophy, and sociology of education,
social justice, diasporic and continental African identities, and ethnography. He has researched and published widely in these areas and among his
books, Internationalizing Curriculum Studies: Histories, Environments, and
Critiques (with Hébert, Ng-A-Fook, & Smith) and The rhizome of
Blackness: A critical ethnography of Hip-Hop culture, language, identity and
the politics of becoming.

Babatunji Ifarinu, M.Ed., (Tunji) is currently the Assistant Principal at
one of the most diverse elementary schools in the country and has taught
a wide variety of students beginning in1997. Tunji provides workshops and

trainings covering topics such as motivating and recognizing the genius in youth, cultural competence, and instruction for culturally and linguistically diverse students. Tunji believes in using "practical and tactical" strategies, while delivering paradigm-shifting information that can be immediately utilized in the classroom or at home.

Mary Lou McCloskey, Ph.D., former teacher in multicultural, multilingual classrooms and author of many textbooks for students and teachers of English to speakers of other languages, has worked with schools, districts, and ministries of education in 36 states and in 39 countries on five continents. She teaches at Agnes Scott College and serves as ESOL Specialist for the Global Village Project, which provides a middle school for refugee girls with interrupted education.

Isabella Alexander-Nathani, Ph.D., is an award-winning writer, filmmaker, and human rights activist. She teaches in the Departments of Anthropology and Film & Media Studies at Emory University and serves as the Executive Director of Small World Films, an independent production studio focused on social impact storytelling. Her latest book (Burning at Europe's Borders: Migration in the Age of Border Externalization, Oxford University Press) and documentary film (The Burning) will uncover the human side of our global migrant and refugee crisis.

Bic Ngo, Ph.D. is Professor of Curriculum and Instruction at the University of Minnesota where she holds the Rodney S. Wallace Professorship for the Advancement of Teaching and Learning. Her research engages critical ethnography and other qualitative methodologies and interdisciplinary conceptual frameworks, including critical, social, cultural and feminist theories to examine "culture" and "difference" in the education of immigrant students, and the implications for theorizing immigrant identity, culturally relevant pedagogy, and anti-oppressive education.

Pedro Noguera, Ph.D., is the Distinguished Professor of Education at the Graduate School of Education and Information Studies at UCLA. His most recent books are Race, Equity and Education: The Pursuit of Equality in Education 60 Years After Brown (Springer). Excellence Through Equity" (Corwin 2015), and "Schooling for Resilience: Improving the Life Trajectory of African American and Latino Boys" with E. Fergus and M. Martin (Harvard Education Press 2014). In 2013 he was appointed to the Kappa Delta Pi Honor Society and in 2014 he was appointed to the National Academy of Education.

Teni-Ola Ogunjobi, MAIR, is committed to serving diverse communities in international and domestic contexts. She delivers high-quality trainings on volunteerism, cultural competence, and communication for multicultural audiences. She has worked in areas of intercultural education, community engagement, nonprofit and business management, grassroots development, and communications/journalism. She attended Howard University and the University of the Pacific. Teni-Ola was a Peace Corps Volunteer and teacher in Mali and Senegal for four years and served the refugee community in Atlanta for four years.

Amy Pelissero, Ph.D., has been the Head of School at Global Village Project since 2013, a special purpose middle school for newcomer refugee girls with limited formal schooling. Amy earned her Ph.D. in Teaching and Learning with a concentration in Language & Literacy from Georgia State University. The subject of her dissertation included refugee women's language and literacy practices and refugee women's education. Amy is certified to teach ESOL P-12 and English grades 6-12.

Enzo Silon Surin, MFA, Haitian-born poet, educator, publisher, and social advocate, is the author of several chapbooks and the forthcoming full-length poetry collection, *When My Body Was A Clinched Fist*, (Black Lawrence Press, 2020). He is the recipient of a Brother Thomas Fellowship from The Boston Foundation and is a PEN New England Celebrated New Voice in Poetry. He is currently Professor of English at Bunker Hill Community College and founding editor and publisher at Central Square Press

Patriann Smith, Ph.D., is an Assistant Professor of Literacy Studies in the Department of Teaching and Learning at the University of South Florida. Her research interests include Black immigrant Englishes/literacies, standardized and non-standardized English ideologies, multicultural teacher education, literacy assessment, and cross-cultural and cross-linguistic literacy practices. Her recent publications include "How Does a Black Person Speak English? Beyond American Language Norms" published by the American Educational Research Journal, "Understanding Afro-Caribbean Educators' Experiences with Englishes across Caribbean and U.S. Contexts and Classrooms: Recursivity, (Re)positionality, Bidirectionality" published by Teaching and Teacher Education, "(Re)Positioning in the Englishes and (English) Literacies of a Black Immigrant Youth: Towards a 'Transraciolinguistic' Approach" published by Theory into Practice, and

"Non-standardized Englishes in Mainstream Literacy Practice" published by Oxford Research Encyclopedia of Education.

S. Joel Warrican, Ph.D., has been in the field of education for over 30 years, with teaching experience at all levels, from kindergarten to tertiary. He is currently the Director of the School of Education at The University of the West Indies Cave Hill Campus. His research interests include multiculturalism and multilingualism, democratizing classrooms and transformative education.

Alex Kumi-Yeboah, Ph.D., is an Assistant Professor of Education in the Department of Educational Theory and Practice at the University at Albany, State University of New York. Broadly, his research examines mediating cross-cultural factors (educational, social, psychological, socio-linguistic) that impact on the educational advancement of Black immigrant students in United States schools. He also studies cross-cultural collaboration and multicultural contexts in online education. Current research projects include exploring African immigrant students' multiple worlds, academic and social experiences in urban schools

Index